3⁰⁰

D1468581

POLO

Alex Brodie, Phillip Elliot, Howard Hipwood and Peter Grace in action.

P O L O

Peter Grace

New York

Maxwell Macmillan Canada
Toronto

Maxwell Macmillan International
New York Oxford Singapore Sydney

TO MY FAMILY
for without them this book would have remained just an idea.

Copyright © 1991 by Peter Grace

All rights reserved. No part of this book may be reproduced or transmitted in any form or by any means, electronic or mechanical, including photocopying, recording, or by any information storage and retrieval system, without permission in writing from the Publisher.

Howell Book House
Macmillan Publishing Company
866 Third Avenue
New York, NY 10022

Maxwell Macmillan Canada, Inc.
1200 Eglinton Avenue East
Suite 200
Don Mills, Ontario M3C 3N1

Macmillan Publishing Company is part of the Maxwell Communication Group of Companies.

Library of Congress Cataloging-in-Publication Data

Grace, Peter, 1938–
    Polo / Peter Grace.
        p.   cm.
    ISBN 0-87605-954-X
    1. Polo.   I. Title.
    GV1011.G68   1991
    796.35'3—dc20   91–20782   CIP

Macmillan books are available at special discounts for bulk purchases for sales promotions, premiums, fund-raising, or educational use. For details, contact:

                Special Sales Director
                Macmillan Publishing Company
                866 Third Avenue
                New York, NY 10022

10 9 8 7 6 5 4 3 2 1

Printed in Great Britain

Sketches by John Board on pages 57, 74, 75, 81, 94 and 194 are reprinted by permission of Faber and Faber Ltd.
Computer diagrams on pages 78, 188, 189, 191, 195, 197, 204, 206–7, 210–11, 213, 214, 216, 218, 219, 220, 222 and 227 were produced by Pippa Grace.
The illustrations on page 46 are reprinted with permission from *Polo* magazine. copyright Polo Publications, Inc., Gaithersburg, MD, USA

Photographic acknowledgements
The author and publishers are grateful to Mike Roberts for the majority of the photographs, including the jacket, and to the following for permission to reproduce copyright photographs: Howard Baker, page 250; Iain Burns, pages 59, 84, 138, 162, 193, 199, 212 and 248; John Garrett, pages 121 and 126; photograph courtesy of Ralph Lauren, page 245; Mario Visual Recording Photographic, page 238; Fernando Topo Martinera, pages 172, 178 and 181, Steve Shipman for *You* Magazine, page 2; *Sunday Mirror*, page 221. Every effort has been made to trace the copyright owners but if there have been any omissions in this respect we apologise and will be pleased to make appropriate acknowledgement in any further editions.

CONTENTS

Intense concentration as Prince Charles turns for the ball.

FOREWORD

by

HRH THE PRINCE OF WALES

KENSINGTON PALACE

Peter Grace seems to have been a familiar figure in the world of polo for almost as long as I have been playing myself. Indeed, now that he has moved the Rangitiki Polo School to his own club nearby, I rather miss the sight of his pupils practicing on chairs as I arrive to play at the Guards Polo Club! I have even played for the Rangitiki Team, in place of Peter, on more than one occasion - although without the benefit of a session on the chairs beforehand...

Sixty years ago my great-uncle, Lord Mountbatten, produced his "Introduction to Polo", but with the enormous growth in the number of people taking up the sport perhaps it is time for a more modern version to help enlighten players on the intricacies of the game.

Peter is generally regarded as one of the best instructors that there is in polo. I believe that this book, with its excellent photographs taken by Mike Roberts and amusing sketches by John Board, will be a tremendous help, at least for the next sixty years, to both present and future polo players.

ACKNOWLEDGEMENTS

After untold hours of work, it is with considerable relief that I sit here thinking of how and where this book was written, and of the many people who, through their kindness and generosity, have helped me with it.

It was written in sections which started with the journeys we took. The foundations were laid in Corvuero in Portugal and the first chapters were written in peace and solitude beside Lake Taupo in New Zealand. It proved impossible to write in England, with the pressures of a rapidly expanding organisation.

The middle sections were written next to the sea in Barbados, thanks to our dear friends Cow and Diane Williams, whose help and support can never be repaid. In Florida by the sea with Thomas Wicky and on the farm in Middleburg I wrote about the breeding and making of polo ponies with Harry, Jenny and Skipper Darlington, and in Malibu Beach the game and its theory developed. In Los Angeles I have Pat Nesbitt and Geoff Palmer to thank for their wonderful hospitality and, in Palm Springs, Jim and Sue Keenan for their constant encouragement and advice. Gradually the pages grew with the list of friends who provided the secluded places where thoughts were turned into words. On the plane back to England the book was finished, but the work had just begun.

A family wedding, with Jane, Bobby, Lolo and Oliver Grace in Long Island and Mr and Mrs Bradley Collins in New York, completed the final reading. The computer corrections were done by Katie, and the floppy discs were printed with the expert help of Roger Mitchell. Mike Roberts, polo photographer par excellence, met every deadline with a smile, and my sincere thanks also go to Stuart Mackenzie and F.D. Walton for their help and patience in sitting for the polo shots.

Pippa, the computer genius, built horses on floppy discs and, after endless hours, she finally emerged triumphant. The people who helped Pippa with this great effort were Alastair Southwell, Jamie Everett, Giles Corbett, Heather Tricker, Giles Toman, DTP – Geoff Belfer, Ali Erfan, Peyman Mestchian, Wayne McIntyre and Tim at Penguin.

I must also thank some of the wonderful friends who have helped me in the world of polo, although some are now sadly not with us. In New Zealand, former Chairman of the NZPA, Hamish Wilson and John McKelvie, who with Bobby Russell and my family encouraged me to take up the sport in the Rangitikei Polo Club. Lord Cowdray for helping me so much when I arrived in England, Adam Winthrop for his friendship and guidance, Peter Thwaites, Alec Harper and the HPA, Sarah Sugden and The Cowdray Park Polo Club, Willie Loyd and Ronald Ferguson, on my arrival at the Guards from Cowdray, and Sinclair Hill for his inspirational teaching.

Many people have helped the family over the years, and in the space available it is impossible for me to thank you all. I must, however, mention Peter Scott-Dunn, Nick Bastian, Bob Hooke, Yves Piaget, Graeme Grant and Doctors Danbury and Furness, whose combined efforts to keep me on the field have so far succeeded; Joan Jackson, Marisa Masters and Mary Rothermere in London; and our club members, including Christian Angerer, Norman and Maryse Bergel, Duncan Boyd, Andrew Hodgkinson, Andrew Marx and Roger Whewell, who have actively encouraged the growth of Ascot Park Polo Club.

I would mention the wonderful work of the experts at Pelham Books, and a special word of thanks to Roger Houghton, John Beaton and Arianne Burnette, whose patience and help were inexhaustible. Finally, I would like to thank my family, for without their continuous support and help this book simply would not exist.

INTRODUCTION

'Let other people play at other things – the king of games is still the game of kings.'

THIS VERSE IS inscribed on a stone tablet next to a polo ground in Gilgit, north of Kashmir, near the fabled silk route from China to the West. In one ancient sentence it epitomises the feelings of the players of today.

Polo is arguably one of the most complex of games. It has proved a constant challenge to sportsmen the world over. When you imagine an ability to hit an object the size of a cricket ball, with a piece of wood 2 inches high and 9 inches long fixed to the end of a thin cane handle over 4 feet long, and make shots that travel up to 150 yards from a horse moving at perhaps 40 miles an hour, you can feel the surge of excitement and tension which is generated by this amazing game.

Imagine yourself out on a ground 300 yards long and half as wide. You and the three other players in your team, all wearing blue shirts, are battling against four opponents in red, each vying for possession of the ball. It's like playing chess at 30 miles an hour – striving and struggling for the ball, your opponent riding you off like a demon, you endeavour to hit the ball up to your number 1 who has galloped into a position where he can strike for goal. He gets hooked and you follow, flying down the line – a crisp swing and sheer exultation as the ball soars between the posts. There's just nothing like polo!

This book has been written in an effort to recreate the thrills and spills of the game, with the aim of initiating beginners and imparting further knowledge to those who are already acquainted with polo. Once you've caught the 'polo bug' you are smitten for life. You have been warned: you'll hear phrases like 'impossible to give up', and 'a game which you'll find very addictive', because you become more and more involved in its continuing complexities and it presents an endless challenge to even the greatest of players. There is always something new to learn about the sport.

In this book I will touch on the many and varied aspects of the game, beginning with arguably the most important – the ability to hit the ball – and progressing through the riding phase, stick and balling, the different exercises you need to master before you can actually get out on to the ground to play, the training of your pony and the various techniques which can be used to improve your polo. After this general introduction, you will be taken through the more tactical aspects of the game, the positioning of the players, the tactics for the many set plays, the rules and regulations and the general format of polo – crossing, fouling, dangerous riding, the line of the ball, hooking and penalties. I will discuss team tactics, the basic direction of the game, the positions of the players, retaining possession, playing as a team and the general run of play. All the set plays and positions will be illustrated to enable players to gain advantage and control the play.

One of the most important aspects of polo is that it is a very sophisticated team game, and this is not surprising when you consider that it was originally played some three to four thousand years ago and is arguably one of the first team sports ever played. Although there are four individuals in each team, the concept of team play takes precedence over that of the brilliant individual, and while from time to time individual brilliance comes to the fore, it doesn't matter how consistently good an individual player is – he cannot often win a polo match on his own.

Author's Note:
Throughout the book 'he' is used to refer to players, stable managers, vets, grooms, etc., but they may equally well be women.

While every care has been taken to verify facts and techniques described in this book, neither the publishers not the author can accept liability for any errors or omissions or for any accidents or mishaps that may arise.

PART
ONE

—

Knee pads, gloves, polo cap and guard, whip, polo sticks, and a polo saddle being used by John Hurt and Charles Dance, who took lessons before the making of White Mischief.

1

EQUIPMENT

IN POLO, as in any sport, the correct equipment is vitally important to your success, and once you have decided to take up the game you should try to obtain the best equipment available. In numerous places around the world polo is played with whatever is to hand, and players love the game to the extent that they enjoy having to make do, but it is so much easier to play well if you have the right equipment.

POLO STICKS

Perhaps the most important aspect of the game is to be able to hit the ball, and the polo stick plays a major part in your ability to achieve consistency. Sometimes called a mallet, the polo stick consists of a shaped rubber handle fitted to a length of cane, with a cigar-shaped head fitted at an angle to the other end. Individual preferences vary considerably, and as you become more experienced in the game your tastes will change. Your first stick should have a medium to stiff cane and a cigar head and should be of a practical length, chosen in relation to the height of your horse (see page 7). It is important to begin with a fairly light stick because the muscles of the arm will be able to handle a lighter stick more easily in the correct plane. As the muscles get stronger, and the body becomes accustomed to swinging the polo stick, increasingly heavier sticks may be used, depending on the strength of the arm.

Polo sticks have been made in many different styles as the game has evolved, and modern technology will play an increasing part in their evolution. In the early days of polo different styles of handle, known as the grip, were used but most of the stick-manufacturers these days have fixed on the rugby grip, and several modifications of this grip are currently available, most stick-makers designing according to their own preferences. Handles, formed from wood glued to the thick end of the cane, are shaped, prepared and finally covered with either rubber or towelling to form the grip. Climate will influence the choice of material:

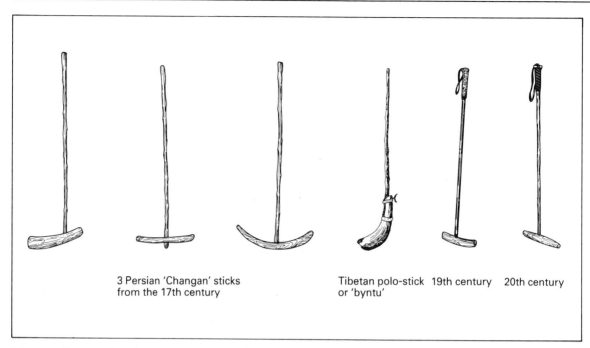

3 Persian 'Changan' sticks
from the 17th century

Tibetan polo-stick 19th century   20th century
or 'byntu'

The polo stick has developed over time . . .

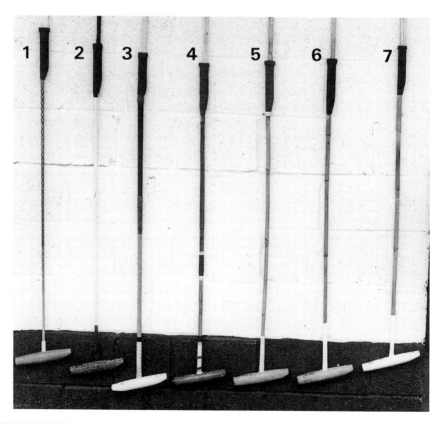

. . . to the ones more commonly used today. The most recent technology has produced the fibreglass and graphite sticks. Shown here are: 1 Argosy Hybrid Composite mallet, Argentine tipa cigar head; 2 Cenataur Classic Carbon fibre and fibreglass cane; 3 Pakistan malacca and rattan spliced cane, skene head; 4 Indian spliced cane with bamboo head; 5 Villamil Argentinian stick, cigar head; 6 Merlos Argentinian stick, cigar head; 7 Mallet Manufacturing Company English stick, cigar head.

if you play in a very hot climate, a towelling grip may be preferable, but these days rubber grips are more universal and players wear thin leather gloves to counteract the effects of perspiration in the hand.

A person with a small hand should choose a narrow stick handle coming to quite a sharp 'V' in the fingers, while someone with larger hands may prefer a wider, flatter grip so that it fits into the hand more comfortably and gives him more control and better direction. The stick handle also has a thong attached to the end which is looped over the thumb to prevent the stick from flying away if a player should lose his grip.

As a beginner your best method of getting the ideal stick is by trial and error initially. Then, once you have found the stick that seems to suit your style of game, take it to the nearest manufacturer and ask him to search his cane stock and try to reproduce it.

Sticks are made with canes ranging from stiff to whippy, and the weight of the head is of vital importance to the 'balance' of the stick. A whippy cane is more difficult for a beginner to handle correctly because of the timing of the stroke, but can be more effective when used by a player who is not so strong, because the whip can impart more speed to the stick head, while a very stiff cane loses its 'feel'. The best beginner's stick has a medium-stiff cane and a total weight of 16–18 oz (450–500 g) with a head weight of 6–7½ oz (180–210 g) for a man, and 13–16 oz (375–450 g) with a head weight of 4½–6 oz (150–180 g) for a woman – heavier, lighter or stiffer to suit the individual. The head is fitted to the cane at an angle because the ball is not hit exactly on a vertical plane as in croquet.

Polo-stick canes, which are from the bamboo family, are grown in the Far East, Malaysia and Indonesia, and are available in two different varieties: malacca and rattan cane. Malacca is dark brown, lighter and stiffer, while creamy-white rattan is stronger, more supple and is better suited for the complete cane. A combination of the two canes with malacca at the top spliced into rattan at the bottom sometimes provides a stick with a good 'feel' – whippy towards the head and stiff at the handle end, which is the perfect 'feel' for a stick: this used to be quite popular years ago, but has been superseded and is now only rarely available. The rattan-only type cane comes with a varying number of joints in the tapering shaft. The closer-jointed ones tend to produce a cane with a better 'feel', because they taper better towards the end to give you the right 'balance' in the stick. These qualities are, of course, personal, varying between both players and professional polo stick-makers, hence the wide variety of sticks.

There are three different shapes of stick head currently available. The cigar head, which has a larger hitting surface, has been designed for general-purpose use and is the best type of head for the beginner. The RNPA (Royal Naval Polo Association) head, flatter and wider at the bottom, imparts more loft to the ball. This head is preferred by players taking penalties or hit-ins from the back line. A skene head is cigar-shaped but has a flat bottom and is a combination of the two heads already mentioned. When selecting a head it is important to have the grain running from end to end, rather than diagonally across the head; this prevents it from splitting.

Stick heads are made from timber which varies from country to country, and wood that is moderately soft and hardwood have proved very successful. Ash and sycamore, and a number of hardwoods such as mulberry, are used, and also bamboo, which in Pakistan they sometimes cover with vellum (thin hide) which seems to last well in dry weather – but it should not be used in the rain as it goes soft. Although different manufacturers have been using and trying various heads over a long period of time, no one material has proved to be outstandingly the best. A hard hitter would generally get better durability from a hardwood head, and one of the better hardwoods available at this time appears to come from Zimbabwe, in Africa. Argentinian tipa wood heads are becoming more popular, but were very difficult to get in England until recently; they seem to have good lasting qualities, and have now been acclaimed as the best available.

Arguably the best polo sticks come from Argentina, but there are two or three stick-makers in England who produce excellent ones, and for years manufacturers in Pakistan and India have produced good serviceable sticks at very competitive prices which have been exported to most polo-playing countries. Recently a New Zealand manufacturer, George Wood, has tried to 'corner' the market, and his sticks, while quite widely available, have met with a mixed reception – sticks I tried at the time of writing had definitely improved since the first ones I saw – and the lighter ones have proved to be quite good for women.

Ray Turner, owner of Salters in Aldershot, England, has a room full of 'patterns' – the favourite sticks of many of the top players – dating back more than fifty years and has made sticks for nearly all the top players in the world since he made his first one in 1942 for the princely wage of 1 guinea a week. He was important enough for George Salter to pay his mother a retainer of 1 shilling a day – refundable if he did not return – when he was drafted into the army, where he spent two and a half years. He has worked at his stick-making bench ever since, at the same time taking over the business. Much of my knowledge of the art of stick-manufacture has been gleaned from his workbench, happily spiced with lots of polo gossip.

Tony Tanner, of Argosy fame, has built up a very good reputation in recent years and exports a considerable number of excellent sticks and polo equipment to the USA as well as catering for many of the players and professionals on the English scene. We first met when I was on a tour to Malaysia and he was living in Kuala Lumpur, and he introduced me to some of the culinary delights of life in the East. I remember numerous evenings spent researching the never-ending varieties of different food always available – even at breakfast time – but marvellous after an energetic day's polo. First we visited the Sultan of Johore's private museum and collection of Rolls-Royce cars during a wonderful Royal Tournament in Johore, where we stayed in the palace overlooking the polo fields. Next came a weekend tournament in Singapore during which I schooled and afterwards won the 'best playing pony' award on a lovely little grey Australian mare.

In Kuala Lumpur we played in a royal match against the Sultan of Pahang's team on a damp clay ground which, the day before, had been covered in 6 inches of water. A polo match appeared impossible until we suggested pulling three V-drains across the field and digging a hundred postholes through the clay pan. We then used hovering helicopters to blow the water away. Flooding had been a problem there for years, and we discovered that, before the topsoil, the thin sand base had been covered with about 3 inches of clay which had been rolled down into a watertight layer and the water could not escape. The field has played very well ever since.

The climax to our memorable polo tour was a Royal Tournament in Pahang as one of the features in a royal wedding celebration which lasted three days. This stands out in my mind as the only time a polo match has been halted at half-time so that everyone could go off for a royal afternoon tea. Over the centuries polo has been known as the sport of kings, for it was often used as entertainment for the royal court. It was wonderful to see that in this busy world, where polo is often put under pressure to meet various expectations, we could for a moment turn back the clock and catch a fleeting glimpse of a former era.

Stick Length

There are several different theories about the correct relationship between the length of your polo stick and the height of the horse. However, most people will find that it is better to change the length of their stick in relation to the height of the pony and, as a guide, for a 15-to-15.2-hand pony, players should use either a 51- or a 52-inch stick. On a taller pony it is much easier to change the length of the stick and keep the swing consistent than to change the swing and bend down lower to the ball. Conversely, on a small pony it is much easier to use a shorter stick than to have to stand up and hit the ball further away from the horse.

When you are selecting your stick length, the following guideline also applies: as you sit on the horse with your stick on the ground, the stick handle should, roughly, come up to the outside bone of your knee, just a couple of inches below the top.

Space-age Technology

With the massive expansion of polo it is perhaps inevitable that the supplies of rattan cane, from which the mallet shaft is made, will become even more scarce than it traditionally has been. Because it takes years to grow before it is harvested, and then additional years stored in bundles to dry out and 'season' properly before it can be used, every player has at some time found himself desperately looking for a supply of mallets, and a favourite one is often irreplaceable. Many attempts have been made over the years to create a synthetic shaft and it is only very recently that anything created through man's ingenuity has come near to equalling the strength, flexibility, shock-absorption ability and lightness of natural cane. As these new materials and the resulting sticks approach the ideal their prices tend to increase steeply: they vary from about the same as a top-grade cane mallet to nearly three times as much.

The majority of players will say they prefer a mallet to be light in weight and stiff but with a little whip in the lower half, and these characteristics are readily engineered into the synthetics. Achieving the qualities of strength and shock-absorption ability in combination with the aforementioned flexibility and lightness presents the greatest problem to the designer. This problem is generally solved using several of the many modern epoxy resin-based materials, plus other materials in combination; the resultant build is termed a composite.

Currently the best of the synthetic products seems to have achieved the required result, and indeed there are bonuses. For example, the generally lighter weight, coupled with a shaft 25 per cent thinner in diameter than that of the average cane shaft, considerably reduces wind resistance in the swing and has a marked effect on manoeuvrability. The shaft recovery time is about one third that of a cane mallet, so the ball fairly zips off the head and should travel around 15 per cent further for a given swing. There are other advantages too, such as imperviousness to climate, precise weight control and exact repeatability – the ability to reproduce the same stick exactly and continuously. The principal disadvantages of the composites are that the shafts are still a compromise between strength and playing characteristics and can break if they get a very severe hook or hit a steel horseshoe hard; and once broken the shaft, unlike cane, cannot be repaired. Nonetheless, the composite-shaft mallet has now evolved to the point where it merits serious consideration by players of all handicaps. Tony Tanner's Argosy composite mallets, I believe, come closest to the best of the cane sticks and have proved ideal for the patron who, like me, needs that extra length to his shot. I have played with them for two seasons now, and my hitting has been better and more consistent than ever before.

Polo-stick Care and Repair

If you do not live near a stick-manufacturer, there are times when you have to be able to do your own repairs. It is possible to rehead a cane at home, and redrill a head to fit it on to a different cane. In these cases take care to fit the cane to the head before glueing and, if it is available, use very thin, 1-inch-wide cotton tape between the head and the end of the cane to aid the fixing. Hold the head on the end of the cane by wedging the cane after putting it through the hole in the head, and use a top-quality waterproof wood glue. Open the head a little at the bottom to take the shape of the wedge, and take care not to use a wedge that is too wide and thus 'explode' the head by pressure sideways from the wedge. Tap the wedge in gently until you feel that it is firm, check the alignment of the head on the handle, then one more tap to tighten it, with plenty of glue, should do the trick.

All the various parts of the stick can be replaced at home if replacements are available, and most suppliers will provide rubber handles, thongs, heads and wedges. If you are replacing a thong, it should be 19–20 inches long depending on the size of your hand (as a guide, a large man's hand may need a 20-inch thong, while a smaller hand, possibly a woman's, one of less than 18 inches). When replacing the thong, take care to put it well down each side of the handle of the stick, and preferably secure it with glue as well as nails or staples. The staple gun is a useful tool here.

a *When fitting a new head to a cane, a wedge should be fitted into the oval hole in the head to expand the end of the cane, as shown.*

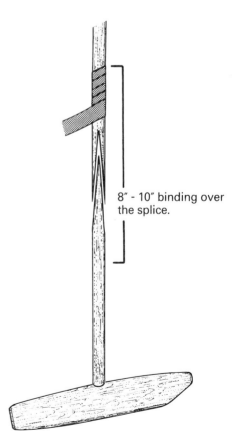

8″ - 10″ binding over the splice.

b *When repairing a stick, a splice should be cut across the line of the head in the same direction as the wedge. The glued splice is then covered with strong cotton tape and painted to seal it and hold it together.*

When fixing a new rubber grip, it is not advisable to glue the grip to the wooden handle. If you do, it becomes very difficult to replace when it is worn. Instead tack it to the top of the handle, by one end, next to the thong, and wind it firmly down the grip, overlapping 50 per cent with each turn. Secure the bottom to the cane with a small tack and cover the end with plastic tape to finish it off tidily.

The more professional carpenter should be able to splice canes together to make use of a broken stick. Cut a 'V' some 3 inches long into the head end of the cane, with the point of the 'letter' pointing away from the head. Then cut an inverted 'V' into the handle end so that it matches up and fits together with the 'V' in the head end. It is important that the top of the 'V' runs across the line of the head and not along it, so that the cane continues to take an even strain throughout its length after the stick has been spliced. Put down the line of the head, the splice would probably peel open as the strain of repeated hitting took effect. Take care to get each 'V' exactly square, so that the handle finishes precisely square with the head and not twisted. Glue the splice and then bind together with strong nylon string, or cover with vellum or wide cotton tape to form a supporting sleeve. A point to note is that it is much easier to drill out the head and use a thin piece of extra cane for the splice rather than using the original broken

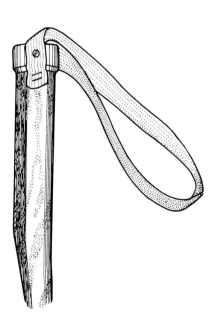

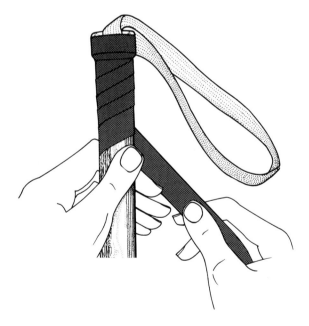

c *The stick handle is made by binding and glueing a second piece of wood to the stick cane and the thong should be attached with both tacks and staples for extra strength.*

d *The rubber grip is attached at the top of the handle with a tack, and twisted tightly down the length of the handle, then tacked at the bottom and finished with plastic tape.*

one, and then you can refit the head in the normal way and thus retain the original stick length.

You must remember that the balance of the stick is of vital importance. To give you some indication, the shaft and handle of an experienced man's polo stick should weigh approximately 10–11 oz (280–310 g) and the head 6–7½ oz (175–210 g), giving a total weight of about 16–20 oz (450–560 g); a well-balanced stick for an experienced woman should have a handle of approximately 8½–10 oz (230–275 g) and a head of 5¾ oz (165 g), giving a total weight of about 14–16 oz (400–450 g), depending on personal preference.

It is also vital to bear in mind that it is not just the weight of the stick but also the speed of the stick head on impact with the ball that imparts distance to the ball. A combination of maximum speed with the greatest weight will hit the ball further than a heavier stick wielded at a slower speed. The new fibreglass shaft with less wind resistance goes through the air considerably faster than cane and therefore hits the ball further.

After the polo season store your sticks carefully for the next year in a cool, dry place, preferably hanging from the thong, and make sure that the cane is vertical. A little linseed oil on the mallet head will stop it from drying out if the climate is very dry.

POLO BALLS

Polo balls were originally made from bamboo root in Persia, India and the Far East, and this material is still widely used in those regions. Different countries tended to use whatever local wood was available and proved to last reasonably well. The balls are painted white for better visibility on the dusty grounds of the Middle East.

Argentina still uses its local tipa wood, which has, for many years, been one of the best sources of wooden balls, while England developed the willow ball, which proved excellent to drive, but did not have the best lasting capabilities. An English composite ball from compressed wood pulp, called the jura-ball, had a period of success during the evolution of the plastic ball, but has recently dropped out of production.

Over the last twenty years, the Americans have developed the plastic ball, manufactured by thermo-plastic injection moulding now refined to the extent that it produces balls weighing within 5 g of 4 oz, and no more than 3½ inches in diameter, which have been almost universally accepted as being the best balls available today.

SPURS

American spurs have proved to be the most popular design in polo, quite heavy so that they sit down on the boots, and with round rowels, about an inch across. These are kinder to the horse than sharp rowels, which are forbidden in polo. It is important that any spur you use should have a rounded end to prevent spur marks on the flanks of the pony. In the heat of the game you can kick quite hard, and it is forbidden to play with anything which might hurt the pony. Round-ended cavalry or English dressage spurs are possibly the most popular if the American style are not available.

WHIPS

Polo whips should be from 36 to 39 inches long depending on personal preference, running down to a fine-tapered end enabling you to use the whip over the top of your leg, hitting the horse on the rump when you are holding the whip with your reins in your left hand. A short whip with a flap on the end, as used in racing, is not very practical for polo.

KNEE-PADS

There are several different styles of knee-pads on the market. Without doubt the long knee-pad stretching from above the top of the knee, with a well-padded bend over the knee itself, and reaching down to about 6 inches below the top of the boot, has proved to give the most effective protection. The knee-pad is secured with three straps – one above the knee, one below the knee and one around the outside of the top of the boot – and strengthened with an extra layer of protection over the front of the knee-cap. In conjunction with a manufacturer, I have designed a knee-pad specifically for maximum protection, flexibility and comfort, while keeping you close to the horse, which is now widely available.

Another type of knee-pad is the short style. This covers only the knee and is secured by two straps, above and below the knee. Finally there is the cricket-style knee-pad which protects the shin bone right to the ankle and may prevent that unwelcome and very painful bruise from a ball, a hard ride-off, or a mallet head on the shin, through the boot.

POLO BOOTS

Boots designed particularly for polo were first developed in Argentina but are now manufactured in England. They have a strong zip down the front to enable the boot to be removed easily at any time. The boots now available in England have been strengthened on the outside especially for polo. Traditionally brown has come to be the accepted colour for polo because black boots used to leave black nugget on the opposing players' white jodhpurs which didn't wash off quite as easily as brown. Historically brown lace-up cavalry boots were worn for polo, and today hunting-style brown boots are fairly common, but more and more people are turning to the style specially designed for the game. Also quite popular in the USA is a high-topped Western riding boot which has been lengthened to form a full-length riding boot particularly designed for polo.

CHAPS

Chaps – zip-on leather over-trousers which are very comfortable and convenient to wear when schooling horses – are available in most equestrian centres. They are not, however, accepted wear in polo for official tournaments.

GLOVES

It is advisable, and essential in wet weather, to wear gloves in polo. They protect the fingers from other sticks, enable you to retain a grip on both the reins and the polo stick, and prevent blisters on the right hand from the continual use of the stick and friction from the handle.

It has proved difficult to find the ideal glove for polo, the problem being the wear in the palm of the hand and around the thumb, and most leather gloves are not durable enough to last for any length of time. Golfing gloves, available from golf club professional shops, have proved reasonably successful, as have racquet ball gloves, though the latter can be a little thick. Strong, thin leather is the best material, and the most successful glove I have found to date is a flying glove, the quality of which seems to enable it to outlast most others on the market. A specifically designed polo glove made in England has also been reasonably successful. Thin cotton gloves are cheap and are reasonably effective for practice, although they don't give quite the same 'feel' on the rubber-handled stick.

JODHPURS

White jodhpurs are officially the correct polo wear, and the stretch-cotton type currently on the market have proved to be the most practical. Beware of jodhpurs which are reinforced on the inside leg with any form of suede or chamois leather: unfortunately this doesn't appear to stand up to modern washing methods but becomes hard and finally disintegrates.

POLO CAPS

Perhaps the most important part of one's polo equipment is the polo cap or helmet. A polo cap is designed for safety and one of the rules of the game is that no player shall play without a protective polo cap or helmet, which must have a chin-strap. In India and Pakistan the turban is frequently seen on the polo field and has been officially sanctioned as the only acceptable alternative to the hard hat. In Britain the new polo caps coming on to the market these days have to meet the British Standards Institute's safety standards.

Polo is a stylish game and designs for polo caps have traditionally reflected this. Based originally on the pith helmet, cap designs have recently tended towards the motor-cycle helmet style because of its greater protection and safety benefits – hence the emergence of the various helmets in America. However, the Duke of Edinburgh polo cap – cloth-covered and stylish – seems to have withstood the test of time and is currently used fairly consistently throughout the world. James Lock and Co., of St James's Street in London, have been selling their internationally recognised Duke of Edinburgh-style polo cap for many years. The Lock Polo Cap is currently available in many different colours, which have largely replaced the original white because they do not show the dirt and keep their appearance for considerably longer.

In America, the USPA (United States Polo Association) have, since 1978, been working on the development of a safer polo cap, and Wayne State University has established, at considerable expense, a testing machine that attempts to simulate the shocks to the head that might be received in a fall. In layman's terms they have developed a severity index (SI), which was originally set at 1500 and has recently been reduced to 1180, giving a person an 85 per cent chance of minimal brain damage if dropped on his head from a height of 2 feet without head protection. Many of the polo caps on the market have been or are currently being tested. At the time of writing, significant advances are being made in polo cap technology and up-to-date information will continue to be made available by the USPA.

Although padding is vital, one of the important discoveries is that a polo cap, no matter how safe, will not protect the wearer from all eventualities, and the objective of the player should be to try to obtain the safest cap available and to ensure it fits properly, with a chin-strap that will not come off or break in a fall. When you are buying a cap take care that the fittings inside it are not fixed with studs or rivets that project into the cap and could prove dangerous in a fall. Also ensure that the chin-strap goes right over the top of the cap, with an adjustment on the top, or that the cap is fitted with a safety chin-strap with a dual-point attachment on each side.

More emphasis should be put on the way to roll in a fall in order to minimise the risk of severe injury, and a section on the art of falling – from painful practical experience – appears later in the book.

My own experience of some twenty-five years in polo and a lifetime of equestrian activity is that if a good cap fits properly, has a secure chin strap and has a face-guard, it will protect a player from most eventualities, not just falls, and if players know the rules and play the game with the basic idea that *nothing* is worth a serious accident, the game will be played in the spirit in which it was originally conceived.

FACE-GUARDS

The controversy over whether the face-guard is right or wrong in polo is on-going. In my experience face-guards have never contributed towards any injury received in a fall or collision and, without doubt, I have witnessed numerous occasions on which they have saved both the eyes and teeth of players, not to mention their good looks. It is my firm and positive opinion that face-guards are essential to learner players and all my family wear them on the polo ground. Since we have been playing we have experienced several incidents where the face-guard has prevented many potentially serious injuries. I myself have worn one since I first saw the wire-style face-guard, when I came to England in 1973. I have since designed and manufactured the face-guard which is currently used on Lock and Duke of Edinburgh-style polo caps, and these are now widely available throughout the world. It is obvious that a face-guard, however designed, cannot protect one from every eventuality in polo. However, the face-guards that are currently on the market have certainly proved capable of preventing the vast majority of facial accidents received in the game from both the stick and the ball, which can hit you so quickly that you never see it coming. At present a new design is being tried which specifically aims to give more protection, particularly for female players, and any such aim is to be applauded.

Pippa and Katie Grace wearing Lock helmets and face-guards designed by Peter Grace.

In the USA where, I understand, a player was seriously injured by the fracturing of the Caliente face-guard, that model was withdrawn from production. But it had been made from a material that could not withstand some of the stresses associated with the game. The guard I have designed is very strong, has proved very successful and, so far, no example has ever been returned to me under any circumstance. While it is not impossible that the wearing of a face-guard could contribute to a freak accident, I have never heard about one, and over the many years that face-guards have now been available in England, they have frequently proved beneficial to a player's safety.

SADDLERY
The Saddle

The correct saddle for polo is determined largely by taste. The important features of a saddle are its ability to assist in giving a rider the correct 'seat', and permitting closeness of the knee to the horse, thus enabling the rider to impart his instructions more clearly. The less padding that comes between the knee and the horse's shoulder, and the freer the leg is able to work around the horse, the better the saddle should be for polo, and this is obvious in the development of the Argentine polo saddle. However, the rider's security is very important and individual riders sometimes prefer a small knee-roll in front of the knee rather than having the saddle completely flat on the shoulder of the horse. I personally find that the Barnsby 407 polo saddle, which has a narrow pommel, a reasonably flat seat and a small knee-roll, gives the average rider greater security, suits my particular requirements and is the most comfortable saddle for my style of riding in polo.

The Argentine saddle is very flat, with only the flap between you and the horse, and very light, having been developed from the English 'hunting saddle' by Argentina's top high-goal players, so it is very well suited to the good rider who is really confident and needs to twist away out of the saddle while still 'feeling' the horse.

Stirrups and Leathers

It is very important to have strong stirrup leathers for polo because of the considerable stress exerted by changes in direction, especially when leaning out to play a polo shot. Buffalo hide is now widely accepted as the best stirrup leather, preferably $1\frac{3}{8}$ inches in width; it does stretch, but continues to maintain its strength.

Stainless-steel stirrups, 5 inches wide, or $\frac{1}{2}$ to 1 inch wider than an average boot, are essential in polo, because of the risk of metal fatigue in other metals – I have had a stirrup break in half, and it was supposedly stainless! In the USA they have developed a safety stirrup which is strong, hinged in the centre of each side and looks quite good but the weight could disturb the very sensitive communication with the horse which is established through the heels.

Girths and Surcingles

Atherstone-style leather girths have proved excellent, and the Argentine folded leather cinch girth enables the player to tighten the girth very tightly to keep the saddle in the right place. Complete leather surcingles should also be used. Neither the girth nor the surcingle should have any elastic inserts because elastic can break unexpectedly. Although widely used in racing, the girth and surcingle do not have to cope with the extremes of stress incurred in polo. At the polo school we have recently tried out some coloured nylon-web surcingles, which are very strong and are proving quite good. Cottage Craft has produced

The Barnsby polo saddle showing where to position and attach the leather surcingle, breastplate and running reins.

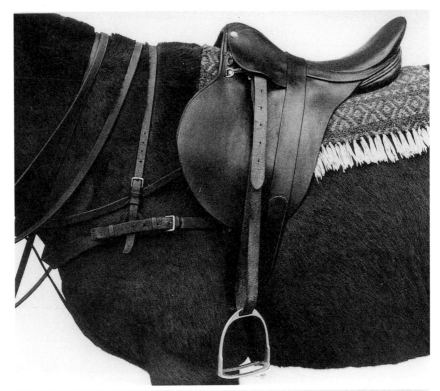

The Argentine Carpincho saddle with nylon surcingle. Note the straighter cut, giving less knee control, and the increased padding in the seat, which reduces the depth of the seat.

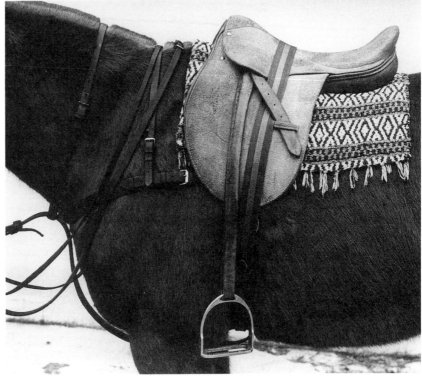

a padded nylon girth which has also shown itself to be very effective. This soft girth is often used to prevent a horse from getting girth galls – sometimes a problem in polo. When a gall develops, as a result of rubbing, a sheepskin sleeve can be put around the girth for extra protection, but the horse should not be ridden until it has healed.

Tack

Other essential saddlery items are: a breast-plate to keep the saddle forward, and a standing martingale running from the girth, between the horse's legs, to a strong cavesson noseband on the bridle.

It is important that all leatherwork in the bridles, martingales, breast-plates and other tack should be of substantial quality to withstand the rigours of polo. Breast-plates should be wide across the chest and adjustable by a buckle, each side of the horse, in front of the girth straps. Martingales should be adjustable half-way between the chin and the neck-strap. An additional adjustment is sometimes put in front of the girth on a buckle which operates up and down the main strap in an adjustable loop to the girth. Buckles should be of good quality and strong enough to cope with the extreme stresses of the sport.

Bridles

All bridles should be basically cob-size, with strong straps and a reasonable length of adjustment down the cheek-strap to accommodate both quite large and reasonably small ponies. Bridles should have double reins of ⅝- and ¾-inch leather to accommodate the bits which are used in polo today. The well-equipped tack room will have an assortment of bits available for the various ponies one might have to play: snaffles, a double bridle, barry and big-ring gags and various pelhams (the difference in severity of action is controlled by the length of the cheek-pieces), a vulcanite pelham and possibly a rubber gag. Bits should range from 4¾ inches for a small pony to 5¼ inches across the mouth-piece. A bit should not be too narrow, otherwise it will pinch the cheeks. A detailed analysis of the individual effects of the various bits mentioned is included on pages 102–108.

Care must be taken to have rubbers on the bits, particularly gags, to prevent a pony's mouth being chapped in the corners by the rubbing of the rings on the bit. An eggbutt gag, which is a fixed-ring gag and has a different action on the horse's mouth from the other gags, is certainly beneficial if problems like this occur.

Nosebands

A drop noseband, a flash noseband (a combination drop and cavesson noseband, with a strap fitted to the front of the cavesson), a rope noseband and a grackle (a special drop noseband used in racing) are all useful additions to the polo player's equipment. Care should be taken to ensure that the drop noseband is not fitted too low on the horse's nose as this can reduce his air intake, which might cause him to start to pull. Another important item is the running rein, which can be beneficial when used on the right pony, but one should always remember that this can be detrimental to neck-reining in many cases.

BANDAGES OR BOOTS

It is essential for polo ponies to have protection on all four legs whilst playing the game and it has been the subject of debate over the years as to which has proved the more effective – bandages or boots. I believe that bandages give the most support and boots give the most protection. Therefore, one should consider the speed and style of polo played when making a choice between the two. As a universal rule, the faster and more open the polo, the more importance should be placed on support. The closer and slower, the more choppy the polo and the more important it is to protect the horse's legs from being hit by either the stick or the ball.

Polo bandages are widely available and, provided they are long enough, thick enough and at least 5 inches wide, they will give adequate protection and certainly more support than boots. Polo bandages must be put on carefully (see page 154) and should not be left

The alternative form of protection for the horse's leg is a thin support bandage (left) worn underneath a protective boot (right). The buckles or velcro ties should always be on the outside with the straps pointing backwards.

on for too long, as they could restrict the flow of blood within the leg.

The new composite boots, made of moulded plastic and obtainable in many colours, are excellent for the protection of the legs – a solid blow with a stick is not even felt through them – and more people are using these for low-goal polo, which involves more body contact and therefore more risk of bruise-type injuries. Composite boots can cause rubbing and may be used over thin bandages if this occurs.

Coronet boots made from leather lined with felt or, more recently, moulded plastic, provide further protection below the fetlock, particularly when used on the front legs, and can save the horse from injury or damage resulting from over-reaching or treading.

Boots are much more difficult to keep clean in the wet weather in which we often have to play in an English polo season, so we have used bandages very successfully over the years in the school. It is very important for the bandages to be fastened with Velcro and not the old-fashioned string ties, which used to cause pressure damage to the tendons if not secured at the top of the leg. In matches it is vital to secure the bandage with bandage straps or plastic sticky tape around the Velcro fastening to eliminate the risk of a loose bandage – on a front leg this can be very dangerous if the horse treads on it at speed.

Tail bandages possibly look the smartest on the polo ground, but these days, for ease of grooming, the tail is often tied up with plastic tape. Certainly the most practical solution to the tail problem for everyday polo is the Argentinian tail knot (see page 158).

HALTERS AND HEADCOLLARS

While basically cob-size, the polo pony's headcollar should be large enough to accommodate the bridle as well, so a cob-size halter is normally big enough, provided there is a nose-strap adjustment; otherwise a full-size halter is advisable.

The lead-rope should be strong enough to stand a pony pulling back, and secured to the halter with a spring clip in case of emergency. It is customary to use string between the pony lines and the halter rope for safety if the pony pulls back. However, this is a matter of preference, depending on whether a pony could cause more problems if he gets loose or if he tries to pull back. A polo pony is trained to stand placidly in the pony lines while waiting for the game.

The Argentine-style headcollar has been developed specifically for polo, with a large loose strap around the nose, held in place by straps up each side of the nose to a ring in the centre point between the eyes. Two straps from the centre ring go just below the ears to a strong and tighter strap behind the ears and fasten with a loop and plaited crown knot below the nearside ear. Though sometimes a little too long for a pony with a small head, these halters fit easily over the bridle and, when specially plaited from strong nylon 'bale string', they are virtually unbreakable and outlast anything else, while securing the horse comfortably. The experienced Argentine gauchos call the English-style

The polo ponies pictured in the snow in St Moritz are tethered with Argentine headcollars. These are made from rawhide and are extremely durable.

Pictured here is the more traditional halter.

halters 'cow headcollars' and do not like using them at all. It is quite amusing in the Ascot Park polo yard, where a number of grooms are trained for polo, to see the experienced gauchos carrying their special bundle of headcollars around with them in case they are 'borrowed', as everyone likes them better once they understand how to put them on.

THE CHAIR AND THE WOODEN HORSE

While certainly not the most essential part of a polo player's equipment, both the chair (my students would say: 'You mean a kitchen chair?') and the wooden horse have proved beneficial teaching aids and training facilities for polo players the world over. A chair is ideal for

Peter Grace giving Bob Hooke his first lesson on the chair. The offside forehand is being 'fine-tuned' with emphasis on the correct shoulder and hand position.

helping you to get your swing in the groove and teaching you the basic body position while hitting the polo ball; and the wooden horse combines the actual sitting on the horse and the body position while in the saddle, which is essential for the correct hitting of the ball.

The ideal chair to use for practising polo is one with solid bars along the ground joining the bottom of the legs: these prevent the chair from sinking into the ground. In the school we are now using two milk crates stacked upside down, one on top of the other, instead of the chair, to make a more stable hitting platform, which has proved ideal.

When using the 'crate platform', the length of stick is important: for a woman it should be 45–48 inches; for a man, 46–49 inches, depending on how tall the person is. With a single crate the stick length should be 35–40 inches.

The primary objective of both of the wooden horse and the chair is to get the polo swing into a consistent groove to establish the best method of hitting the ball. Consistency can then be related to direction and distance. Selecting the correct length of stick will enable the body to twist into a consistent position on either the horse or the chair.

2

HITTING

BECAUSE POLO is about scoring goals and winning, hitting is arguably the most important facet of the game. Certainly in your early polo you will probably derive greater pleasure from hitting the ball well than from anything else in the game. I have vivid recollections of some possibly lucky, but certainly marvellous shots in my early polo career which gave me untold pleasure and I am sure all of the players who get bitten by the 'polo bug' have the same recollections.

The importance of consistent hitting cannot be over-emphasised and therefore this introduction to the subject will be both detailed and precise. Polo is a game of precision, and the learning process leading to a correct swing must be followed very precisely. If you have a problem with your swing at any time, revert to the chair (see page 40) and practise your movements until they are precise.

The teaching method I have proved over a number of years on the chair is described here in a number of steps, which, if followed to the letter, will enable you to learn the correct method of hitting a polo ball from studying this book. As it is easier to read from a chair than the back of a horse, I suggest that the time taken to perfect the swing before you get on the horse will be more than repaid by your progress later.

HOLDING THE POLO STICK

There are several steps involved in holding and swinging the polo stick correctly and these are outlined below. To save repetition, the instructions given here are complete – for both riding and practising on the wooden horse or the chair. The important thing about the polo swing is that, no matter where you do it, the swing remains the same, and as you follow the instructions and suggestions given here, the repetitive nature of the learning process in polo will become apparent. This is essential to programme your mind (the 'polo computer') so that the correct actions and reactions instinctively occur during the various plays in the game.

The Thong

To put the thong on correctly, take the polo stick in your left hand, holding it vertically in front of you just above the grip, with the stick head pointing down, away from you, towards the ground. Place your right thumb through the thong, away from you, and pull the thong out sideways to the right so that the thong and the stick form a right angle. Tuck your fingernails in towards your tummy button and, passing your hand in between the thong and the stick, take hold of the stick as though you were shaking hands with it. The thong will then be around the back of your hand without a twist in it – if you have a big hand and the thong becomes twisted because you have put it on incorrectly, it may be too tight.

The thong is *not* used as a support around the wrist to enable you to hold the stick tighter. It should be quite loose so that you can swing correctly and fold into the follow-throughs and the balancing motions which will evolve as you learn to swing the stick properly.

The Grip

As in the illustrations, the polo stick is held very similarly to a tennis racquet, with the 'V' of the finger and thumb pointing down the line of the shaft and out through the end of the stick head. Take the polo stick as though you were shaking hands with it. The thong is looped around the thumb and then curled around the back of the hand to the top of the stick so that the thong acts only as a secondary method of holding on to the stick if your grip becomes dislodged.

(Left) The position of the grip for the offside fore-hand and nearside back-hand. The 'V' between the finger and thumb points directly away from the end of the handle of the stick. The little finger should rest on the ledge as shown.

(Right) The thong should not be tight and should not twist as it goes around the back of the hand. The handles shown should be much wider under the fingers to give a better 'feel'.

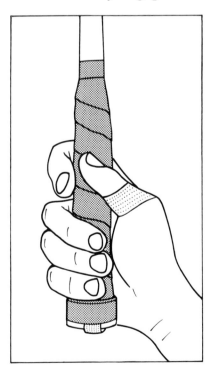

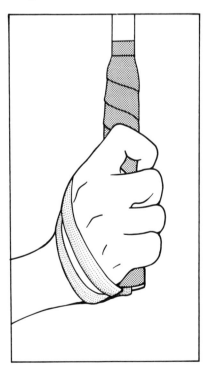

The Little Finger

It is essential to maintain the correct grip on the polo stick, and, as you hold your stick in the 'carry' position (see below) the little finger should feel the ledge at the bottom of the handle at all times to ensure that the stick is the correct length in your hand. There is no other way to tell that your hand is in the correct place or has slid up the handle of the stick, leaving it perhaps 2 or 3 inches shorter in your hand. In the latter case you would miss the ball without knowing the reason why. You have to rely on your little finger: there is no other way that you can programme this information into your 'computer'.

There is a school of thought that believes in holding the little finger curled up under the bottom of the stick so that you can hold the stick in the three remaining fingers, thus achieving a greater whip through the ball in the 'two' position (that is, when the head makes contact with the ball). Unless you are very strong, you will find that the stick has a tendency to over-cock at more than 90 degrees in the 'one' position (when your arm is braced back behind your head, before you begin the descent into the 'two' position, see page 30) and therefore your consistency of hitting will be affected because you will not be able to bring the stick down in the same plane with every swing. Also, there is a tendency to lose the stick off the vertical plane when it becomes over-cocked in the 'one' position, with the action of the arm and wrist becoming unco-ordinated, and the stick head drops outside the correct plane over the top of the ball.

The alternative grip for the offside backhand and nearside forehand. The stick twists clockwise half an inch in the hand and the thumb moves half-way around towards the flat side from the back. Take care not to twist the stick too far and put the thumb straight on the flat side.

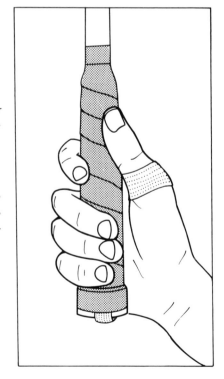

The Alternative Grip   Although not essential, the alternative grip for the nearside forehand and the offside backhand is well illustrated. The stick twists about 15 degrees anti-clockwise in the hand, with the sharp edge at the front of the grip coming further around into the bend of the fingers, and the thumb moves around the grip to a position down the 'corner' of the back of the grip, as shown. The weight and strength of the thumb in this position adds considerably to the power which can then be generated into the stick head, thus greatly increasing the distance achieved with these shots.

The 'Carry' Position   When you are cantering around the ground, the most convenient position in which to carry the stick is in front of you with your forearm horizontal and the stick comfortably carried about a foot in front of your nose and slightly to the right, straight up and down, and held in a relaxed manner in your hand. From this 'carry' position you can make a balanced swing for any shot, and if the ball suddenly bounces sideways, you can get the stick down on either side of your pony very quickly to hit the ball. You can also rest the stick on your shoulder to relax the arm, but never start the swing from the shoulder because you will lose the balance of the stick.

THE BASIC SHOTS   There are four main polo shots, two on each side – the offside forehand and backhand, and the nearside forehand and backhand. Together with cut shots and pull shots, both forwards and backwards, on either side

This diagram shows where to hit the ball in relation to the horse.

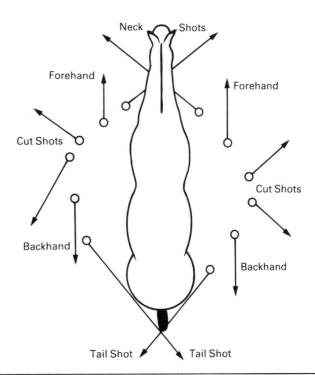

Neck   Shots

Forehand   Forehand

Cut Shots   Cut Shots

Backhand   Backhand

Tail Shot   Tail Shot

of the pony, and one or two shots that are played square of the pony, they comprise the repertoire of shots which will be covered in this chapter.

The basic shots will be broken down into three positions – 'one', 'two' and follow-through – to enable you to follow more readily the concise instructions to hit the ball, and the action photographs which

a The offside forehand. *Stuart Mackenzie begins his wind-up after dropping his stick backwards past his shoulder from the carry position.*

b *His horse is collected as he concentrates on the ball.*

e *Stuart hammers the heel of the hand down through the ball, uncocking his wrist just before impact –* **the 'two' position** *– as the stick passes his toes. The ball zips away . . .*

f *. . . as the arm begins the follow-through. The arm flows along the line of the shot, up to the horizontal, and . . .*

accompany the descriptions will illustrate the body and arm positions that you must achieve.

The Offside Forehand   Probably 70 per cent of all of your polo shots will be played with the offside forehand, so it is of paramount importance in your game.

c *The stick is balanced as he prepares to punch it back.*

d ***The 'one' position.*** *Lifting his stick high, he twists his body into the brace position with his left shoulder over the top of the ball. The wrist is cocked at a 90-degree angle, with the elbow locked firmly straight.*

g *. . . the elbow begins to bend to take the speed out of the stick. Note the right shoulder position at the extent of **the follow-through.***

h *The wrist and the grip relax in the follow-through, allowing the stick to rotate in a small circle, as the elbow folds back into the carry position.*

The 'One' Position

From the 'carry' position you pull the stick back past your ear, trying to keep your head as still as possible, punching your arm backwards in a line over the top of the pony's tail and into the air as high as you can while still remaining comfortable. You twist your body into the 'brace' position, so that your left shoulder points towards the ball and you bring your left hip forward with your right foot down the line of the girth in the stirrup and your weight over your right leg, while your left heel twists outwards from the horse, forcing your left knee into the flap of the saddle to hold you on the horse. Your stick is held at a 90-degree angle from your straight arm; this is called the 'one' position (see page 29d).

Of vital importance is the absolute straightness of your elbow and the 90-degree angle of the stick to the arm, while the stick must be held vertically in your hand. Your shoulders should be twisted parallel to the line of the horse so that your stick in the 'one' position is in a vertical plane over the top of the line of the ball.

The 'Two' Position or Hitting the Ball

Unlike in croquet, the polo ball is hit with the side of the stick and you will have noticed that the head of the stick is fixed to the handle at an angle, so that you can get the head parallel with the ground while the stick is held in your hand at a slight angle to the ball. When holding a polo stick correctly, your fingernails will be on the side of the handle on the same plane as the front face of the stick head and thus they become the direction finders for your offside forehand polo shot.

To hit the ball: from the 'one' position proceed to drive the heel of your hand down through the line of the ball, parallel with your horse, rolling the wrist at the bottom to hit the ball with the front face of the stick (the 'two' position), pushing the stick through, so that your arm comes up into the horizontal position in front of you to begin the follow-through, before you relax the grip on your stick a little. You flow straight into the follow-through, holding the stick firmly between the first two fingers and thumb, relaxing the heel of the hand, and letting the stick roll around in another rotation, again parallel with your horse, bending your elbow and folding your arm down and back into the 'carry' position.

The ball should be hit approximately 18 inches to 2 feet wide of your big toe when your foot is in the stirrup in the correct riding position. As you screw down to hit the ball, your foot goes down the girth. This will get your leg into the proper position and you should hit the ball about 2 inches forward of the line straight into the ground from the point of your right shoulder, especially if you wish to loft the ball when taking a penalty.

Balance the Stick

All of the better players in polo have developed the art of timing the ball to a high degree, and in the offside forehand they often use a preliminary wind-up which I call 'balance the stick'.

Once the basic swing has been mastered, it is time to try to put together this preliminary wind-up, which changes a 'reverse' movement – pulling the stick back past your ear – into a forward, flowing movement in the same direction as your horse is travelling, thus increasing the speed of the stick head at point of impact with the ball, and therefore increasing distance and the ability to loft the ball.

The analysis of timing is essential to an understanding of why this action is effective. The basic timing of all the shots remains the same. If you read out loud: 'Balance the stick, one and one, two and follow-through,' the time you have taken to say it is the same as the timing of your stroke to hit the complete forehand shot. (The timing for the backhand is much the same, though the stick does not pause in the 'one' position.)

Balance the Stick Action

From the 'carry' position, drop the stick head back past your shoulder and, keeping the hand low, roll the wrist and let the stick flow around in a circle, pulling the arm back into the 'one' position as the stick comes up past your ear. The pause – 'and one' – to gain the maximum extension of the arm in the 'one' position sets you up to hit the ball to perfection.

Practise it initially on the chair or the wooden horse without the ball, and say it out loud in time with your actions to achieve the correct timing. Move on to the horse when your shot is flowing smoothly, and get it right, again without the ball initially, so that you 'programme the polo computer' first. The timing will then remain the same, and with stick and ball practice on the horse you will soon relate the timing to the distance you need to be from the ball as you start to 'balance the stick'. This distance must increase as you approach the ball at a faster speed in the game.

The Offside Backhand

First remember to change the grip, putting the thumb down the corner of the stick. This shot is the offside forehand in reverse. Start with the follow-through to where you hit the ball in the 'two' position, and then flow up into the 'one' position to complete the follow-through for the backhand. The shot stops there and you fold back down into the 'carry' position.

To take you through the shot: from a low hand in the 'carry' position, drop the stick head forward next to the pony's ear, rolling the wrist forwards and tucking your elbow in, and lift the hand up above the height of your nose as the stick rotates around parallel to the horse in a tight, vertical circle over the top of the line of the ball. As the stick comes up and over the top, start your main down-swing by hammering the heel of the hand hard down the line of the ball, rolling the wrist at the bottom as you hit the ball, with the knuckles pointing 15–20 degrees wide of the straight line backwards. Let the arm follow through

a The offside backhand. *F.D. Walton is seen here, coiled up in* **the 'one' position**. *His body is braced with his knees gripping the saddle. His eyes are fixed firmly on the ball, looking over the top of his shoulder and his wrist is cocked at a 90-degree angle. The stick should not stop in this position, but flows into the main swing.*

b *He has begun his down-swing, his elbow is still bent ready to release the power at the last moment and he is driving the heel of his hand down through the ball, with the point of the stick cutting through the air first. His wrist remains cocked until two feet from impact when he is ready to roll it through. He then uncocks his wrist and powers the stick head through the ball.*

and your body twist back and upwards into the 'one' position for the forehand shot.

It is important to avoid hitting the ball straight backwards to ensure that the players coming down the line behind you are not able to meet the ball.

Don't hesitate to follow through nicely and smoothly and let the shot flow. Remember that in this shot you should try not to hit the ball at the top of the swing by twisting the stick head across the line of your horse and folding your wrist in towards your knee. You should 'hammer' the heel of the hand through the ball and the stick automatically rolls at the bottom to hit the ball out 15 degrees, with a natural shot. When you want to check whether your arm is functioning properly, think of the karate chop – backwards and down through the line of the ball – bracing your wrist and hitting the ball with the heel of the hand. This will achieve maximum power through the ball and hit it as far as possible for the effort and energy expended.

The firm and crisp use of the wrist in this manner, as in all your shots, will enable you to time the shot much better, because you retain

c *The ball is hit behind the heel of the player –* **the 'two' position** *– with the elbow locked and the player's head steady as he watches the ball.*

d *As he completes the swing with* **a follow-through**, *you can see his body position and his head have remained constant, and he is now coming up to the 'one' position of the forehand. His wrist has rolled right through the shot, ensuring that the ball travels in the desired direction.*

complete control of the stick and the stick head at all times.

The straight back shot and the tail shot are executed by hitting the ball fractionally later and rolling the wrist further through the ball. Remember that the direction finders in the back shot are the knuckles, and you hit the ball in the direction in which your knuckles are pointing at the time of impact. Having decided whether you want to cut or tail the ball some 10 yards before you get to it, you time your shot accordingly. For a cut shot the ball should be hit level with your stirrup and about 3 feet wide, and for the tail shot, as late as possible behind your stirrup, swaying backwards through the ball and letting your wrist roll around the back of your pony. And don't forget to follow through in every shot with a nice big sweep and a supple body, letting the arm flow in the direction you want the shot to travel.

The Nearside Shots

To enable you to understand the mechanism of the nearside shots, there is a simple exercise which has proved very effective in training the body to understand the position it has to twist into, so you can swing parallel with your horse and hit the ball on the nearside. These shots are certainly a little more difficult to begin with because you have to twist right across the line of your pony to hit the ball. It is essential, therefore, that you obtain maximum twist of the hips, which hold you in the saddle, and your shoulders, to enable you to swing the stick parallel with your horse.

The 'Open/Closed' Exercise

Practise while you are sitting on a quiet pony, if necessary getting your groom to hold the horse's head; better still, practise on a wooden horse. Let go of the reins, twist your hips and put your left arm straight back from your shoulder towards the pony's tail. Put your right arm with the stick cocked at 90 degrees vertically up in front of you, over the horse's ears. This is the 'open' position. Swing the stick downwards in a line parallel with the pony, skimming the ground at the bottom, and right up to the top of the swing backwards, letting it come forward on a vertical plane in front of your nose, pointing up towards the sky at a

An important exercise for the two nearside shots is *the 'open'* . . .

. . . *and 'closed' exercise*. It helps the body twist position on the horse and can be practised on the chair, the wooden horse or a very quiet horse.

45-degree angle, with your hand next to your left eye and your elbow tucked in so that your forearm is pointing up to the sky as shown. There is a right angle at your elbow, between your upper arm and your forearm, and another right angle at your stick, between your forearm and wrist, and the stick. This is the 'closed' position. It is the uncocking and straightening of all these angles at the bottom of the swing which imparts the maximum speed to the stick head and delivers the power that you generate as you hit the ball.

At the same time as you swing the stick around into the 'closed' position, bring your left arm under your right arm and push it across to the right-hand side of the line of the pony, as though you were neck-reining away from the shot (see page 100). You started in the 'open' position; you are now in the 'closed' position.

Do the exercise ten times, swinging your stick from 'open' to 'closed' and back to 'open' again, moving your left arm accordingly. Let the stick flow, on a vertical plane, parallel with the line of your horse. The benefits of this exercise can be explained in two seconds – you are doing both the backhand and the forehand swing on the nearside in one exercise, and you will train your body very rapidly to feel and absorb the positions you have to get into to hit the ball effectively, both forwards and backwards. It is an essential part of the programming of your 'polo computer'.

Both of the shots on the nearside are hit when the ball is positioned about 18 inches further forward than on the offside. This is because your right shoulder comes forward as you twist your body into the nearside shots. It is very important to hit both of the nearside shots early.

In the photographs of this exercise you will see the position your body has to achieve to obtain maximum benefit.

The Nearside Forehand

The 'one' position you must achieve for this shot is the 'closed' position in the exercise described above. From the 'carry' position, twist your body to the left, bringing your right shoulder forwards and pushing your right arm across your body, so that your elbow is pushed over to the left of the line of your body, with your right shoulder pointed towards the ball. Your upper arm should be parallel with the ground and the forearm should be pointed nearly straight up towards the sky. The wrist should be cocked at 90 degrees, and the stick should be held with the thumb down the shaft as in the offside backhand grip (see page 27), at 45 degrees to the ground. The stick should be pointed parallel with the line of your horse and not very far outside the line of your shoulder. Your left arm must push the neck rein over to the right to hold the horse away from the ball. Remember that to achieve the maximum benefit from the swing, the stick should travel parallel with the line of the forward momentum of your pony.

From the 'one' position, the stick head travels right over the top, and

a The nearside forehand. *The player is coiled into the 'one' position. His right shoulder is turned well round, pointing at the ball, with his left twisted back towards the pony's tail, and his rein hand is held steady.*

b *Beginning his down-swing, the player drives the heel of his hand down the line of the ball while keeping his wrist cocked and the head of his stick travelling through the air point first. The player's head is well positioned directly over the ball.*

by forcing the heel of the hand around and then down through the line of the ball, rolling the wrist at the bottom, you will impart maximum impulsion to the ball. Then let the stick flow forward and up into the follow-through position, allowing the wrist to break and cock up into a 90-degree position at the top of the swing. This takes the speed out of the stick and you fold down into the 'carry' position from there.

The Nearside Backhand

If you have practised the 'open' position in the 'open/closed' exercise described on page 34, you have already done the simple nearside backhand action. Start from the 'open' position, with your hand up in front of you and the stick cocked in your hand at 90 degrees, flowing directly back over your left shoulder, in the same plane as the direction of your horse; this is the 'one' position for the backhand. As you flow into the 'closed' position, you complete the offside backhand shot. Practise going from the 'carry' position to the 'one' position several times before you start your shot, remembering that the higher you lift your hand, the more power you will get into the shot as you drive the heel of your hand down through the line of the ball, rolling your wrist at the bottom to hit the ball and cutting it 15–20 degrees wide of the straight line backwards from the horse. (See pages 38–39.)

c *The stick head is rolled through the ball with the player's head remaining stationary above, and the ball is hit well in front of the player's toes.*

d *The stick flows into a lovely follow-through.*

Don't forget, as you let the follow-through flow round past your shoulder, to bend your wrist outwards so that the stick head doesn't come over the top and hit the horse in the ear. The follow-through can also be folded round underneath the left arm and over your back, particularly if you wish to pull the ball around your horse's tail.

The Argentinian Wind-up

The wind-up makes this shot possibly the most elegant in polo and, if practised, it can be carried out very successfully by most players. It is easier to do if you are naturally supple; if you find it difficult, stick to the simple swing. It is not easy to do justice in words to this lovely flowing motion that moves with the forward momentum of the horse, and the ball may be hit 20–50 yards further too because, with this wind-up, the speed of the stick head is considerably increased at the point of impact with the ball. It also looks really 'professional'.

The initial motion is achieved from the 'carry' position by putting the arm slightly to the right, bending the elbow and allowing the stick head to flow sideways and backwards in a circular motion away from your left shoulder but not down below shoulder level. As the stick comes behind the shoulder in line with the forward momentum of the pony and over the top of the ball, you start to put the power into the shot,

a The nearside backhand. *The start of the Argentinian wind-up. The head of the stick flows into a position over the ball as the body twists around into position with the shoulders parallel to the horse. The right elbow is bent and the rein hand is steady. The rein hand in this photograph should be pushed further to the right to neck-rein the horse away from the ball.*

b *The arm and stick are lifted higher as the power starts to 'flow' into the stick head, with the elbow remaining bent. The player's head must stay very still over the ball,*

directing the stick head over the top and downwards by driving the heel of your hand down the line of the ball, rolling the wrist at the bottom and thus achieving the backhand cut shot out 15–20 degrees to the left from the straight line parallel to your horse.

It is important to understand when performing this shot that the balance point of your stick is centred on the balance point in the shaft, rather than up and down in a line with the stick head over the top of the ball. The stick is very easy to control in any direction if its balance point moves in the same direction as your forward momentum.

c *Stuart begins to hammer the heel of his hand down through the line of the ball. Again note the stick head travelling through the air point first. Although his brace position is allowing him a clear swing through the ball, he should perhaps have more contact with his left knee and the saddle.*

d *The lovely follow-through seen here is for the nearside backhand around the tail. The right shoulder has been pushed round after the ball as the body is rotated through the shot.*

To achieve the maximum power in the swing, the stick should be balanced at all times and, as you shift the balance point in this swing from half-way down the shaft to the stick head by the input of your power, the head should be flowing on to the plane vertically over the top of the ball. It is the 'whip' generated by the transfer of balance and the straightening of both wrist and elbow through the ball which generates the extra power. The actual striking of the ball and the follow-through are the same as before.

Having taken you through the four main shots, we will move to the wooden horse, or the chair, where you can first put those shots into practice and begin to get your swing 'in the groove'.

USE OF THE CHAIR

To maximise the benefit of the chair, you need a bag of about fifty balls, the correct length of stick (45–49 inches; or, if using one milk crate, 35–40 inches) and a position which gives you about 75 yards of hitting range. A tennis court with tennis balls proves very effective for winter practice, and a 27–31 inch stick to collect the balls is also useful.

Take up your position standing on the chair with your feet slightly apart as though you had a horse between your legs; your feet should be square to the front of the chair and your toes about 3 or 4 inches behind the front legs of the chair. When you start to swing your polo stick you must assume that the legs of the chair are the legs of the pony and therefore all your swings should be parallel with them. It is also a good idea to position a 'goal post' directly in line with the side of the chair so that you can practise hitting accurately. Before you begin to hit the ball, loosen up with some practice swings.

Where it all begins – Katie teaching the offside forehand.

When you have loosened up, put the ball about 18 inches out from the chair; it should be level with your toes if you are practising the offside forehand, or level with your heel, or a little further back, for the offside backhand. On the nearside, both shots are hit from about the same spot: 6 inches in front of the left foot and about 18 inches out from the chair.

Practise hitting the same shot until you are happy with it, and if you are just beginning, take alternative swings with and without the ball. When you try to hit the ball, you don't concentrate as carefully on the swing, so if you are teaching yourself, swing for quite a long time and ensure that you get your swing 'in the groove' and comfortable before you start actually to hit the ball.

Progress through each of the four main shots, working through your bag of fifty balls for each one, if possible, but you should have at least twenty goes at each shot before moving on to the next if you are to gain the maximum benefit from your practice.

USE OF THE WOODEN HORSE

The wooden horse has proved to be an important facility in the training and development of the correct polo swing. It enables a player to hit more shots in a short time than any other facility, and speeds up reaction time, hand-eye co-ordination and the ability to handle the stick. The wooden horse is a very adaptable animal – you won't have to feed it, and it can be fitted into almost any average-sized room. My own experience of using one for training, with a 42–inch stick, has proved that there is no problem with adapting to the bigger stick when starting on the horse outside.

In a good climate, of course, the horse can be open to the sky and you have to move only your saddle in and out. It is advisable to cover an outdoor wooden horse with a roof in England, with a ceiling high enough to swing a full-size stick. The standard specifications for a wooden horse are given on page 43.

While pages 27–40 give specific details of the various strokes, and the photographs show the techniques for hitting the polo ball from a horse, there are particular aspects of hitting which can be developed and improved by practising on the wooden horse. The main object of using the wooden horse is to develop your polo swing. So, before you start, make sure that your stirrups are the correct length. Avoid the temptation just to climb on the horse, swing your polo stick and hit the ball. You are not going to achieve your objective unless you take the trouble to go through the steps listed below.

Once you are mounted, and have your stirrups adjusted, start to swing your stick and loosen up. Perhaps do some limbering exercises, twisting and bending. Below are several excellent exercises to perform on the wooden horse. They help both to make you supple and to get your body into the right position to enable you to do the strokes correctly.

Peter Grace using the latest in high technology – the computerised mechanical practice horse – to work on his tap shot at Ascot Park.

Stuart is seen here teeing up the ball for a nearside forehand shot on the traditional wooden horse at the Guards Polo Club. Many of the good players use the wooden horse frequently to perfect their swing and speed up their reactions.

1 Put your arms horizontally out from your shoulders and alternately swing your left arm to your right toe and your right arm to your left toe.
2 Twist your hips, pointing your arms alternately forwards and backwards horizontally, and parallel with the horse.
3 Bend your body forwards and backwards alternately, touching your head on the pommel and on the back of the horse.
4 Reach round to the back of the saddle with each hand in turn, twisting the hips to strengthen the 'brace' position. Both the right and left knees tuck in behind the knee-roll on the saddle flap and anchor you in the saddle while you lean out to hit the ball. An amusing riding

Dimensions for the con-
struction of a traditional
wooden horse. Imitation
grass may be used to
cover the floor.

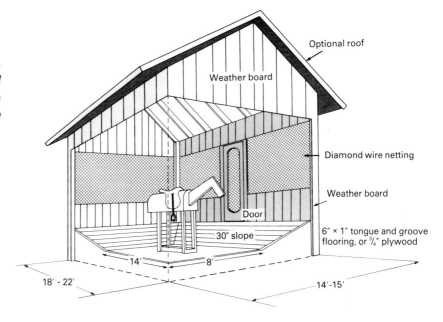

Optional roof

Weather board

Diamond wire netting

Weather board

Door

30° slope

6" × 1" tongue and groove
flooring, or ³/₄" plywood

14'

8'

18' - 22'

14'-15'

instruction, 'Squeeze zee knees', exactly illustrates the objective. Take
care not to strain too hard if you are not very fit.

Now, having loosened yourself up, swing your stick parallel with the
horse on both sides so that you accustom yourself to the height of the
wooden horse and feel the swing of the stick. You should check the
length of your stick – when it is resting on the ground, it should come
up roughly to just above the hard bone on the outside of your knee. It is
usual to use a slightly longer stick on the wooden horse which doesn't
give as you lean over to hit the ball – the wooden horse is built
fractionally smaller than the live version, so you will achieve this effect
if you use the same size stick. If you are making your own wooden
horse, ensure that it is about 2 inches lower at the wither than the real
horse on which you normally play.
    When you start to hit the ball, place it 18 inches to the left of your
right toe and tap it straight forwards to establish a rhythm in the roll of
the ball. Every wooden horse varies in construction, and you will find
that the ball rolls in a different way on each one. Try therefore to take a
minute or two just to relax and understand the way the ball is going to
roll before you really start to hit it.
    When you are ready, place the ball precisely and prepare to hit it
with a full swing. Starting with the offside forehand, practise the shot
at least twenty consecutive times before you move on to the next shot
you want to practise. Be sure to play each of the main shots enough to
increase your consistency before moving on to the next. Both forehand

shots should be hit accurately and straight. Both backhand shots should be cut into the corners of the cage of the wooden horse. Be precise in trying to gain accuracy and consistency in all your shots.

On the offside forehand it is the fingernails, and on the backhand the knuckles that control the direction of your shot, while on the nearside it is reversed – the fingernails control the backhand and the knuckles the forehand. While swinging on the wooden horse, concentrate particularly carefully on hammering the heel of the hand down towards the ball as you swing the stick down, rolling the wrist so that the fingernails control the ball in the right direction, just before you hit it. Don't brace your wrist back and try to hit the ball at the top of the swing, in the 'one' position.

The stick head should point in a forwards-and-backwards direction parallel with the horse for most of the time during the polo swing. Only at the bottom, as you hit the ball, and at the top, as you actually bring the stick back past your ear, should the stick head turn to a lateral position. This is possibly best explained by putting the stick down and opening your hand flat, with the thumb sticking out sideways at 90 degrees. In the swing, the hand should travel with the thumb pointing upwards, straight up in the air at the back of the swing, rolling the wrist at the bottom, to straight up in the air at the front of the swing. If you do this several times, you will feel the bones in your arm lining up with your hand correctly and, as they come through at the bottom of the swing, your hand will be square across the horse to hit the ball, and then the wrist will continue to roll through to the horizontal position in front of you, when the thumb is pointing straight up into the air and the wrist starts to break into the follow-through.

Combine this action with the whip generated by the uncocking of the wrist, while squeezing the stick tightly just before you hit the ball, and you will achieve maximum power and speed in the stick head and therefore hit the ball the maximum distance.

You will frequently hear: 'Don't hit the ball too hard.' In my opinion that is not necessarily good advice. Once the swing is disciplined and the stroke is in the correct plane, you should try to hit the ball as hard as you can if you want to hit it as far as possible. Your swing should then be controlled by the distance you need to hit the ball, and there should be no restriction on the power that you can put into any particular shot, always remembering that rhythm, timing, smoothness and control parallel to the horse come before power. In recognition of this, I award a bottle of champagne to anybody I am training who can hit the ball 100 yards from the chair, and I hope I don't get besieged with letters from people telling me that they have been able to hit a ball that far! You have to take a lesson at the polo school to prove it in front of the expert eye. If you are successful, I'll be delighted to 'pay up'.

The 'Brace' Position

While practising on the wooden horse, take care to ensure that you achieve the correct 'brace' position in the saddle when pulling the arm back into the 'one' position before you hit the ball. This means that you must twist your hips on the horse to hold yourself correctly in the saddle and achieve the tightest seat while hitting the polo ball. The hips should twist to approximately 45 degrees off the line of the horse, as you get into the 'one' position for each shot, with the outside hip forwards. The weight should then be down the inside leg – always the leg next to the ball – and the outside leg should be twisted outwards from the horse to accommodate the twist of the hips, with the knee squeezed firmly into the saddle to hold you on to the horse. Try not to

The perfect brace position *for the offside forehand. Note the right foot is correctly pointing almost forwards, forcing the knee into the saddle. The left leg is twisted into a firm bracing position and the shoulders are well round.*

point your inside toe out at a greater angle than necessary. In order to achieve the right brace, some instructors recommend twisting both toes in a parallel direction so that the inside toe sticks straight out from the side of the horse. This takes the inside knee away from the saddle and therefore you lose essential contact with the horse, and it can run over the ball. You can also hit your toe instead of the ball.

One of the main points to remember about riding, particularly in polo, is that whatever you do with your body should not interfere with the contact that you maintain with your horse through your hands. The better the player, the more capable he is of dissociating his riding from any effect that his strokes may have on his horse. As long as he remains balanced and at one with the horse, he can hit the ball in any direction, while simultaneously obtaining control over another player using his horse as an extension of himself.

The 'High-Tech' Swing

To help you to understand the concept of the correct hitting of the ball, try the following: perform half-swings with the thumb pointing backwards as you take the stick back, sideways as you come through the line of where you would hit the ball, and forwards with your arm coming up to 45 degrees and cocking the wrist a little each way. This will give you the correct plane on which your arm should travel in order to hit the ball properly. It is essential that the bones of your arm travel in the same plane as the polo stick head to deliver the maximum power to the ball, and they must do so both before and after you hit the ball. This theory has been proved by computer plotting of the swing of two top polo players, Memo Gracida and Podger el Effendi, and a 1-goal player, Allan Connell, which is illustrated on page 47.

Playing the Ball

Once you have completed the necessary practice for all the main shots on the wooden horse and you are happy with your consistency and accuracy of hitting, you should relax and enjoy the fun of 'playing the ball'. This means playing every shot you know as the ball rolls into the correct position around the horse. You must speed up your reaction and concentrate on the preparation for each shot very quickly. You should play the rolling ball. You should also play each shot instinctively as the ball gets into the position for that shot. This part of your training is essential in speeding up your reaction time so that when you start to play for real you instinctively start to prepare yourself for a shot much earlier. The good players seem to have so much time to accomplish the plays they set themselves up for and this is achieved by anticipation and fast, instinctive reactions to any given situation.

While playing on the wooden horse, take care that the ball doesn't come back at dangerous angles from any part of the cage and hit you on the rebound. When you play the ball, it is great to have it occasionally jumping up into the air because it sharpens your instinctive reaction to hit the ball in the air – the good player can hit the ball absolutely

Two pictures from a com-
puter study of the polo
swings of Allan Connell,
Memo Gracida and
Podger El Effendi. (top) A
frontal view – every
fourth frame was used so
that the elapsed time
between each impression
is about one twentieth of
a second. Note how far
the high-goalers lean out
and observe especially the
evenness of Gracida's
stroke. Also note their
lack of mobility in the
right knee and thigh and
the line between their
shoulder and hip. Con-
nell, on the other hand, is
far less steady. The stick
head comes off the plane
as each player 'balances
the stick'.

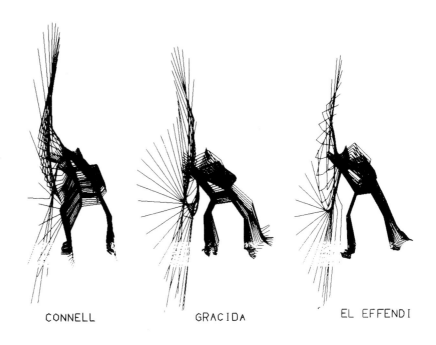

CONNELL   GRACIDA   EL EFFENDI

(bottom) A side view of
the same sequences.
Compare the three hit-
ters' wrist angle, the angle
of their mallets at the
stretched-arm position
and the elbow position in
the final phase of the
stroke. Also note the ball.
The first image was shot
prior to impact and the
other two afterwards. In
Connell's case the mallet
head travelled faster than
the ball even after impact,
which shows the impor-
tance of uncocking or
'snapping' the wrist firmly
and very fast through the
ball.

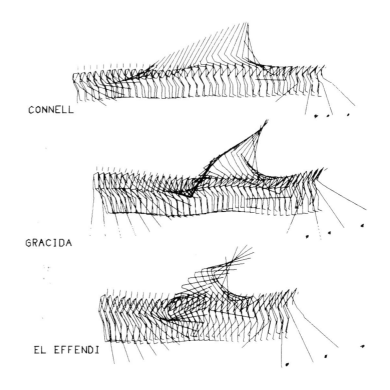

CONNELL

GRACIDA

EL EFFENDI

anywhere at all. This can be practised on a wooden horse if the ball flies, but do take care, particularly with a hard ball, because if you do hit yourself in the back of the neck it will be uncomfortable and could be dangerous. On the small wooden horse I use a soft plastic ball to avoid any possibility of injury.

POINTS TO REMEMBER – THE WOODEN HORSE

- When you start to hit the ball, perform each of the four main shots at least twenty times consecutively – forehands and backhands on each side. This really establishes your swing 'in the groove'.
- Concentrate on making your swing as vertical as possible over the top of the ball.
- Ensure that your arm in the 'one' position is absolutely straight.
- Be sure that your wrist is straight so that the stick is cocked and forms a 90-degree angle with the arm in the 'one' position.
- Pause in the 'one' position in the offside forehand so that your arm becomes completely still and the stick is balanced directly over the top of your head, more or less over the top of the ball.
- If necessary, take alternate swings, one hitting the ball, one without the ball, to concentrate on the swing.
- Concentrate on hammering the heel of the hand, not the finger-nails, down through the ball. Only towards the bottom of the swing does the stick automatically start to roll with the arm and you hit the ball squarely.
- In the offside forehand it is the fingernails and in the backhand it is the knuckles that control the direction of the shot; the reverse is true for the shots on the nearside. As you hit the ball, point these 'direction finders' exactly where you want the ball to travel and follow through along that line, as near as possible.
- In practising the basic forehand shots, you should endeavour to hit the ball straight. However, in practising the backhand shots, the ball should be cut at about 15–20 degrees to either side. You then learn instinctively to hit the shots in the right direction.
- The follow-through should be along the line of the stroke and must not come across the line of the body. The little twirl on the end of the forehand is vital to the direction of the follow-through and to ensure that the stick does not come across the line of the body.
- It is the uncocking of the wrist at the bottom of the swing just before the impact with the ball which generates the maximum speed to the stick head and therefore the maximum distance to the ball.
- Do not let your wrist pass a line between your shoulder and the ball before you have hit the ball, otherwise you will hit it into the ground.
- Remember always that, to hit consistently, your little finger must be able to feel the ledge at the bottom of the stick at all times.

SHOTS FOR THE MORE ADVANCED PLAYER

After practising the four basic shots, you will want to move on to the shots which turn the amateur into the budding pro. Practise these shots first on the wooden horse, if available, and always take care not to hit your horse in the legs.

The Under-the-neck Shot

Play the under-the-neck shot from either side of the pony the same as the basic forehand except that in the 'one' position you should be pointed 45 degrees out to the side of your right shoulder for the offside shot, and slightly across the line of your pony for the nearside shot, because this is the direction in which you want to hit the ball.

When riding to the ball, ride 1 foot closer to the line of the ball than in the ordinary forehand. You hit the ball about 1 foot earlier, further in front of you, and drop your chin down towards the mane of the horse to enable you to reach the ball.

In the 'one' position your arm should be pointing in the opposite direction from that in which you wish to hit the ball and, as you get better, you will find that you can hit the under-the-neck shot square or even backwards on the opposite side as some of the really good players do. In attempting this shot don't forget that you must ride your horse over the top of the ball to enable you to hit in the reverse direction. You must also hit the ball even earlier than before, and take care the flow of the stick is wide of the left foreleg of the horse, as you fold your arm under the horse's neck.

Tail and Cut Backhand Shots

In the tail shots on each side, hit the ball as late as possible and roll your wrist through the ball to put it around your horse's tail. The offside tail shot is a very important one in setting up a positional play for your team.

The cut shots are played much earlier and, depending on how square you want to play them, you should try to have the 'one' position as square as possible to the line of the horse, so you have to lean out of the saddle and hit the ball considerably wider than normal.

In all of these shots the basic swings remain the same, and it is only by practising on the wooden horse or stick and balling on your pony (see page 59) that you can understand how to let your movements flow and thus achieve the correct timing.

Tapping the Ball

What lifts the good player above the average is an ability to control the ball to a position where he can hit the big shot effectively. Tapping the ball is essential to a good game of polo.

While you must hit the ball away as soon as possible, it is pointless to swing at it and miss, or to hit it to the other team. You should control the ball to a position where you can hit it away, with exactly the right direction and strength, to find your team-mate. Remember to keep a firm wrist and always tap the ball at least 5 yards to enable you to retain possession of it. The good player rides and taps the ball instinctively, but this can be practised, and during stick and ball you

a **The offside under-the-neck shot**. *The player balances the stick.*

b *He begins to move the stick out to the right with the same basic swing as for the offside forehand. Note the arm moves approximately 45 degrees wide of a line parallel to the horse's mane.*

a **The nearside backhand tail shot**. *The player is starting to do the Argentinian wind-up.*

b *For the nearside shots the whip is held flat against the horse's shoulder. The player is beginning to rotate his body into the 'one' position.*

c *Punching the stick out into the 'one' position, he leans forward in the saddle while gripping tightly with his knees.*

d *The follow-through flows under the neck of the horse with the wrist rolling firmly through the ball for extra control and accuracy.*

c *The face of the stick is too open and the player's wrist, though cocked at a 90-degree angle, is braced too far back as he prepares to hammer the heel of his hand down through the ball. His elbow has straightened too early and his body hasn't yet fully twisted around in the saddle.*

d *The player has rolled his wrist well to tail the shot and has rotated his body into a good position to hit the ball, with his shoulders parallel to the horse.*

should spend a certain time each day tapping the ball to control it, concentrating particularly on mastering a tapping cut shot which enables you to change the line and therefore retain control of the ball.

Remember to change the angle of the ball and then the angle of your horse. Also, remember to ride independently of hitting the ball so that the forward momentum of your horse relates to the forward momentum of the ball and the direction of it. To control the ball and the play at the same time, your 'computer' should feed in all the essential information – the directions of the players (particularly in the opposing team) and the direction in which you need to control the ball to enable you to pass it to one of your own team.

The swing should be quite short and very crisp for tapping the ball accurately; avoid the tendency to tap the ball too late rather than too early. Pull the stick head back to just behind your horse's hind leg, your wrist cocked at about 45 degrees and very firm, then push your arm slowly forward through the line of the ball, uncocking your wrist firmly through the ball and letting your wrist roll up into a half follow-through position. The stick should flow parallel with the horse and preferably down the line of the ball.

To achieve maximum tapping consistency, your stick needs to travel down the line of the ball, and you change the line of the ball, then your horse. Once the ball has been cut or pulled, you change the line of your horse and proceed straight to the line of the ball. When controlling the ball it is vital to watch it carefully, so assess the positions of the players early and then watch the ball while you tap it and then proceed to hit the big shot.

It is essential to hit away as quickly as possible. If you can hit the big shot, never tap the ball. On the other hand, if the ball hasn't rolled kindly and you need to control it before you can hit it away, control the ball first, but then hit it away as soon and quickly as possible.

The Square Shot

Once you have mastered the above shots there are others that are worth practising. One such shot is the square (or flick) shot, which can be played on each side of your pony. For the offside square shot you put your thumb down the flat side of the stick handle and the 'one' position requires leaning forward, pushing your arm across under the neck of your pony as far as you can. You must hit the ball early – very early – to avoid hitting your horse as he brings his front leg forward in the gallop stride. On the nearside, the arm goes under the neck of the pony from the left, while you lean well out to the left and cock the wrist in the backswing, then play the forehand square under the neck, leaning forward as before. (See pages 54–55.)

These shots are valuable to use when scoring a goal from fairly close in front and while travelling parallel to the goal line, and should be hit with the intention of making the ball travel about 20–25 yards. They should be played very crisply with an extremely firm wrist.

Alex Vilella demonstrating a beautiful body position for the square shot on the nearside. The best his opponent can do is hope he misses it. Rangitiki won this match with Alex and it is easy to see why with style like this.

The Millionaire Shot

The millionaire shot (aptly named because it is customarily played by the patron of the team in order to score goals) can be very useful but should be played with great care to avoid hitting the pony in the legs. Timing is very important and possibly, as you hit the ball, you should aim to hit the ground at the same time to prevent your stick from travelling into your pony's legs. (The millionaire may have enough ponies for this not to worry him so much!)

Trick Shots

Occasionally you will see a very good and athletic player playing a shot after he has been ridden over the ball in an offside swing that goes right round the back of his pony, hitting the ball between the two horses when he has been ridden off, and hitting it forwards. This amazing shot enables the player to retain possession of a ball which he would otherwise miss completely.

Another useful shot, again accomplished with practice, is the shot behind your horse's hind legs forward and to the right, executed when you have been ridden over the top of the ball from the nearside. You must lean way back and drop your stick down the line of the ball – you

a The square shot from left to right. *Starting with the stick hand dropping under the horse's neck, the player leans forward in the saddle, pushes the heel of his hand as far as possible to the left and rolls his wrist into the 'one' position.*

b *As he starts the down-swing, Stuart places his head directly over the ball to maintain concentration during this difficult shot.*

e *The face of the stick opens into the 'one' position before the wrist is rolled firmly through the shot.*

f *The follow-through is almost into the 'one' position for the nearside under-the-neck shot. Stuart has used a lot of wrist strength in this shot.*

c *After hitting the ball to the left, the shoulders are rotated as the follow-through is stretched down the line of the shot. Note the position of the thumb down the shaft, which gives added power.*

d *Preparing the stick face for* **the square shot from right to left.** *The body position in the saddle is very important. For each shot the player twists his body into the brace position.*

may not be able to see it at the time, but you instinctively know where it is, and hitting this type of ball is part of the difference between the three- and the eight-goal player!

Take care when trying these shots that you don't twist so savagely that you throw your horse off balance and bring him down.

**HITTING
TECHNIQUES
Hitting at Goal**

The good player will regularly practise hitting at goal. An excellent way of doing this is by setting up two sets of quite narrow goal posts 100 yards apart and taking the ball down in a series of half-shots, repeatedly scoring goals at each end. Goal-scoring ability is mainly a matter of confidence, and the more you practise, the more confident you will become.

When approaching goal, make the last shot at goal as easy as possible, but take care not to cross the line and therefore foul anybody who is coming hard behind you in an effort to prevent you from scoring. The approach to goal is of prime importance: try to centre the ball as early as possible. It is obviously much easier to hit at goal from 30 yards directly in front than 5 yards from the back line and 30 yards wide of the posts, and yet even good players make this mistake.

When hitting the cut and under-the-neck shots at goal, endeavour either to cut the ball away or pull it under the horse's neck inside the far post rather than the near post. The good players will always hit the ball wide on the opposite side, whereas the low-goal player hits the ball wide on the nearside. Aim to hit the ball about 2 yards inside the far post on each of these shots.

Lofting the Ball

The principle of lofting the ball is to ensure that the trajectory of the stick head at the point of impact is slightly upwards, rather than slightly downwards. Therefore you must uncock your wrist and force it through the ball faster, and slow the speed of your arm down a little before impact. Remember that the higher the handicap, the slower the swing, and this is a very obvious feature of the polo swings of the very good players, particularly when they take penalties and therefore wish to loft the ball. The whip generated by the uncocking of the wrist through the bottom of the swing, just before the point of impact, will increase the ability to loft the ball.

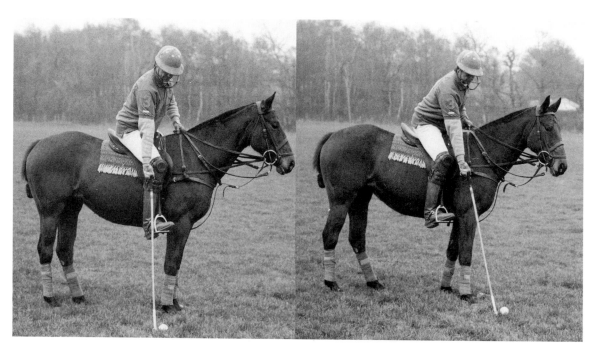

a The lofting technique. *It is very important that you strike the ball in such a position that your eye, shoulder, hand and stick head are in a straight line parallel with the ball should you wish to hit a superb shot straight along the ground.*

b *If you require a more lofted shot, strike the ball further forward, slowing the arm to let the wrist push the stick head in front of the arm and hitting the ball just on the way up from the lowest point.*

Secrets of Long Hitting

The most important feature of long hitting is the player's ability to time his shot. This, coupled with the maximum wind-up extension, and the uncocking of the wrist timed to achieve the maximum speed of the stick head through the ball, provides the basis of the long hitting swing. While strength plays a big part in long hitting, it is not necessarily the major requirement.

Most good players 'balance the stick' as the first movement in the powerful offside forehand shot, to achieve the perfectly timed stroke.

The Rolling Ball

Always remember to hit down the line of the rolling ball to improve your consistency. If you can meet the ball down the line and play all your shots with the basic swing down the line of the ball, you will greatly increase your chances of hitting the ball.

Note that when you wish to change the angle of the ball you should ride straight and change the angle by cutting or pulling the ball, then change the angle of your horse. If you try to change direction on your horse at the same time as hitting the ball, your 'computer' will not be able to function as effectively and you therefore considerably decrease your chances of hitting the ball.

Always meet the ball with a full swing exactly down the line. The elbow should be straight.

MEETING THE BALL

The Percentage Shot

During a game it is very important to remember to play the shot which gives you the greatest percentage chance of success. If you have to score a goal at an acute angle, establish very early in your mind which shot you intend to play and then prepare your body to play that shot earlier than normal. Try to swing down the line of the ball to play the shot and cut or pull the ball accordingly.

Watch the Ball

Probably the main reason why players miss goals is that they lift their eyes off the ball to look at the goal just as they are about to hit the shot. You should know, particularly when approaching a goal shot, precisely where the goal is and, as you come to the shot, especially in the last 5 yards, you should watch the ball until after you've hit it. Try to follow through with your arm directly towards the centre of the goal.

Remember the direction finders – the fingernails for the offside forehand and nearside backhand, and the knuckles for the nearside forehand and offside backhand. It is very important to remember instinctively those direction finders when heading for goal.

Ride Correctly to the Ball

Riding correctly to the ball is vital. You will improve your hitting consistency immensely if you concentrate on riding properly to the ball – 18–30 inches away for most shots – and then proceed to let your swing flow down the vertical line of the shot, following through in the direction in which you wish the ball to travel.

The Wrist Action in the Polo Shot

The major fault in all hitting, and especially in tapping the ball, is to 'flap' at the ball with a floppy wrist. This completely eliminates the power that is naturally generated in the arm and the pendulum swing of the stick and consequently, when you hit the ground or mishit the ball, it goes 2 feet instead of 5 yards and you lose possession. You must brace the wrist firmly and uncock it in the right plane, driving the wrist through the ball in a straight line from the shoulder to the stick head.

To help you understand this, try putting your hand at your side with your thumb sticking out sideways from your hand and just flap the wrist forwards and backwards. You will then see that the wrist has no power in it whatsoever. In the same movement, if you swing your arm backwards like a pendulum, roll and cock the wrist a little, again with your thumb sticking outwards, your thumb comes to the top pointing up towards the sky and, as you swing your arm forwards, you roll the arm and uncock the wrist so that the thumb again comes up towards the sky. This shows you the power you can achieve and is the best indication of how your wrist should operate when you are hitting and tapping the ball. The same basic wrist action applies to almost any shot in polo.

Play on the Boards

When approaching the boards, which surround some polo fields, with the ball, remember that the line will change as the ball hits the boards and make allowances.

If you are being ridden off, control your man further away than normal to give yourself room to run into the ball and hit it after it bounces away from the boards. If the ball is lodged against the boards, hit with a very firm wrist, and just inside the line of the ball, so that you hit it with the outside of the stick head. If possible, check up, tap the ball out and then play the big shot away. Take time while stick and balling to accustom your ponies to the boards, and always take a young pony over them two or three times as you come on to the field at the beginning of a chukka.

Beware of the unexpected when playing near the boards. With practice it is possible to create some clever plays as the line changes off the boards.

STICK AND BALL

'Stick and balling' is the term given to the methodical practice necessary when you graduate from the wooden horse to the polo pony out on the ground. The correct use of your 'stick and ball' time is essential to improve your play in the game. There are two main reasons to stick and ball: to improve your hitting technique until every shot is timed and hit to perfection; and to correct any problem which you may have with your horse.

When starting your stick and ball after loosening up, you should perform each one of the main four shots at least ten times consecutively, until you are happy with its consistency and accuracy. This is essential because, if you just go to the ball and hit it with whatever shot you happen to choose, you won't increase the efficiency with which you hit any of the shots. At the same time you are training your horse methodically to go to the ball perfectly, to play each of the shots in the same manner.

Once you are happy with the four main shots, continue to stick and ball with whatever shot you particularly need to set yourself up on the line to play the next shot. While stick and balling, remember that your thinking should be the same as if you were playing in a game. Don't change the line, continue on the same line along which the ball is hit and ride correctly to the ball for each of the shots. If the ball runs to the nearside, don't switch your horse hard left and then back right again; ride smoothly past the ball and play it on the nearside.

The more smoothly your horse goes, the smoother your hitting will be and therefore the more consistent and more accurate it will become. If you ride your horse on an 'S'-bend to the ball, it is most unlikely that you will hit it, because you throw your balance in different ways too quickly and the horse probably won't take you in the correct manner past the ball, or you won't swing down the line of either your horse or the ball. Your stick should travel on the same plane as your horse, in order to improve your consistency.

When training your horse, initially tap the ball away to the right in a circle, tapping it about 20 yards each time. This gives your horse the confidence to flow to the ball in the correct plane. It also helps you to become consistent in the control of the ball. Use a firm half-shot when tapping the ball.

This exercise plays an important part in giving a young pony confidence to go to the ball correctly and should be carried out on each side to ensure equal training of the young horse. Don't forget that the horse often cannot associate what you do on the offside with what you do on the nearside; the two halves of the horse's brain understand things independently, and one controls the left side of him while the other controls the right.

To maximise your polo practice time in an effort to improve your game, concentrate fully on only one technique at a time, preferably until you have mastered it and got it to a degree where you are satisfied with your play. Considerable improvement can be made in your game if you use your mind to work through the various aspects that you want to improve. Concentrate on them individually over a period of time and, as one is corrected, switch to the next – don't try to work on all aspects of your play at once. Mind concentration, when you are completely relaxed, is amazingly effective in improving your game, and has been proved so in many other sports. I have frequently found that polo students, who go away with certain problems which they think about, come back having worked out the solutions to them and find their improvement amazing from one day to the next.

POINTS TO REMEMBER – SUCCESSFUL HITTING

- The follow-through is important for two reasons. First, it takes the speed out of the stick so that you fold back into the 'carry' position in a stylish, relaxed manner without imparting to the horse the forward momentum you put into the shot; you thus make a smooth transition to the 'carry' position or into the starting position for your next shot. Second, it prevents you from following through across the line of your horse and up to your left shoulder – a common fault which prevents you from achieving a consistent and accurate forehand shot – because your swing becomes oval, around the line, rather than straight through the line of the ball.

- You must ride correctly to hit the ball each time and then you will achieve the consistency and accuracy for which you strive.

- In your hitting you should aim for consistency first and distance second. It is better to hit consistently and accurately 50 yards than 100 yards one minute and 30 yards the next, possibly not in the right direction. The team has great difficulty in reading the game if its high-powered player does not hit consistently.

- The most important thing about consistency is to develop the swing which is parallel with your horse's direction and with the line of the ball.

- Maximum distance in hitting is achieved by imparting the maximum speed of the stick head to the ball, not by increasing the weight of the stick. Also, a heavier stick is much more difficult to swing in the correct plane.

- Remember that the offside forehand encompasses the greatest number of shots that you will do in polo: the cut shot, the under-the-neck shot and the tap to control the ball for your big shot.

- When stick and balling, practise tapping the ball, because in a game you use this technique to control the ball to set up for the next big shot. To tap the ball properly you should always keep a firm wrist. Don't ride too close to the ball, and tap the ball in front of your big toe. If you are tapping at speed, always tap the ball a minimum of 20 yards to retain control, otherwise 5 yards is sufficient.

- It is essential to realise that, in all of your polo, certain shots give you a greater percentage chance of success than others, and you should therefore always go for those shots. This is of vital importance when playing your goal shots – there is often an option, and you must instinctively go for the 'percentage' shot. Practise this on the stick-and-ball ground in pairs.

- As you approach the ball you need to know, about 10 yards away from it, exactly what you intend to do with it when you get there.

YOUR FIRST GAME OF POLO

Confidence or your instructor should tell you that you are ready for your first game of polo. You should be confident in your ability to hit the ball reasonably consistently while stick and balling, and you should be confident in your ability to control your horse at all times, and in speeds at least up to three-quarter pace.

Before you play your first game, you should come out with an umpire or a coach and spend some time watching a game as the second umpire on the ground. You will thereby learn what actually happens before you charge in and try to play.

While I never rush a player to start playing the game, the whole object of anybody learning polo is to get out there and play, and once that confidence point has been reached I don't hesitate to let him begin. Too much time is often spent stick and balling when the player is ready to get into the game and start to enjoy it.

Many times I have been told that there is nothing quite like your first game of polo, and I can still remember going out on to the polo field for the first time and riding round wondering where on earth I should be. I watched the game go up and down past me and, after a chukka or two, I think I roughly knew what was going to happen next, but trying to guess where I should be in relation to that game was absolutely another story. I hadn't seen much polo at that time, so it was all brand-new; I should have gone out with an umpire first.

The Benefit of Coaching

In those days instruction in the game was virtually impossible to find and any player coming into the sport was basically given a horse and a stick and told to get on with it. Now I can probably teach in a week what it took me years to learn, and I would advise all players coming into the sport these days to try to get some coaching and help: the nearest polo club secretary will be only too happy to point you in the right direction. Trying to teach yourself to hit the ball in the correct manner instead of having lessons could well take you as long as three years, and even then you will probably learn so many bad habits that you will need the next three years to correct them. At Ascot Park the chukkas are always umpired, usually by a coach, who will explain a foul to a new player if he doesn't understand.

The importance of coaching in the game of polo is rapidly gaining acceptance in almost every country in the world. Polo schools have been springing up even in Argentina, the Mecca of the game, and it is interesting to note that, with the rapid increase in the popularity of the sport, schools and clinics – particularly in the USA – have been widely attended. More and more I am being approached by players who have been playing the game for some considerable time and have achieved quite high handicaps, but who have some problem with one aspect of their game and feel that the expert eye of a qualified coach might be able to help them resolve it. Sometimes just by correcting one or two small problems – possibly in the swing or in the way he thinks during the game – a player can play at least a goal better than his handicap, will be much more valuable to his team and will get more personal enjoyment and satisfaction from the game. Women particularly can benefit from such training, as I have found from coaching them at the school. Correct swinging of the stick is more important than strength when hitting a polo ball, and it is amazing how far some women can hit the ball when they swing the stick correctly. My daughters, for example, can hit a 60-yard penalty better than I can.

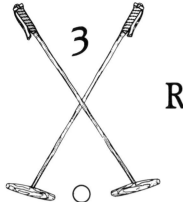

3

RIDING

BECAUSE THIS IS a specialised book on polo, it will not dwell on riding instruction. In these days of freely available riding lessons, the person who is interested in playing polo but is unable to ride should take riding lessons with a qualified instructor. It is not essential to ride well before you learn to play polo but, as you improve in the game, riding becomes more and more important. An illustration of this point is Sinclair Hill, the retired Australian ten-goal player, who when he was nine-goals took his first ever riding lessons with a top dressage instructor because he thought that he could become much more at one with his horse by learning the various aids used in dressage. Six months of these lessons improved his riding and his ability to communicate with his horse, and he went from nine to ten goals.

Starting from the assumption, then, that the person wishing to play polo has done at least some riding, the most important thing for him to work on initially is confidence in the saddle. Confidence is probably one of the most important aspects of the game of polo, and confidence in riding can be obtained only by actually spending time in the saddle. The more time you are able to spend, the more relaxed you become and therefore balanced and in harmony with the horse. This is basically achieved while out hacking, preferably with an instructor or somebody who is a better rider than you, who can give you the basic assistance to get you sitting in the right place in the saddle, and using the correct aids to do the particular exercises you must do with the horse. I use hacking as the main basis from which to work in the overall schooling pattern established for my own ponies. While walking or proceeding at whatever speed suits you in a hack you can achieve a considerable number of the basic responses required from a polo pony which are essential to his ability to understand your instructions in the game.

SPECIFIC EXERCISES FOR POLO

To ensure that your body is capable of achieving the flexibility and suppleness required for riding – particularly in polo – make a habit of performing the exercises described on page 42. These can be done on a wooden or a still horse or on a quiet pony at the walk – have him going on a reasonably loose rein in a straight line. Otherwise, your groom could hold the pony still while you are doing the exercises.

Exercises on the Ground

The best exercises to do on the ground are those which increase the twisting capability of your hips and pelvis and spine, and also strengthen and stretch the inside riding muscles.

1 Standing with the legs apart and knees straight, bend forward to touch the left toe with the right hand, then straighten up and, with arms horizontal, twist as far as you can to the right. Then perform the same exercise on the opposite side. Do each side ten times.
2 Standing straight, with legs well apart, bend alternate knees, putting the weight on the inside of the straight leg so the tension is taken down the inside riding muscle of the straight leg. This exercise is particularly effective for stretching and strengthening the riding muscles. (Another excellent exercise for this is to squeeze a soccer ball between your knees up to twenty times each day.)

SPECIFIC RIDING FOR POLO

Possibly the main difference between riding for polo and most other forms of equitation is that in the latter your seat is always square with your horse and the slight movements you make, known as 'aids', are used to produce the various athletic movements you want from the horse. In polo, however, your riding has to be completely flexible because a considerable amount of your time is spent not necessarily square with the horse, but loose and free, particularly in preparation for your shots, and twisted so that your body is travelling in a different plane from that of your horse. The graceful movements achieved by good players while hitting the ball, often at high speed, are a delight to watch, and the elegant combination of horse and rider plays a major part in the spectator's enjoyment of the game. For the experienced rider new to polo this difference is possibly the most difficult thing to understand initially, but the exercises described above and on page 90 will help you to achieve the positions required.

The basic polo riding style can be adapted from that which is most comfortable for the individual. It should be based upon a deep seat, nice and relaxed, and with the heels well down, muscles firm in the leg, and the body weight balanced on the thighs and slightly forward in the seat of the saddle. With the shoulders square to the horse and the heels just behind the girth, the left hand should make light contact with the horse's mouth, and be very flexible and independent of the body. The elbows should be bent at an angle of about 15 degrees and an almost straight line should be maintained at all times between the shoulder and the horse's mouth.

Your riding is done with the left hand on the reins because, with the stick in the right hand, you very rarely use your right hand on the reins. These days most polo ponies are played in double reins, and the best way to hold the reins is in the palm of the hand with the index finger separating the top pair of reins, one on each side, from the bottom pair. Just the one finger separates the two pairs of reins, so they are very easily adjustable: hold them in the right hand and slide the left hand forwards or backwards or release either pair of reins between the fingers to adjust the tension as you proceed. Spend some time practising the adjustment of your reins so that you rapidly gain confidence in handling them.

Your seat should be deep in the saddle, with your back slightly arched and your shoulders upright and relaxed, to help you to 'cruise' at any speed. As you increase speed forwards, your shoulders lean forwards in front of the point of balance and your heels go back, applying the request for impulsion with equal force just behind the girth, to drive your horse forwards faster, at the same time pushing the rein hand forwards to lighten contact with the mouth.

To slow down, the reverse applies: the shoulders swing back through the balance point, which is basically a line between your heels, your bottom and your shoulders. Your weight swings back, your hands lift up and apply slight pressure to the bottom or stopping rein, and the pony slows down or stops. Remember to apply very smoothly as much gentle pressure to the reins as you need to achieve the speed required.

To turn left or right, with one hand on the reins, you use a contra-rein movement, and the tension is taken with the outside rein along the pony's neck, pushing the pony's shoulders away from the rein. Meanwhile you exert pressure with the inside leg down the girth and the outside leg back 1–2 feet behind the girth, bending the horse slightly round your inside leg and applying impulsion with the outside leg so that he maintains his fluid movement in whichever direction you wish to turn.

The two ways of turning are: (1) an extended turn around in a big circle, where you use your neck rein forward with impulsion and your outside leg to drive the horse around as fast as he can run, with a minimum of collection; and (2) a short, tight circle where tension is exerted on the neck rein, so you collect the horse and your body comes well back, behind and inside the balance point and you turn sharply around, using the outside leg forcibly to push the horse into the corner and maintain impulsion into a firm and collected hand. The more you collect the horse, the more sharply you can turn.

SPECIFIC AIDS FOR POLO

The aids you have in polo are the left hand on the reins, a whip and a pair of spurs, and the use of your legs and your voice. Aids are used in polo in a more definite manner than in other forms of riding, but should always be applied smoothly and kindly to enable the horse to understand them more readily.

As in all riding the correct balance is of vital importance in polo and is essential to the smooth progress of the horse in the game. The voice can also play a considerable part in the smooth progress of the horse and, if used consistently with the same words and tone, the horse rapidly understands, you will save strain on his mouth and enable him to comply with your wishes gently and to maintain a relaxed attitude. The voice aids commonly used are a 'kissing' noise made with the lips or a clicking with the tongue to make the horse run faster, and 'Whoa' to slow him down. 'Steady' is an important word in my vocabulary too. The intonation of the voice is the important thing, not what is actually said, but it needs to be consistent for the horse to react correctly.

The horse should be encouraged to cruise regardless of its speed, and your body should reach the same position, just behind the balance point, at whatever speed you are cruising, which will make the pony relax. He thus quickly understands the need to maintain this speed, whatever it might be.

In polo as in all your riding your hands work in conjunction with your legs and voice to communicate your instructions to the horse. These, coupled with balance, are the aids you have for communication with your horse.

The Correct Use of the Whip

The correct use of the whip is to carry it and have it ready for the very infrequent times when the pony may need a little assistance or encouragement to, say, cross a stream or face an alarming situation or, on the rare occasion that he is totally disobedient, to remind him firmly but not unkindly who is 'boss'. This is more pertinent in the reschooling of horses – particularly thoroughbreds – than in the training of the young horse. But the wise jockey always carries a whip in case it is required. The whip is a very essential part of neck-rein training, and its gentle use down the neck of the pony reminds him that he should go away from the pressure of the rein.

The time when I believe firm but not unkind use of the whip is essential is to change the mind of a horse that bucks. When a horse starts to buck from sheer cussedness and not from high spirits (there is an important difference), you should continue to punish him with the whip until he stops. This is the only method I have found which actually retrains the horse and finally cures a bucking problem. You have to change the horse's mind and, unless he is bucking for some external reason, such as a girth pinching or a saddle hurting, or possibly pain in the back, making him realise that it is more uncomfortable to buck than not to is the only way to break this very bad habit.

The whip can also be used to advantage when a horse starts to run off the ball. As a gentle reminder to make him keep straight, a tap down the shoulder will assist the leg in ensuring that he approaches correctly to the ball, and responds to the leg and neck-rein properly.

It is the practice among some polo players and pony schoolers – especially the better ones – to carry a whip whenever they ride. There are times where this is definitely a bad thing for a horse, and the whip should be left behind. Bad use of a whip is worse than no whip at all, and occasionally just carrying a whip is enough to upset a horse.

I recall years ago a lovely American thoroughbred called French Camp which finally came to me having totally rejected the game of polo and, after almost everybody else had tried to re-educate this horse to the sport, he was destined for the scrap heap. After two years, a double bridle and using all of the various methods outlined in this chapter, I played that horse in high-goal polo, and at the peak of his ability. Because of his previous experiences, in retraining him I had to throw away the whip; until I did that, I was never able to gain the horse's confidence and start him on the right track.

As all good jockeys prove, the whip should be used gently to 'encourage' the horse to ever greater ability. It cannot be used to 'force' him to achieve his maximum potential, or 'make' him pay attention. Too many players take to the whip unnecessarily and in seconds destroy the confidence which correct schooling may have taken hours to build.

The incorrect and unnecessary use of the whip is intensely disliked in polo, and it brings the game into disrepute. It always creates a stir in the crowd when a player makes unnecessary use of the whip to try to make his horse perform better, or more probably to chastise it for doing something that was often his own mistake. That form of chastisement, if occasionally necessary, should be done kindly and calmly on the schooling ground and never on the polo field. It is the responsibility of umpires to warn the player concerned and to ensure that it does not recur in the game.

The Rein Hand

Polo is a game of control – you must control your horse before you can control the ball – and the rein hand is the link in the chain of communication between you, your horse, the ball and the game.

Whatever you do with your rein hand must be totally different and dissociated from what the rest of your body may be doing at any time. The instruction to slow down or turn may have to be given while you are busy tapping the ball to control the play or riding your opponent off the line.

To cruise at any speed, the line of your rein hand should be in a straight line from the bit to your elbow. The tension you apply to the rein controls the speed. As the horse stops, he lifts his head and you lift your hand to maintain that line. Hold the reins in the palm of the left hand, with the first finger separating the top pair from the bottom pair on each side, and the loose ends hanging down the left shoulder of the horse in front of your knee. Adjust the tension on the reins by holding all the reins in your right hand with the polo stick, loosening the left-hand grip and sliding the left hand forward (straightening the elbow) until it is in front of the martingale strap, then adjust the tension on the top and bottom pairs by squeezing the one pair while letting the other pair slip through the fingers. Practise this each morning when you get on the horse, until it is second nature to have the right 'feel' of the reins.

While the right 'feel' varies with each horse, a 'cruising' feel should be nice and light, very even and constantly responsive to the action of the horse's head. You should *maintain the same tension* no matter what the rest of your body is doing. As your horse goes faster he drops his head down and forward, and your hand follows his nose. As he stops, he lifts his head, and you take up the tension – only as much as you need – and lift the hand up to maintain the correct line.

Push the rein hand across to the right as you play the nearside shots, and, if necessary, lengthen the reins a little to make it easier as your left shoulder goes backwards for the 'one' position of the forehand and the follow-through of the backhand.

Occasionally one sees ponies being played with just one bottom or stopping rein on a pelham or a gag bit. I am very much against this because the tension on the bottom rein should be required only when stopping the pony. The player is totally without a balancing rein for the pony to feel its mouth and thus remain confident while going forward. Without the top rein, which could also be considered the neck-rein, the stopping rein has to take the strain whenever pressure is applied to turn the pony in the game, so he rapidly loses the confidence to go forward and finds it difficult to turn with forward impulsion and speed. While it is possible to school a pony with only a bottom rein, if he is losing confidence, to play him with only the bottom rein will rapidly undo all the good confidence-building work which you have put into the horse, and finally will have the effect of destroying both his mind and his mouth unless you are a particularly good rider and have exceptionally good hands.

It is essential to build up a very light contact in your relationship with the horse's mouth through the reins, ideally finger-light, and therefore the top rein or balancing rein is essential. If, for any reason, the horse is not responding enough to the bottom rein, use of a running rein should be considered. But to take away the balancing rein is really the last thing you should do, particularly in the game.

The Running Rein

The running rein runs from your hand down each side of the horse's neck and, from the outside, passes through the snaffle ring and back under all the straps to the girth. It can be either crossed over the top of

Prince Charles shows the correct use of the running rein. This big, strong pony is going beautifully into the bit, having won the ride-off.

the withers in front of the saddle, to the opposite sides, or passed down along each side, and slid on to the front girth strap. In certain circumstances it can advantageously be taken down to the girth between the front legs, each side of the standing martingale strap.

As its name implies, this rein runs through the top snaffle ring on the bit and therefore, as it is pulled, applies increasing tension to the bottom or checking rein. It is of most benefit when a horse is big and strong and therefore naturally, without any bad habits or for any detrimental reasons, applies too much pressure to the reins for comfort by leaning on the bit. In a case such as this the running rein is ideal as it helps to lighten the feel on the hand which is crucial to the smooth transitions of both speed and direction in the game.

**Quick Acceleration
and Quick Stopping**

If you want to squeeze speed from your horse, don't throw your weight forward and hope that he will come with you. Try to understand that, as when squeezing a tube of toothpaste, you don't squeeze the tube at the top! You must drive the horse from a reasonably deep, firm and balanced sitting position, squeezing with your legs forcibly behind the girth, and giving rein with your hand forward, to encourage him to stretch out quickly.

The reverse – quick stopping at speed – is just as important and involves swinging the weight back, pushing the heels down into the ground to force the weight through the centre of gravity of the horse, which is basically just behind the saddle, and really trying to force him into the ground against a fairly firm hand which is lifted up to increase the action of the bottom, stopping rein.

Remember, however, that quick stops and starts are tiring both on the horse and rider and take considerable energy to perform. Bear in mind that there are only a certain number of stops in a pony in each chukka and in each season, so it is important to ride your pony within his capabilities in each chukka he plays. Conversely, I have discovered that horses which are difficult to stop can be encouraged to change, if ridden with sympathy. Once they start to play properly their confidence and willingness to perform suddenly blossoms into an amazing ability to play the game. Playing in the arena has helped the attitudes of some of our horses considerably.

The Rein-back

The rein-back is a very valuable polo pony exercise, particularly useful for 'lightening' the horse's mouth. The aids from the stop position are to squeeze both legs down the girth, forcing the impulsion of the horse equally forward into a firm and resisting hand and thus asking him to go backwards rather than forwards. To encourage the horse to start to rein back, you may have to give a little with the hand initially to start the impulsion forwards, then ask him to walk backwards by slowly increasing the pressure of the hand. 'Feel' the horse's mouth – give and take the tension on the reins, rather than pulling with a constant pressure. This movement can progress into the 'roll-back', an excellent movement for collecting the pony and used in the training of cattle-cutting quarter-horses in the USA. The pony collects himself and turns on his hindquarters at a canter, with encouragement from pressure applied with the foot down his outside shoulder.

**Aids for
Changing Legs**

In understanding the aids required to change legs at the canter, it is important to understand the actual gait of the canter. The gait is in the form of 'three time'. When the horse is cantering in a circle the first leg to come down is the outside hind leg. The second and third legs come down at the same time and they are the other hind leg and the diagonal front leg. And the last leg to hit the ground is the leading inside front leg. In this case the horse would be described as cantering on the left or right leading leg, the leading leg being the last he actually puts on the ground in that stride and thus the furthest in front. Therefore to change legs you must change the hind leg first to enable the horse to change his front legs in the correct manner. To endeavour to change the front leg first would result in the horse cantering disunited – in other words, leading with one hind leg and the wrong front leg. Always try to avoid making a polo pony canter in a disunited manner as he is very much more likely to slip and fall over on a corner.

One of the most important parts of a polo pony's schooling is to teach him to canter immediately on the inside leg when required to do so. It is therefore vital that he learns to change legs automatically when a change of direction or a change of weight is applied. Changing legs at the canter, also known as a flying change, should be practised every time you take the pony out for a schooling session, particularly in the early stages of his training, once he is physically capable of performing the movement. It may take some time before the young pony gains the co-ordination required.

The correct time to change the horse's leg is when he has all four legs off the ground. If, just before this time, a diagonal aid of slight tension on the right rein and the left leg back behind the girth is applied, in conjunction with the weight of the body swinging slightly forward and to the left, the animal should put the right hind leg down first and end up by leading with the left leading leg. As the reins are held in the left hand, this means normal neck-reining to the left as you lean over. Remember that pressure with the left leg back behind the girth will force the hindquarters over to the right, and should have the effect of bringing the horse's right hind leg to the ground first.

These aids can be reversed to produce the right leading leg and, if the timing is correct and the horse understands what you require, he will quickly learn to give you the leading leg you ask for.

One point of confusion concerning this aid is that normally the rider's inside leg is down the girth and the outside leg is back. In producing a change of leg in the horse, the inside leg initially goes back to apply pressure to the hindquarters to force them outwards and therefore ask the horse to put down the outside hind leg first.

Once the horse is cantering on the required leading leg, the correct aids can be applied for impulsion and balance. The inside leg moves forward down the girth to support the horse and the outside leg moves backwards for impulsion. If the horse is going straight, the outside leg is on the opposite side from the horse's leading leg.

When working with a green horse, or a horse that doesn't understand your instructions initially, try to work in an enclosed school and use a corner to bend the horse a little one way or another, simultaneously employing the aids to get him to strike off at the canter on the corner. You will thus be instructing him to strike off with the inside leg and he will rapidly associate the aids that you give him with striking off with whichever leg happens to be on the inside of the circle.

So long as your aids remain the same, you will reasonably rapidly gain the required response from your horse to change his legs according to the direction of your body and hand, and the pressure of your legs. The horse is trained by consistently repeating the same aids.

Any horse undergoing training for polo should spend considerable time cantering on the right leading leg. Because most horses do their work initially in their breaking-in period on the left leading leg rather than on the right, the majority tend to bend more easily to the left than to the right. If your horse has this tendency, you may have to give him extra schooling on the right to compensate.

Remember, too, that instructional work should be done equally on each leading leg, because the horse can't readily associate what he does on one leg with what he should do on the other.

One further important point to remember is that the horse will learn faster if taught with calm patience. Frequent periods of time relaxing at the walk, on a long rein, during schooling can be beneficial in helping him to maintain a calm attitude to his work.

SCHOOLING THE PONY TO WIN

The following exercises and schooling methods are directly concerned with riding the pony better in the game, and thus improving his ability to play. They need to be practised while schooling so that, in the heat of the game, the pony's ability to play is not jeopardised by any lack of knowledge.

As you are now preparing your horse to play the game, this section of schooling should be done in conjunction with other ponies – several, if possible. It will help him get used to concentrating on his work in the presence of other horses doing various things around him. He will have to learn to think of what you are asking despite the distraction of other horses – as in the game – and this is very important in the conditioning of his mind.

The techniques described below are of vital importance to your game and should be practised on the stick and ball ground with another player to enable you to go out and play polo instinctively better. The pony needs to practise all the necessary movements just as much as the rider in order to gain confidence in the rider's aids and judgement and his ability to achieve what he sets out to do.

Riding Off

Riding off is a major part of the game of polo and its importance cannot be over-stressed. Players learning polo in the army used to practise the technique without sticks, so that they could concentrate on learning the correct procedure, and occasionally we resort to this in the polo

The two techniques for riding off are well illustrated here. Number 3 is using his body to lean in and apply pressure, whereas his opponent is leaning out, forcing his horse in with his seat.

school when players tend to chase the ball. From a team point of view, riding off becomes of paramount importance in the overall team strategy and the flow of the game.

To train yourself and your pony to ride off you will need the help of another pony and rider. Start to canter parallel with them, gradually using your neck rein and your outside leg to push your horse over until it comes against the other horse. Place your knee just in front of the other rider's so that your horse has about 6 or 8 inches' lead on the other horse and therefore can exert his superiority over him. By the use of your outside leg to maintain impulsion, and by pushing your neck rein over and forward, using your shoulder only, not your elbow, and keeping your body forward to maintain increased impulsion, you will encourage your horse to push the other horse off the line and win the ride-off. You will thereby control the area of ground or the line of the ball, whichever is essential to your team.

When practising your riding off, concentrate on the correct timing. In other words, your horse should be progressing at no more than a 30-degree angle to the line on which the player whom you intend to ride off is travelling. Your forward momentum should be approximately the same and, as both horses come together, you should

'DISLIKES IT TO BEGIN WITH'

a *Preparing to ride off when training the young horse.*

b *Picking up the man. Allow the young horse to win at first to give him confidence.*

'APPRECIABLE SHOCK'

endeavour to place your knee in front of the other rider's so that you automatically gain control of the ride-off.

Watch particularly carefully the other rider's hands and his horse's shoulder. If you concentrate on these two things, you will be able to time the ride-off to perfection. You will immediately see if the other rider starts to check up if his hand starts to lift, and by watching the progression of his horse's shoulder you will pick up the forward speed and momentum of the horse.

Concentrate, too, on the line of his approach because you should be more or less parallel with that line as you make contact with the other horse. It is also essential for you to control the important part of the ground, or the line to the ball, at the same time as riding your opponent off. Otherwise he will beat you and dominate the position you have been striving for.

Riding off is also a strain and the 'bang, boom, bump' type of polo is very wearing and bruising to a horse, quite apart from being annoying to a good player. There is no game of polo worth injuring a pony for. Instead of resorting to the bump, 'escort' your opponent off the field. The good player seldom has to ride hard – he anticipates well enough to 'escort' his opponent to wherever he foresees he should be next, simultaneously controlling the area of the field which is essential to him.

Learning the ride-off takes considerable practice, but in time it becomes a major part of your game, and its successful performance is one of the main differences between the learner and the better player.

Hooking

Of almost equal importance is the art of hooking a player's stick as he is in the act of hitting the ball. It is a crucial part of polo because it prevents the ball from travelling and offers an opportunity to gain possession, which is critical in the flow of the game. You will, of course, need another player with whom to practise hooking.

When practising, the player who is to do the hooking must ensure that his pony is on the same side of the other horse as the ball. It is a foul to hook across the line of an opponent's horse to try to stop him from hitting the ball. It is also a foul to hit above the height of his shoulder or when he is not in the act of swinging at the ball.

The hooking player, then, should approach his opponent at about a 15–20-degree angle from the same side as the ball and, taking care not to put his horse's head in the line of the other player's swing, should lean out and hook his opponent's stick about 2–3 feet above the ground, while his opponent is in the act of striking the ball. A high-goal player is often able to hook his stick and hit the ball in one movement. This can have a major impact on a play in the game because no one has anticipated it, and such a rapid change of possession, and therefore a change in direction, often leads to a goal-scoring opportunity, if your team is quick enough to capitalise on the change of play.

In approaching to hook, say, an opponent's offside forehand, you

While an excellent play outside, in arena polo this hook is too high and therefore a foul. The hook must be below the horse's rump in the arena and below the player's shoulder outside.

'KEEP AT HIM'

should have your stick on the nearside of your horse, pointing down the neck. This makes it easier to control the line of your hook unless you are coming very fast, when a good player might swing under the neck of his own horse to hook an opponent's stick. Hooking with your stick down the nearside of your own horse gives you greater control of your horse's head in relation to the line of the other player's swing, and makes it easier to get the timing right. However, it is harder to win the ball as well on that side.

After hooking, it is possible with practice to come away with the ball by tapping it and controlling your forward speed in relation to that of the ball, thus not only preventing the other player from hitting the ball, but also controlling it yourself and turning the play completely. It is perfectly legal in polo to hook both a forehand and a backhand on either side of your opponent's horse, provided you are on the same side of his horse as the ball.

a *Stuart is attempting to hook by leaning under his horse's neck to catch his opponent's down-swing. He could also hook with his stick on the nearside of his horse if he were riding fast enough to move alongside.*

b *He connects with the cane.*

When trying to hook a forehand and hit a backhand at speed, a good player will assume exactly the same line as the player in front of him, about a length behind. As the first player swings to hit the ball forward, the second player will time his forward swing to hit the first player's stick firmly and knock it off the line, thus preventing the hit. At the same time he will reverse his hitting action and drive his stick hard down through the ball, hoping to hit a short backhand and change the line enough to deny the following players possession of the ball, so giving his team the opportunity to pick up the new line.

It is legal to hook an opponent's stick from directly behind him, but you must not come from the wrong side at the same time as hooking: the umpire will invariably call a foul unless he is on the exact line himself and reasonably close to the play. Although the timing may be legal at the moment of the hook, both your opponent and the umpire may not see it as a legal play if it is done in the same split second.

Changing the Line

If you are on the right side of the ball and able to reach it before the player who is coming down the line, and can control your horse without crossing his line, you may tap the ball across his line before he arrives, but you must not cross the line before he goes past you on the old line. You may then assume the new line, provided nobody else is following him at speed, and he will not be able to swing on to the new line without fouling you.

Meeting the Ball

It is very important at times to try to meet the ball in the game. Remember that two players following the line of the ball and riding each other off have superior right of way over everybody else. But if only one player is coming down the line of the ball and you are able to meet it on its exact line or approaching from *his* right-hand side of the line, you may meet the ball, right hand to right hand, provided you can reach it before the other player and your horse is travelling parallel to his before you hit the ball. If you can meet the ball safely, you should think very quickly, move quickly and smoothly, totally under control, and meet the ball with your stick flowing straight down the line of the ball if possible, not across it. Your success rate in meeting the ball on the line would probably be about 80 per cent, whereas trying to meet it across the line is likely to result in a failure rate of 80 per cent.

Great care must be taken to avoid crossing the line or even getting too close to it. The umpires must be sure that you have not caused the other player any interference or that there has been any risk of danger in a manoeuvre such as this. Young ponies need to be trained to meet the ball – and other players – with confidence, otherwise they may get frightened and weave across the line when under pressure in the game.

If you are at all to the right of the line as you face it, you must not

a Meeting the ball. *A Two players have complete right of way following the ball. B White 3 rides his opponent off the line. allowing 4 to meet the ball. C Because white 3 has pulled out, his 4 can meet the ball correctly. D The correct play is the tail shot from white 3. White 4 has deliberately gone wide ready to pick up the new line, but must give way if anyone is coming fast down the old line.*

b Coming into the line. *A Incorrect. There is not enough distance between the players – white 4 must allow black 1 to hit the ball, then ride him off. B White 4 has entered the line safely at the correct speed and allowing enough distance. Black 1 must play on the nearside.*

c Riding off. *In the example on the left, white 4 must check up and ride the oncoming 1 across the line, as in the diagram on the right. He must be very careful if black 1 checks to avoid the ride off. Both players must come together at more or less equal speeds and at no more than a 30-degree angle to each other.*

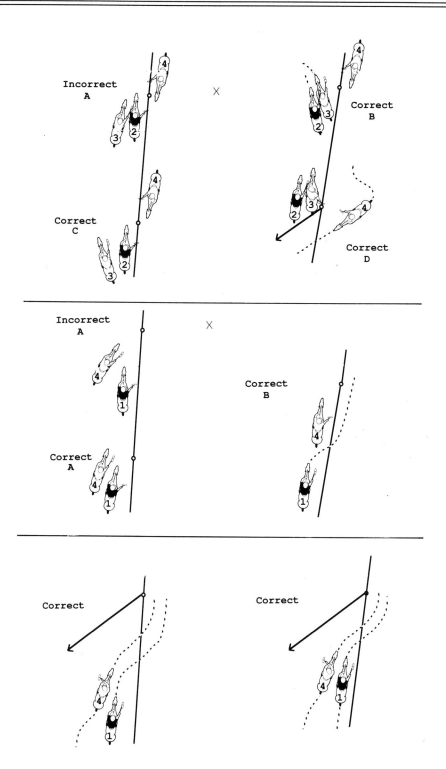

meet the ball. *Turn away*, going in the direction you anticipate the next shot will be hit. Try to pick the player up as he comes down the new line of the ball and ride him off, thus getting the next shot.

Although players vary in their approach, it is probably better to meet the ball with a full firm swing than to have your stick down and try to tap the ball with a small swing. You can adjust the full swing very quickly if the line changes, but you cannot adjust the mallet to try to stop the ball as fast when you are just holding it still.

A good player can come to the ball from beside – not on – the line so long as he is under perfect control and, if he can get to the ball, he can either change the line, or hook his opponent's stick as he swings at the ball. Be careful to avoid crossing the line, which could be very dangerous at high speed.

A player approaching the ball from the side has the choice of changing the line of the ball, in which case he must allow the attacking player to continue through on the old line before he assumes the new line, or he can hook the player's stick as he goes for the ball and then assume control of the ball by changing the line. Again, if players are following down the line fast, they have the right of way to go through on the old line before an attacker can assume the new line. It is essential for a player, when meeting the ball, to ensure that there are not two players riding each other off coming down the line. One player cannot meet two players coming down the line, and he should stay to one side while they ride each other over the ball. He may then assume the line as long as no more players are following behind.

Stick and Balling in Pairs

When you are stick and balling with another player, it is a great opportunity for you to increase your understanding of how the game flows and how you pass to another player. Start off side by side, with one ball. The player without the ball calls for a shot and rides in the direction in which he wants the shot to be hit. The player with the ball then proceeds to hit it 10 yards in front of the other player so that he can canter on to the line and pick up the ball. The player who is going to hit the ball should assess where the other player is riding each time and put the ball 10 yards in front of him, enabling him to canter on to it and pass it back to his friend. The hitter should remember, when going to the ball, to play it a little further away from the other player rather than too close.

This teaches you several things: how to pass the ball in the game, how to ride to collect the pass and, of vital importance, how not to change direction when the player in possession is approaching to hit the ball. At the same time it teaches your pony to go correctly to the ball for you to make the shot you need to pass the ball correctly.

It is essential during a game that when a player is within 10 yards of hitting the ball, his team-mates continue riding in the same direction.

His assessment of their various positions will be made by then and he will decide where he is going to put the ball in relation to the various directions in which they are riding. He will also have worked out who is winning the ride-offs and which of his team-mates will be in the best position to take the pass. In a match he should always name the player to receive the ball, to avoid the chance of both of his team-mates going for it.

It is the player off the ball who makes the opportunity for the next play in the game and therefore, when you are stick and balling with your friend, assuming that he is the player off the ball, you want to use him as the objective for your practice in passing and setting up a play. This is also where your anticipation in the game begins. It is relative to the position of your pony, your impulsion and your riding at any moment in the game and thus the direction in which you are intending to ride next, because that is the anticipated direction in which you think the ball is going to travel.

It is essential at this time for you to concentrate on riding precisely to the ball – in other words, 2 feet to the left of it – to enable you to control the ball, hitting it cleanly 10 yards in front of the other player. Don't try to hit the big shot every time, and remember that you cannot hit the ball very far if you wish it to travel at a 90-degree angle to your horse. Position yourself and the ball to enable you to make the shot in the correct direction. Use a firm-wristed tap to control the ball and set yourself up for the big shot.

Lastly, spend time playing against each other, attempting to keep the ball away from each other and in little circles or short runs, trying to avoid being hooked or ridden off, and still come away with the ball. All this will develop skills essential to the game and it is great fun to practise them in pairs on the stick-and-ball ground. It speeds up your reactions, and gets both your horse and your body tuned to play the game.

A large number of techniques have been covered in the last part of this chapter and the practising of each one on the stick-and-ball ground is of vital importance to the overall improvement of your game. However, don't try to practise everything at once. Take things slowly and you will improve more rapidly.

BALANCE AND THE ART OF FALLING

All good riders have a natural ability to balance with the horse and you very rarely see them off balance, no matter what the horse does. In polo this becomes of greater importance when related to the body positions which must be achieved, particularly in order to play the more difficult shots with maximum power and agility. Confidence and balance are together among the most important factors for polo players, and these are generated and improved only by hours spent in the saddle, riding, schooling and stick and balling.

RIGHT

If you are involved in an accident always roll as you fall.

Never put your arm out to save yourself. Always release the stick quickly and take extra care to collect your horse when playing near the boards.

WRONG

The art of falling is to realise when you have *completely* lost your balance: the horse has gone one way while you were going the other, and you are too far out to get back. If you let go and roll – two actions carried out simultaneously – in most cases you won't get hurt: the horse goes one way and you go the other. The physical action of falling can be practised at home, or in a gym on a tumbling mat, and it is worth the effort if it saves you from spraining or breaking something in an unfortunate fall that will inevitably happen.

The instinctive reaction to falling from a horse is to put out your arm, which is totally wrong, and this must be changed to the instinctive roll. Curl up the body and try to land on or behind the shoulder, and roll away, possibly twice, in the direction in which you are thrown. You thus take the force out of the fall and end on your feet, or, in the game, either holding the reins or lying on the ground – if the latter, the umpires will stop the game. Remember that if you get up and run after the horse, the opposing team could score at the other end, and the umpires cannot stop the game unless you are in danger. If you stay down, they must stop in case you have been injured.

CARE ON A WET PITCH

Although it is not everybody's idea of fun to play polo in the rain, occasionally – and possibly more often in England than anywhere else – we do have to play in wet weather. There are certain precautions which you should take automatically when playing in the wet to ensure the safety of all the players in the game.

First, turn that little bit more slowly. Steady your horse on a straight line before you start to turn. Don't go for a dangerous play which may necessitate your turning very rapidly or losing control. Think more quickly and ride more slowly than usual. Watch the ball carefully as it tends to bounce more in the divots.

Get your groom to ensure that all the horses' hind shoes are fitted with steel studs. Avoid, if possible, playing the pony that bounds or is for any reason unsteady. If he shakes his head or does anything to throw himself off balance, he is much more likely to fall over than a steady, easier pony. Remember: the game won't be as fast, so you can ride a slower pony that turns more easily to much greater effect.

4

TRAINING THE POLO PONY

So far in this book I have concentrated on polo from the point of view of the player. Now it is time to concentrate on the horse for, without horses, we couldn't begin to play the game. This chapter will discuss the basic work programme involved in bringing a horse from his winter turn-out condition up to the peak of match fitness, the feed required through the various stages in that programme and the schooling exercises necessary to enable him to play at his peak.

Although your groom may possess superior schooling capabilities, it is a good idea to do as much schooling of your pony yourself as is possible, for you will gain much benefit from doing so. The more you personally school your pony, the more he will grow to understand and respect the instructions you give him and the more quickly he will obey them in the game. Greater familiarity between horse and rider brings considerably greater pleasure to both – and the better the player, the more important this becomes.

THE BASIC TRAINING PROGRAMME

The basic care of the polo pony during winter will play a major part in his fitness in the early spring and summer; his health and general condition will depend on your ability to produce him in peak condition early in the season.

Let us presume that the pony is in reasonable condition, but not over-fat, when brought in from the paddock after being turned out for the winter. Check his feet, and get the vet to inoculate the horse for flu and tetanus. At this time the horse's teeth should be looked at and treated if necessary – they need rasping at least once every year – and he should be wormed. If possible, arrange for the blacksmith to shoe the horse the day after he is brought in from the field and then he will be ready to proceed quietly with his daily routine.

The exercise routine outlined below relates specifically to trained polo ponies. The young and green pony will be discussed in a later section of the book.

Week 1

In the first week care should be taken not to do too much. Half an hour a day, increasing to three-quarters of an hour, of quiet walking and jogging with a little trotting is ideal. Exercise if possible on reasonably firm ground.

There is a widely held belief, particularly in England, that all the preliminary exercise should be done on hard, preferably tar-sealed roads, because in February and March the ground can be so soft or uneven that horses might strain their tendons or ligaments. I personally prefer an even but softer surface, and suggest keeping off the road altogether if possible, and working in the dry part of a field or a manège. I have seen more foot problems, pedalostitis and navicular in England than anywhere else, and I believe that the risk of this can be increased by constant jarring on tar-sealed roads.

Week 2

Exercise can be increased gradually to a point where two intervals of five to ten minutes of trotting can be included in the total of about an hour and a quarter each day.

It is common practice in the English polo world for a groom to ride one and lead one, two or often three ponies out on exercise together; in Argentina it is not unusual to see a gaucho with five or six ponies riding up to the polo field. In England, however, polo ponies are very valuable, and unless your groom is highly qualified I feel the risk to the horses from traffic accidents or unexpected surprises, causing them to pull away from the groom and bolt out of control, perhaps on a road, is too great. Except where the exercise field is enclosed and absolutely no

When exercising it is possible to ride one and lead one or two polo ponies, but take care on a narrow road.

danger exists if a horse should break free, I suggest that the groom rides one and leads one pony, alternating between the two on successive days to achieve maximum benefit. Remember that no saving in time is worth the risk of injury to anyone.

Care should be taken not to feed the horse too well in the first two weeks of stabling. The winter feeding ration of one feed in the evening and as much as half a bale of hay a day should gradually be built up to a third of a bale of hay and two feeds a day consisting of about 3–5 lb of feed in the morning and 5–7 lb in the evening. Do not build the feed up too quickly as the horse needs time to adapt his digestive system to the change from the winter to the summer feeding programme. More information on feeding is given in Chapter 7.

Week 3

Week 3 shows a continuation of the exercise programme with a further gradual increase in the speed and length of the trotting sessions to fifteen minutes each time. The total length of the exercise period should now be about an hour and a half, and the two sessions of trotting should be divided by an interval of at least ten minutes of walking. Week 3 also sees the start of cantering: two or three times during that week the horse can be allowed to canter for up to five minutes.

In Argentina horses are often exercised twice a day, and high-goal ponies, because of their high-protein feed intake, will benefit from this routine. Most low-goal stables, however, exercise the ponies only once a day, in the morning, and take out individual horses for schooling in the afternoon.

Specific schooling for the individual horse commences in week 3. This is done completely separately from the basic fitness exercising and should comprise gentle schooling two or possibly three times during the week, in sessions of initially no more than ten minutes and gradually increasing and varying, depending on the strength of the individual horse. Don't forget: always warm up your horse gently before you school him, then relax him on a long rein afterwards, so that he will benefit to the maximum from your schooling.

Week 4

I start to play my own ponies *slowly* in chukkas during week 4. The rider's ability should dictate whether the ponies are played now or in week 5. If there is a possibility that the player might go too fast, an extra week of exercise should enable the pony to cope with any unexpected pressure. The average player who comes down from the city to play his first chukkas of the season is not aware of this potential problem, and in a recent example that I witnessed a very good horse was asked to turn 'inside out' by her owner – he was so keen to get into fast polo. She nearly managed it too, she was that good, but sadly strained a ligament in trying and was out for a couple of months.

If ponies have been turned out for only short periods of time – for instance, up to a month – they can be played considerably earlier. A good rule of thumb is a week of work for a month out in the field, but you should always consider the individual circumstances carefully and, if in doubt, give the horse extra time.

If the ponies are played in chukkas during week 4, their work load should be adjusted to take into account the exercise they are receiving during chukkas; in this case their actual exercise period should not exceed one and a half hours. (This need not include time taken in actually walking to or from the exercise area or the polo ground.) Take care not to overwork the horse early in the season.

The feed should be changed during weeks 3 and 4. Gradually reduce the hay to about a quarter of a bale, fed half at night after the main feed and half late in the morning – after exercise, if the horses are worked in the morning. The morning feed could be increased to 7 lb, the evening feed, depending on the individual animal, to 10–12 lb. A maximum of about 15 lb hard feed each day should be suitable for the average polo pony as a maintenance ration, and possibly 3–4 lb extra, spread over three feeds, if the pony needs building up.

The overall condition of the individual animal is important in establishing the correct feeding programme. But possibly of more importance is the horse's temperament. If the temperament is hot, the concentrate feed should be lower in quantity and definitely lower in protein content than if he is placid. A change in the bulk of the feed may be compensated for by a proportional increase in the amount of hay. One of the secrets of successful training is to balance the feed intake with the work load, and this is by no means easy without considerable experience.

Week 5

Week 5 sees the start of easy match polo – most match ponies are given at least a month, preferably five weeks, to acclimatise themselves and get reasonably fit before they play any really serious polo. I always bring all my match ponies in at least a month before I expect them to play in their first matches, and I am careful not to ask them for a stressful performance during their first or second match.

The weekly training programme now ceases to exist and each individual pony is trained primarily from polo game to polo game. Of course, the daily basic training programme of up to an hour and a half of exercise, which can consist by this time of a programme of ten minutes' walk, ten minutes' trot, ten minutes' walk, ten minutes' canter, ten minutes' walk, ten minutes' canter or trot and then ten minutes' walk, with twenty minutes' leisurely hacking, should certainly be enough. This should then be reduced according to how much polo is being played. Every exercise period should always conclude with five to ten minutes of walking to relax the horse.

We now have three different programmes to combine over the six days of exercise each week: the regular fitness programme, schooling whenever necessary and polo.

Experience is essential to know what an individual horse requires to keep him in peak condition. In fact, the object is not to keep an animal in peak condition but to train him from match to match and try to keep him bubbling at just under his peak so that he plays consistently very well rather than brilliantly on one day and only at 80 per cent the next. One of the secrets of success in polo these days is to produce a team mounted on ponies that play as well on the last day of the tournament as they did on the first. This is possibly one of the hardest things to do.

SIGNS OF AN UNFIT PONY

When a pony starts to pull nearing the end of a chukka, it is a fair indication that all is not right. If the pony pulls up blowing, with frothy white sweat up his neck, or is distressed in any other way, in all probability he is not quite fit enough, and if he doesn't catch his breath quite quickly after the chukka his overall fitness is definitely suspect.

At the end of a fast chukka a fit pony should catch his breath in two or three minutes and be breathing reasonably easily by the time he gets back to the pony lines. If that is not the case, and particularly if the pony is distressed, the groom should not tie him in the lines but should lead him around for five to ten minutes. This is quite crucial because it helps prevent a build-up of lactic acid which causes the horse to 'tie up' in the muscles and might eventually result in azoturia. Walking the horse removes the build-up from the system by keeping a good blood flow through the tissues, thus preventing a potential problem. The groom should always check for any leg problems after a game.

Conversely, a pony might play the second chukka better than the first, showing perhaps that he needs to be well warmed up and schooled before he plays his first chukka. For numerous reasons not all ponies will play two chukkas of polo and this should be taken into consideration when the work load of each individual pony is assessed.

My match ponies play only one chukka in a match if I can possibly arrange it. I believe that the second chukka is the time when stress catches up with the animal and problems occur. On the other hand, at certain times it might be necessary to play a pony for two chukkas, and then care should be taken towards the end of the second chukka not to stress the pony unduly, unless it is absolutely essential to the outcome of the match. If at all possible, I will always play two ponies half a chukka rather than one pony twice – the strain is then halved and, with it, the risk of injury.

THE HIGH-GOAL PONY

The high-goal pony is asked for peak performance more times in each chukka than if he were played in low- and possibly medium-goal polo. This results in the onset of a secondary phase of exhaustion level in the pony and certainly imposes a greater strain on the animal as a whole. He therefore requires special training as he needs to be fitter before he starts his high-goal programme than is necessary for a horse playing a lower level of polo. He also needs to be 'clean in the wind' – able to cope with the greater requirement for oxygen – so he must be galloped to open the chest and to encourage him to breathe properly.

The programme of training outlined on pages 83–87 can be applied to most polo ponies and will enable them to play consistently at 95 per cent of their peak performance, which is the average optimum level. However, in specific training for the top string of horses in any team which has to mount a high-goal player and needs to be performing at maximum capacity for a longer period in the season, extra work needs to be done.

Interval Training

Interval training – a special fitness programme – produces progressive loading on a horse's capacity for performance. By doing so it applies enough stress to the system to improve his ability to handle such a threat. Thus the horse's system can gradually be strengthened by a natural response to the increased loading so that eventually he can cope with the stress periods in the hardest of chukkas.

The objective of interval training is to achieve the horse's maximum fitness with a minimum of wear and tear on his legs and joints. After the first month of slow conditioning, the programme is extended to include, every three or four days, a period of canter work which gradually increases during the next two to three weeks. In extensive tests it has been shown that it takes three to four days for a horse to recover fully from a strenuous work-out, and that he could beneficially be rested in the paddock for the first day after each one. To work tired limbs under pressure any sooner is to invite the possibility of strain or injury. If left longer, the horse's muscle tension relaxes and he therefore fails to improve his fitness as quickly as required.

Hacking, a relaxed ride through the countryside, is great for the horse and rider, who can do whatever they wish depending on the surface of the track. For the other two days it is ideal for the balance of the work programme in the six-day week. The canter period is broken into three, separated by two relaxation periods of walking. After the first canter, the horse should almost fully recover his wind and pulse rate in the first walk and only half-recover during the second. You are thus extending his heart and lung capacity and therefore increasing his overall fitness in a similar but more specific way than has already been outlined for the basic training programme.

Initially intervals of three minutes can be used, both at canter and walk, increasing to possibly eight minutes at canter and still three minutes at walk. However, each pony will vary in his requirement. The cantering speed in these work-outs should be about 400 yards a minute, increasing in the last minute of the second and third gallops to 500 yards a minute. As the horse reaches full fitness, a 'blow-out' – at 90 per cent of full speed gallop for one to two minutes – each week, possibly during or just after a chukka, is important for improving the pony's wind.

A horse at almost full speed gallops at about 1100 yards a minute. A quarter-pace canter will be up to 400 yards a minute, and a half-pace about 600 yards a minute. It is work at maximum speed which injures horses, so the less top-speed work a horse can be given, and still kept bubbling at just under peak performance, the better. A horse only needs six days' work each week; in some cases, if he is turned out on the field, five days of schooling and hacking, or possibly four plus a light hack, will maintain him in fit condition.

The exercise programme outlined above is for work done on the flat. If hill work can be incorporated, the horse will achieve better collection and fitness with markedly less work, but again this needs to be balanced with the amount of polo being played to maintain fitness at the desired level. A horse cantering uphill suffers considerably less strain to the legs, Conversely, cantering downhill produces a greater jarring effect so should be limited, and if the ground is hard you should not canter downhill but slow to a trot.

It is important always to match the feed intake with the higher work load and, depending on the temperament of the individual horse, the oat and/or protein content of the feed should be increased. Mineral supplements and plenty of salt should be used, particularly in hot weather, to replace the sweat the animal produces under the extremes of exercise he is now undergoing. There is a school of thought that recommends up to three months of basic exercise before starting increased exercise such as interval training, and another three months at that level before stressing the horse to the maximum. In my opinion such a slow build-up is not essential: practical experience has shown me that horses can achieve their peak of fitness more quickly. If this were not the case, ponies in England would never be turned out during the winter, and most racehorses would have problems too. However, while I am convinced that a horse brought in in the middle of March can be playing matches by the beginning of May, certainly his peak won't be achieved until the middle of June.

A word of warning is necessary here regarding treatment of the pony: if he is over-fed and under-worked – and remember that we are talking about a very quick, high-goal pony with capabilities of extreme manoeuvrability – it is possible that the average groom with only low-goal experience might not be able to ride him confidently. In such a situation the horse could well be at risk of injury because of the groom's lack of control, so if in any doubt ensure that the animal is led on exercise rather than ridden. In most instances the pony that is led is much easier to handle than the badly ridden, more excited horse.

Again on the subject of the pony's welfare, it should be stated that the training programme outlined for the high-goal pony is aimed at an animal that is 100 per cent sound. As has been explained the programme stresses the pony to a very high degree to produce it in peak physical condition, and not all ponies are capable of taking this. Care should therefore be taken to adapt the training programme to the individual horse, not vice versa. Such a programme can over-stretch the capabilities of many horses, and they will play much worse if they are too fit than if they are a little more relaxed.

KEEPING MATCH PONIES IN THE FIELD

When I arrived in England in 1973, I was very surprised to find that just about all the match ponies played in England were kept in boxes throughout the summer. My training, having been rather different, showed me that it was certainly possible, and in some ways more beneficial, to keep match ponies out in the field. The risk of having a pony injured by being kicked or by running into a fence was outweighed by the fact that he would be far more relaxed if kept outside and would play much better polo because of it. In recent years, since the Falklands War with Argentina and the arrival of more Australians, New Zealanders and Americans in English polo, this practice has become much more widely accepted. Certainly I have proved in my own organisation that the difficult pony is much easier to play from the field than if he has stood in a box for twenty-three out of twenty-four hours a day and so comes out on to the polo field bubbling over with surplus energy and behaves like a jumping bean. This type of pony can become almost unplayable from a loose box and is ready to boil over at the slightest provocation. In fact I have had several that, as a result of their highly-strung temperament, were quite difficult with the grooms in the box, and horses such as these really do need to be played from the field and kept on a very low-protein feed supply.

SCHOOLING EXERCISES

While considerable schooling can be done during the course of a pony's daily exercise, he needs specific schooling to tune him to a high degree and bring him to the peak of his polo-playing ability. The following exercises all have particular benefits and make the horse easier to handle on the field.

Polo is a precision game and all of the exercises in this section are about training the horse to be precise in his response to your increasingly lighter aids. They also teach him the familiarity essential between horse and rider to enable him to understand, at speed and under the pressure of the game, what the rider wants.

Exercises are best done, when appropriate, with another horse as a pivot point; this has the added advantage of helping the learner to accept any exercise more rapidly because he always wants to turn towards the other horse. Remember that anything that you can think of to make the pony want to do an exercise, rather than having to force him to cooperate, is far more beneficial and achieves the objective much more rapidly.

It is very important to keep the horse calm and responsive during your schooling. If at any time a horse gets excited, he will cease to learn properly, and time should be taken to settle him down by walking him on a loose rein, talking to him and letting him relax. While a horse learns by repetition, his learning threshold is, depending on his intelligence, from three to ten minutes maximum. After this period of time it is unwise to continue trying to teach a pony something new during the exercise session in question.

On the other hand, constant repetition of schooling exercises already learnt is not a wise move if the pony is doing them reasonably well. He will simply think that by increasing repetition you are punishing him rather than asking him to improve on his performance. Short, sharp and sweet is much more preferable to a long, arduous grind. I have used the latter only on rare occasions when I have had to try to change a horse's attitude from being dominating and uncooperative, which resulted in a complete rejection of anything that the rider asked, into a more gentle acceptance of the request.

When you are retraining, it is vital to achieve this acceptance and compliance. The pony's mind must be changed if he has been allowed, by whatever means, to dominate the rider. Non-cooperation is an impossible attitude for a horse to have if you are going to train him successfully for polo or anything else. Only by perseverance can you achieve compliance to the point where you are always obeyed. There is no other way and, if you don't win that battle, you may just as well give up on the horse.

Willingness to accept what you ask marks the difference between a good horse and a bad one, and a horse should always be encouraged to accomplish the requested exercise to an even higher degree than expected. One of the main attributes of the top equestrian is his ability to find out why a horse responds to a command in a particular manner and thus form a rapport which builds a mutual confidence. This will ensure complete acceptance by the horse of the commands the rider chooses to give.

Bearing in mind that the athletic requirements of the horse in polo supersede those of any other equestrian sport, the basic dressage aids which produce the suppleness and the responsiveness essential in a dressage horse are also used to assist in the training of the polo pony. The difference, of course, is that a rider has to be so much more supple and athletic himself in polo, whereas in dressage he sits very still and the indications and aids become almost unnoticeable except to the horse.

In schooling the polo pony there is no substitute for time spent in the saddle. The horse needs it to enable him to understand more readily the rider's commands, and the rider certainly needs it to enable him to sit deep in the saddle, to be relaxed and to learn to handle his horse with the confidence that is so essential to the animal's continued improvement. It is vital to concentrate on the smoothness of your riding at all times, both when schooling and later when playing your horse.

You must also remember the difference between riding for schooling and riding when playing the game. In riding for schooling it is crucial that every movement is absolutely precise; whenever your pony makes a mistake, you must start again, getting him to do the exercise correctly and with confidence. In a game, of course, this is impossible, and his movement or his reaction to any given situation will be instinctive, as will yours.

It is on the schooling field, the stick and ball field and in slow chukkas that you create those instinctive reactions to any circumstance, and so it is there that your reactions and those of your pony must become instinctively correct. You must insist on accuracy and you get that by persevering with patience. Work on your pony's weak points one by one, not collectively. As you improve each weak point to an acceptable standard, so you will improve your total ability in the game. In this way the benefits of schooling your own ponies will soon become apparent.

A pony is almost always either left- or right-legged, just as human beings are left- or right-handed, and he will turn and manoeuvre better one way or the other. This will, in the beginning, necessitate more work on the pony's difficult side. Having achieved equal flexibility, however, it is no longer necessary to maintain considerably excessive work on the pony's difficult side. More or less equal schooling on each side should, from this point on, achieve what you require and as the pony grows in his experience and knowledge of the game his own intelligence will help when it comes to understanding and executing your various requests. The word 'requests' is used deliberately here for, as a pony becomes better and more experienced in the game, it is important that your demands, which you initially had to insist were carried out correctly, evolve into requests for feats that he is delighted to perform for you because of the rapport you have established with him.

As well as being invaluable in schooling, the following exercises will prove useful for warming up just before play. Give your horse a couple of minutes' exercise and then five minutes of stick and balling and you will have him really tuned to play the ideal chukka.

Exercise 1: Turning into the Boards, a Fence or a Wall

A polo pony needs to be able to stop short and turn quickly. This exercise is ideal to produce exactly that on the polo field. You need a fence or hedge, preferably 40–50 yards long. The initial exercise should be done at the walk, then the trot and, as soon as the horse has learnt what he should do, at the canter.

Take the horse straight down the line of the fence, parallel with it and about 2 yards away from it. Check up straight, turn into the fence using your aids with a very light hand and come straight away along the fence in the opposite direction. If necessary use your whip gently down the outside of the neck, tapping to encourage the horse to turn quickly. Move along 25 or 30 yards from the previous turning point, turn again into the fence, using your whip down the outside if necessary as before, and then proceed back to the starting point. Change your whip each time to the outside before you turn, regardless of whether you use it or not.

As the horse starts to put this exercise together, speed and the distance between turns can also be increased to enable him finally to stop, turn and canter away. Speed can be increased to about three-quarter pace before checking up, turning into the fence and galloping away again.

Your aim during this exercise is to teach the horse to respond rapidly to your instructions, turn quickly in a collected manner and canter away with the correct leading leg. There should be no trotting stride before the cantering stride begins. The horse should learn to respond with precision to the increasingly lighter aids of the rider.

Exercise 2: Stopping Straight and Reining Back

Both stopping straight and reining back are essential in a polo pony. Starting slowly and working up to quite high speed, take the pony in a straight line, make him stop and then rein back three or four paces before proceeding again in a straight line.

It is very important for a pony to be able to stop on a straight line.

STOPPING ON A STRAIGHT LINE

a Stopping and turning against the boards. *This exercise can be used as a schooling technique and to give the pony experience with the boards. The player is beginning to check up here.*

b *Turning into the boards encourages the pony to turn on its hocks. Use the boards, a fence or a wall to lighten the contact with the mouth.*

a *When turning to the left the feet are pushed forward with the shoulders leaning slightly back to encourage the pony to check up.*

b *The player swings his weight over the left or inside leg, and neck-reins to the left. The right or outside leg moves back and squeezes firmly, providing impulsion to turn the horse tightly around the horse's left hind leg.*

c *Push away again quickly to avoid any trotting paces.*

d *Having leaned back to collect and check the pony on the turn, the player's body is then forced forward through the balance point to give maximum impulsion to the horse. Note the rein-hand position and the delicate contact with the horse's mouth.*

c *He squeezes with the legs and leans slightly forward while giving rein to accelerate away.*

d *The polo pony requires strong hindquarters to withstand the rigours of the game.*

As the pony learns to do this exercise kindly, first at the walk, so you increase the speed, possibly moving straight into a canter and then to at least half-pace, again asking him to stop smoothly, head down and collected, and then reining back at least three or four paces in the same straight line.

Exercise 3: The 'U'

While most polo-pony schoolers have their own favourite exercise, this contains almost everything that is required and can be varied to produce just about any movement in the game.

It is best done around another horse or, if that is not possible, towards and away from a barn. The ends of the 'U' point away from the other horse or barn, and each time you get to the end of the 'U' you turn outwards.

Using another horse, position him at the bottom of the 'U' as your pivot point. Starting from his right side as you both face the same way, trot away from him in a straight line for about 30 yards. Then collect your horse, turn quite sharply right in a semi-circle and proceed to trot back towards and round behind the pivot. Next trot away from him again in a straight line parallel with the first one to about the same distance, where you turn left, in another semi-circle, proceeding back at a canter around behind the pivot horse. You then repeat the whole process.

The 'U' exercise requires two people, unless the turns are made towards the barn instead of around the pivot horse's position. Alternate as necessary between one tight turn and one flowing turn. Start slowly and increase your speed as your pony's flexibility increases. Collect and tighten the turns gradually. When cantering change to the left leading leg at X and back to the right at Y.

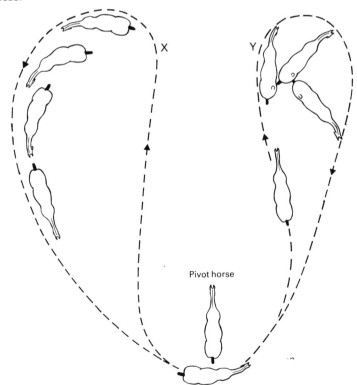

Pivot horse

As you are now cantering, you will have to give your horse the aids to change legs just before he gets to the corner, so that he is balanced on the right leading leg as he turns right. You then again canter round behind the pivot horse with the right leading leg, turning right and going up the second side of the 'U' once more. At the end point of the 'U', you turn left, so the change of legs has to be produced just before the corner as before.

Do not proceed into the canter until your horse is sure of exactly what you are intending to do. There is no point in trying to do the exercise at the canter and fighting with the horse when, if you take it a little more slowly, you can ease him into it and get his compliance much more readily.

Once the horse is flowing through the exercise and changing legs in the right places at a reasonably confident half-speed canter, you can begin to tighten the corners, turn on the hocks and increase the speed. At the same time you should lengthen the sides of the 'U' so that you can in fact produce all the movements required in a game of polo, even to getting to the end of the 'U', stopping, turning immediately and galloping back towards the other horse. You can, if you wish, execute a running turn on the other side, varying the movement, the collection and the speed.

Exercise 4: The Figure-of-eight

The figure-of-eight exercise is of great benefit and can be varied in size so that flying changes, acceleration and deceleration, very tight turning and larger, smoother circles can all be incorporated at the canter,

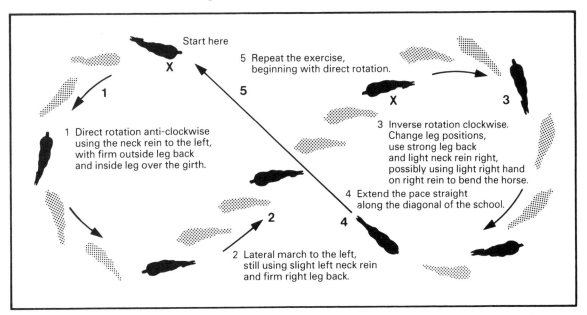

The figure-of-eight exercise at all paces encourages a response to pressure from the leg aids. At the canter change legs at X.

increasing to three-quarter pace and decreasing to a very collected canter – all of which are ideal movements for polo.

The initial movement should be in a circle about 30 yards across, smoothing round straight as you come to a point, leave the circle and change the legs, then turning in a circle of the same size in the other direction. Again, arriving at the same point, leave the circle, change the legs and complete the first circle again. Do the exercise smoothly and consistently before you start to vary it with increases of pace and the tightness of the turns. Ensure that the horse changes legs correctly each time, both back and front, so that he remains united each time you change legs and direction in the exercise. If necessary, collect the horse down to a trotting stride to allow him to change behind.

SCHOOLING WHILE HACKING

Hacking plays a major part in the schooling programme because it relaxes a horse and he is then in an ideal frame of mind to learn. I do a considerable amount of my preliminary schooling at various speeds while out hacking. Bear in mind, however, that you should only ask the pony to do what he is capable of doing. With younger horses particularly you should increase your demands very gradually and each time ask them something new within their capabilities, so building the learning curve little by little.

It is very important to remember to do equal work on each side of the pony in all your schooling, but especially while hacking. All of the exercises should be done first at the walk, then the trot and, lastly, at a canter, when the horse has grasped precisely what you want, so that he remains calm throughout.

When schooling out hacking, you should carry a whip to assist with the aids. A little tap – with the emphasis on the word 'little' – sometimes just helps the horse to maintain his attentiveness to your instructions. I also prefer to train my ponies with spurs because it makes them respect my commands more quickly and means that I need to use my legs much less firmly. I prefer all my horses to respond to the lightest of aids that can be given in any circumstance. You will also find that ponies will go more smoothly with lighter aids and they learn to respond more kindly.

Changes of pace and transitions from walk through trot to canter nicely and smoothly, and with no resistance, are very easy to achieve while out hacking. The horse can also be trained to strike off with a particular leading leg while hacking, by bending and using the aids described on pages 65–72.

Make the horse bend away from your legs on each side alternately by bringing your heel back and forcing it behind the girth firmly into his side. He will gradually move away from your leg and start to bend around your inside leg, but keep him walking straight along the road. This is the start of a half-pass in polo and is crucial in the suppling of

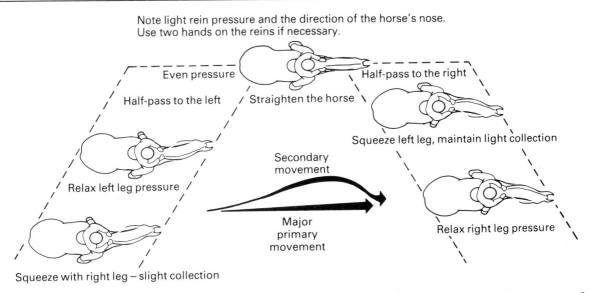

Note light rein pressure and the direction of the horse's nose.
Use two hands on the reins if necessary.

Even pressure

Half-pass to the right

Half-pass to the left / Straighten the horse

Squeeze left leg, maintain light collection

Relax left leg pressure

Secondary movement

Major primary movement

Relax right leg pressure

Squeeze with right leg – slight collection

Moving away from the leg. Use this half-pass exercise to improve the horse's response to the pressure of the leg.

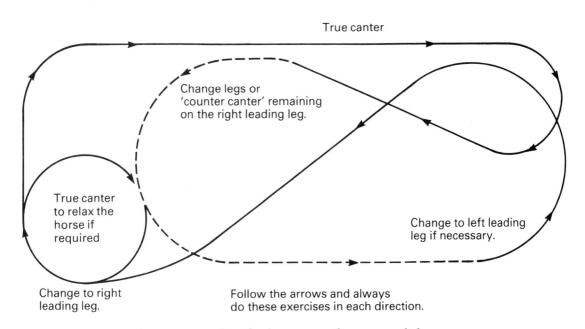

True canter

Change legs or 'counter canter' remaining on the right leading leg.

True canter to relax the horse if required

Change to left leading leg if necessary.

Change to right leading leg.

Follow the arrows and always do these exercises in each direction.

This schooling and suppling exercise is beneficial at any speed to improve balance.

your pony in readiness for play. It should be done on alternate sides at the same pace, and he will rapidly understand exactly what you want.

Unfortunately in England we don't have access to the ranch work which is available in many other countries of the world where they train polo ponies. Working with cattle is one of the easiest ways both of giving a horse the rudiments of polo training and exercising him. It keeps his interest up and he seems to learn more quickly and remain more relaxed. It is not uncommon to ride the stock horse for eight to ten hours in a day, and this makes any hot-natured animal settle down.

MAXIMISING YOUR GROOM WHILE SCHOOLING

To maximise the benefits of your groom while you are schooling, bear in mind the horse's learning threshold of three to ten minutes. You only need to ride the pony yourself for a period of, say, fifteen to twenty minutes. If your groom is warming up your next pony for the ten minutes before you need him, having cooled off your last pony for five minutes after you have finished schooling him, you will maximise the use of your groom during your schooling period. Instead of being able to school one pony in an hour, you will school three, bearing in mind that each horse will probably be schooling with a different programme and to a different level of ability.

Remember, too, that however good your groom is, he doesn't actually play the pony in polo for you, and you should endeavour to do as much of the schooling of your own ponies as possible. The more you personally can do with your horses, even if you don't ride so well, the more readily they will accept your style of riding, and therefore the more you will be able to contribute to the game.

NECK-REINING

It is of prime importance for polo to retrain the average horse which has been trained to ride with direct reins – that is with two hands holding the reins – so that he becomes accustomed to the rider holding the reins with one hand and to the very different feel and directions transmitted to him through his mouth as a result. When the rider holds the reins with one hand, the main difference for the horse is that he feels an indirect rein rather than a direct one, when he is asked to turn, the result being that his nose will point slightly the wrong way. Horses that have been trained to follow their noses around a corner suddenly find a totally different instruction, and it is quite confusing to them.

Initially a whip should be carried for this exercise. Holding the reins in one hand, encourage the horse to go forward, pushing the reins over to one side or the other and using the whip gently down the outside of the neck as a little added incentive to get him to go away from the whip and thus start to neck-rein. Be patient: only by very slow practice will a horse learn to understand this indication, which is totally opposite to what he has learnt to feel from the reins before.

When the horse turns on a direct rein, the inside rein is used to lead him around the corner. When a rider is holding the reins with one hand, a contra-rein indication means, as its name implies, that the wrong rein is tensioned and, in a double action, pushes/pulls the horse around the corner. Because of the nature of the way a horse turns, when his neck turns outwards and the weight of his head actually turns away from the circle, his shoulder falls the other way and he turns more quickly; hence the benefit of contra-reining and turning with one hand. It just happens to be essential to the polo riding style because the stick is held in the right hand. Possibly the one horse that can turn inside a polo pony is a cutting horse, and many of the exercises used to train cutting horses are also ideal in general to collect and train a polo pony, and to increase his manoeuvrability. They are also useful for keeping the pony's head in the right place.

In all training it is important to keep the pony perfectly balanced and that means without putting his head too high. Obviously some ponies carry their heads higher than others, but a perfectly balanced pony normally carries his at an angle of about 45 degrees from the wither and bends beautifully at the poll, at the top of the neck, without becoming over-bent and getting too far behind the bit. If this can be maintained throughout a polo pony's exercising and schooling, he will come into the game much more quickly and kindly, with the result that he will play much better.

The method of training the cutting horse encourages him to keep his head low and watch the animal or the man he is working on. Cutting

Neck-reining to the left. This should be done equally each way to begin with, and then more frequently in the direction the horse finds more difficult as he progresses.

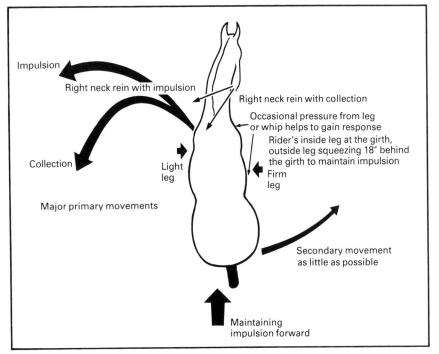

Impulsion

Right neck rein with impulsion

Right neck rein with collection

Occasional pressure from leg
or whip helps to gain response

Rider's inside leg at the girth,
outside leg squeezing 18" behind
the girth to maintain impulsion

Firm
leg

Collection

Light
leg

Major primary movements

Secondary movement
as little as possible

Maintaining
impulsion forward

horses are trained to work with quite a slack rein, and this is ideal for the polo pony too. Because of the very fast forward momentum a polo pony achieves, the rider has to pull the reins quite hard at times and this is bad for the low head carriage of the horse, but the polo pony that can stop and turn with the lightest of reins and indications obviously achieves the manoeuvre to greater perfection than a horse that arches his back and puts his head up in the air.

As the pony's response to the neck-rein increases, so you will finally be able to turn him around in a little circle on a complete axis away from the rein. You must maintain the impulsion but sideways instead of forwards, and the pony will pirouette right round, sitting on his hind legs. Cutting horses are encouraged to do this by the use of the outside spur gently tapping on the shoulder. This aid can also be used with the whip when training the polo pony to neck-rein. Neck-rein with either impulsion or collection; when turning from quite a high speed, neck-reining is normally used with collection to turn the horse more quickly. If, however, the pony is being turned slowly, or neck-reined in a ride-off, you need to ride with impulsion to win, and the position of the hand in the neck-rein varies according to the tension on the rein.

If using the neck-rein with impulsion, the rider must push the rein hand at least 6 inches further up the mane and further out to the side than when using the neck-rein with collection. Pull back a little on the rein and then pull it over in the direction you wish to turn. At the same time use the leg aids to help push the horse into the turn and thus maintain the turning momentum. Work in an enclosed school is ideal for helping to collect the polo pony without having to use too much rein. The rein tension is crucial in any horse's training, but it becomes of vital importance in the training of a good polo pony.

CORRECT BITTING

There are several schools of thought regarding the correct bitting of a horse. My own is based on my experience of making and remaking polo ponies, plus the useful experience of having trained dressage, show jumping, steeplechasing and event horses before I ever played polo. A bit used in the correct manner is the quickest method of relaying your instruction through the reins to the pony.

It is possible – though totally undesirable – to relay all your indications solely through the bit. This is not possible with any of the other aids you have. It is vital to have the right bit in your horse's mouth, and to help you choose the appropriate one their characteristics are outlined below.

The Snaffle Bit

The snaffle is a very mild bit with an 'action' that relies on the pressure you apply to the bars of the horse's mouth and to the cheeks which are squeezed together as you pull the reins, so forcing him to open his

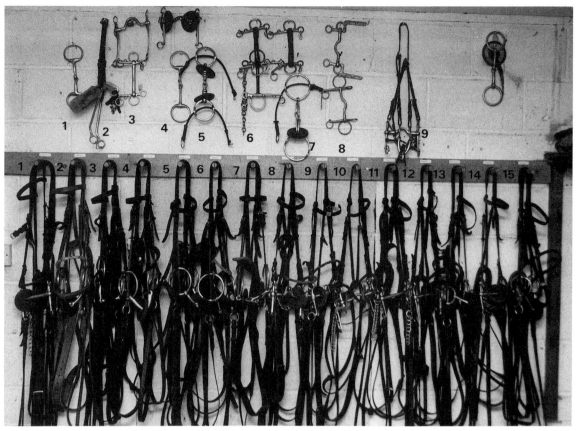

Horses react differently to the various bits used for polo. The bits seen here are: 1 eggbutt snaffle; 2 hackamore; 3 (top) western bit, (bottom) mullen mouth pelham; 4 double bridle with (top) bit and (bottom) weymouth snaffle; 5 roller gag; 6 vulcanite and straight mouth pelhams; 7 (top) vulcanite pelham, (bottom) barry gag; 8 military pelham, port pelham; 9 weymouth bit and bridoon double bridle. The bridles hanging below them are: 1 straight bar pelham; 2, 3 and 5 big-ring gags; 4 big-ring gag with thick mouthpiece; 6 and 7 barry gags; 8 coscojero; 9–12 various pelhams; 13 fixed-ring gag; 14 pelham; 15 gag.

mouth and possibly lift or throw his head in evasion. It is this bit that all racehorses are encouraged to use because, being mild, it encourages a horse to move into it and go forwards without becoming frightened that its action in his mouth might be painful. The snaffle is the first bit used on most horses to encourage them to go straight and give them confidence as they are being broken in and beginning to learn.

The Eggbutt Snaffle

The eggbutt is a fixed mouth-piece snaffle. The ring does not run through the mouth-piece freely and it exerts slightly more downward pressure on the bars of the horse's mouth. The eggbutt is therefore possibly a better snaffle to use in the initial training for polo. The eggbutt mouth-piece also protects the corners of the mouth.

The Big-ring Gag

Possibly the bit that has the widest use in polo, the big-ring gag is a very effective bit for stopping the pony which may not be quite as well schooled as he could be. By its action of lifting the head up, opening the mouth and pinching the cheeks all at the same time, it has the rapid effect of arching a horse's back and making him sit back on his hindquarters.

A pony which is schooled to a higher state of flexibility might be able to stop much better with a lower head carriage than necessarily might be achieved with the gag bit. On the other hand, I have ridden many ponies which stop better with the head in a higher plane, and a gag bit is therefore the best one for them to play in.

It is essential on bits where the ring runs through the mouth-piece to have cheek-protecting rubbers which prevent the corners of the mouth being trapped in the mouth-piece holes and so pinching and cutting. This is particularly important in the big-ring and barry gags which are used for polo. It is also beneficial on most pelhams, where slight pinching can occur as the bit moves in the horse's mouth.

The Barry Gag

The barry is a split mouth-piece gag with the joints offset in the middle of the mouth-piece. Both of the jointed mouth-piece bars are quite thin and, because of that, have a moderately severe effect on the horse's mouth. The barry gag is particularly good for a horse that takes a hold on the bit and is therefore not so responsive in the heat of the moment, particularly towards the end of a chukka.

I have found the barry gag an excellent bit for the more difficult pony which possibly has been asked the question too young or too often and decides not to obey the request of the rider. It has proved very beneficial in several of my reschooling programmes because its action prevents a horse from grabbing the bit and tends to make him relax his jaw.

The size of the ring is quite important in a gag and has a bearing on the downward pressure on the bars of the mouth. It also has an effect on the speed of release of the gag, which is quite important in maintaining the forward impulsion of the horse. Rings can vary in size from approximately 2 to 4½ inches, and the bigger the ring, the more severe the action.

The Weymouth Gag

The weymouth is a fixed-ring gag similar to the eggbutt snaffle with gag cheek-pieces. It has a considerably greater effect on the bars of the mouth with downward pressure than the other gag bits already described, and it could be much more suitable for the horse that puts his head too high in the air but is still more responsive to a gag bit than a pelham.

The cheek-piece, i.e. the round strap that runs through the rings, connecting the top rein to the head-piece, is very important on a gag bit. The gag action should release rapidly when the rein tension is released, thereby getting a considerably quicker reaction from the horse. Originally rolled-leather cheek-pieces were used in gag bits, but recently nylon has been substituted and this gives a far more rapid release to the action of the bit.

The Pelham

The pelham bit has a non-flexible straight-bar mouth-piece which extends right across the mouth. The cheek-pieces pass through the ends of the mouth-piece and move freely, but are held in position by a ring at each end called the snaffle ring. The cheeks extend down in varying lengths – the longer they are, the more severe the bit – to a bottom ring, called the curb, where the bottom rein connects. The snaffle rings on the cheeks have a hook on each side which holds the adjustable curb chain. This passes under the chin of the pony and creates a lever action which is applied to the bars of the mouth by tension on the bottom rein. The curb chain should be adjusted so that it begins to apply pressure when gently pulled by the curb rein to 45 degrees from the line of the cheek-piece of the bridle. On all bits the top rein, or snaffle rein, is always the 'go' or balancing rein and the bottom rein is the 'stop' or curb rein.

There are many different mouth-pieces in the pelham family, ranging from thin and straight to fat, curved and twisted; they may be made of rubber, fitted with a roller, or even jointed in the middle. All have a different action and therefore create a different reaction from the horse, and if one doesn't work, another might.

A gag pelham, which might seem a total contradiction, is also available; this has a use on a horse which begins to 'take hold' of a pelham towards the end of a chukka.

The Snaffle *versus* the Pelham

In establishing whether one should start with a pelham or a snaffle bit of some kind, the question must be asked: 'What is the natural head carriage of the horse?' If his head is held quite high in a normal carriage, you could perhaps try the pelham action initially to lower his head carriage and bend his neck at the poll, thus encouraging collection. If, however, his head is kept fairly low, the lifting action of the gag may prove to be beneficial and act as more of a collection aid. The problem of putting a pelham in a horse with a naturally low head carriage is that he very rapidly gets 'behind' the bit and becomes over-bent, and then has difficulty in achieving the movements you require. Once a horse is over-bent with a pelham he tends to lean on the bit, and it encourages him to become 'dead' in the mouth and then, of course, very much less responsive.

Remembering that the first bit a horse should work in is, because of its very kind nature, a snaffle, the minute your schooling requires your pony to come slightly 'off' the bit, a thick mouth-piece, short cheek and therefore mild pelham may well be the first schooling bit that you try. (When a horse is described as 'off' the bit, it means that he drops his bottom jaw and releases the slight tension you have taken on the bit with the rein. As he drops the bit, so you give with the hand, to develop the correct feel on the rein.)

The Vulcanite Pelham

Pelhams in general vary in their severity, depending on the shape of the mouth-piece and the length of the cheek-pieces. Possibly the mildest of all polo bits is the short-cheeked vulcanite pelham. That and a rubber snaffle, which is thick, soft and pliable, have extremely kind actions on the horse's mouth, and for a naturally light-mouthed, responsive horse there are no better bits to try than these. A rubber mouth-piece pelham, which is also soft and flexible, may be even kinder on a horse's mouth, particularly if he doesn't pull. However, the thicker bar in a vulcanite pelham is the reason for its mildness. It exerts the pressure over a bigger area of the bars of the mouth than the thin straight bar of an ordinary pelham.

The Port Pelham

One of the reasons a horse might start to pull is that he gets his tongue over the bit. A port pelham has a bend in the centre of the mouth-piece which prevents the horse from doing this quite so easily. It also has a place for the tongue to sit and therefore applies slightly different pressures to the horse's mouth – pressure on the tongue being also a part of its action.

Horses that have the right feel in a pelham, but still pull a little, often go very well in a port pelham with running reins, and this combination has proved useful in horses which tend to toss their heads in resistance to the bit. It is also worth trying a double bridle to cure this type of problem – one will prove much better than the other.

The Coscojero or Argentine Pelham

The coscojero or Argentine pelham features a quite high closed port in the centre of the mouth-piece with a roller in the middle so that the tongue has something to play with, and the action of the bit rolls over the tongue rather than depressing it straight into the bottom of the mouth. It often has slightly longer cheek-pieces than the average straight-bar pelham and has proved very effective on horses as they get older and become less responsive to an ordinary pelham bit.

I have several older ponies in my stable which go very kindly in this bit, and one pony which is totally unplayable in anything else. The port particularly prevents the horse from getting his tongue over the bit and the roller seems to keep the mouth far more moist than is the case with an ordinary pelham.

The Western Bit

This really is the single bottom-rein, pelham-action bit in which the mouth-piece varies depending on the style of the bit. As its name denotes, it is the chief bit used in most western riding and, for the same reason as the pelham used with one bottom rein, is not ideal for the horse's mouth. On the other hand, partly because of its length of mouth-piece and also because the western bit is not often fitted with a curb chain, it has a beneficial effect in schooling and can be used to get the stop-turn action seen in the cutting horse.

Some horses do tend to throw up their heads in avoidance of this bit and, as it usually lacks a curb chain, it doesn't necessarily have the required effect for this type of evasion. Its beneficial aspect is that it is often used with a very loose rein while the rider sits balanced and deep in the saddle, so the horse quickly learns to understand a very light application of the rein, which is of course the prime objective in bitting the horse. After schooling in the western bit, a horse should play well in a coscojero.

The Hackamore

A hackamore is a bitless bridle that works by applying pressure to the nose. Although it is currently illegal to play a pony in a hackamore, this is a very effective schooling bit for the re-education of some horses with pulling problems. A small check hackamore can be made legal with the addition of a snaffle bit, but I would hesitate to play with this type of bridle in anything other than practice chukkas. The horse which throws his head about or lifts his head up violently when asked to stop or, as a result of previous mouth damage, has rejected the bit, can in many cases be reschooled in a hackamore.

Recently I bought a horse which, when you asked him to slow down and collect, threw his nose violently to the left in an effort to avoid the bit, and almost fell over. The horse had a particularly light mouth and was very sensitive, but after a period of reschooling in a hackamore, he came back into top polo and was played successfully by an eight-goal player.

The Double Bridle or Bit and Bridoon

The double bridle or bit and bridoon is possibly the most under-used bit in polo and possibly the most effective. More frequently used in the USA, often in combination with the running rein, it has a very kind action, although not all horses go well in it, and even with considerable schooling, you may find that, once the pressure is on, another bit is more effective in the game.

The double bridle is widely used in the world of dressage and has a very fine effect on the collection of the horse. It enables him to balance on the top rein, which is attached to a small snaffle bit, and brings into play the stop rein which is based on a straight-bar pelham action with a variable length cheek-piece. But the curb action doesn't take effect until actual pressure is put on the bottom rein. The two actions are therefore quite separate and enable the horse to go forward with more confidence than sometimes is the case with an ordinary pelham. At the same time he will be more responsive to the pelham action because he has remained fully sensitive in the mouth and doesn't have the insensitive feel that the straight bar can give if pressure is constant from a firm strain on the snaffle rein affecting the bars of the mouth.

This is my favourite of all polo bits, for if a horse performs well in it he can often be fine-tuned to brilliance. Its main benefit is that it has the horse beautifully balanced in the forward impulsion mode and therefore ideal and ready for collection when the signals are given. By carrying his head in the right place the horse is capable of responding much more readily and kindly, which is the optimum for a polo pony.

In graduating from the snaffle, this is probably the first bit that I would try, particularly for a big horse, because he is already in harmony with the snaffle and therefore half-way towards accepting the new bit.

Mild or Severe Bitting

Occasionally, in controversial debate on the subject of severe bitting in polo, the question arises of the harsh action of gags and long-cheek pelhams on the horse's mouth when used with rough hands. The importance of kind hands in any riding, not just in polo, cannot be stressed enough. Hands can do a lot of damage used in the wrong manner, whereas if used correctly they will never have a detrimental effect on the horse whatever the bit. As has already been explained, hands are the first indication to the horse of a rider's wishes, and any player who thinks his hands are letting him down should take lessons to learn the right 'feel'.

There exists a misconception regarding the use of the severe bit – a gag *versus* a snaffle, or a long-cheek pelham *versus* a vulcanite pelham. The true reason for using a severe bit is to make the horse considerably lighter and therefore more responsive to the bit, whatever it might be. It is much more important to worry about whether the bit is the correct one for the horse and is used properly than whether it is severe or not severe. I endeavour to train all of my ponies to react to the lightest of hands rather than to take a firm hold on a mild bit. Players taking up polo should concentrate primarily on their hands and rein contact as they begin to 'feel' their pony. Remember always in this connection that 'Light and smooth is beautiful', and polo is a beautiful sport.

THE YOUNG PONY

This chapter has so far considered only the made polo pony. In this section attention will be focused on the young pony and the major differences in his preparation for the game, beginning after the breaking-in stage at approximately two and a half years old.

All of the discussion in this section presumes that the rider is capable of doing the various exercises and manoeuvres outlined. If this is not the case, a rider should take care never to attempt anything that he might not be able to achieve, for in polo a learning player cannot easily teach a green horse. Both fail to progress, and once a pony picks up bad habits they become very difficult, if not impossible, to correct. Remember that a horse learns the wrong habits just as quickly as, if not more quickly than, the right ones, and once he has learnt something the process of changing his mind is considerably more difficult than teaching him the correct way in the first place. This is the prime reason why it is easier to breed, break and train a horse at home than to buy one which has been taught something different and possibly alien to polo, and which you then have to retrain to the sport.

In assessing the young pony, it is of course beneficial to know his previous history – what to look for when buying a pony is discussed in Chapter 6. However, all young ponies need similar treatment initially, and the treatment outlined below is specific to the young pony in combination with the full fitness training and exercise programme already described on pages 83–100.

A newly broken pony needs to gain experience – experience in almost everything that he might be confronted with. Therefore time under the saddle is of paramount importance to him – not time to make the animal tired, but time to make him understand. Just as a child has to go through a schooling programme to give it understanding in general, so does a young horse.

The major problem you are faced with initially is to get the horse progressing forward in a straight line. To help him learn this it is wise to go out hacking with an older, more sensible animal in front of or beside you. The young horse 'follows the leader' and soon picks up from the other horse what he should do, as well as learning the individual instructions from his own rider.

The young horse will be basically extended in paces and unable to flex into any form of collection, and he won't understand any aids other than what he has been taught during the breaking-in stage. While out hacking, therefore, you are faced with an animal which needs to be shown everything and *slowly*. Slowly introduce him first to the rein, then the leg and your seat, to push him in a confident progression forwards with impulsion. Keeping the rein relaxed, encourage the horse to go into the bit and obey the legs with independent pressure. When educating the young horse to the leg aids, independent pressure is applied by squeezing the legs – one at a time or together – repeatedly to make the horse understand what you mean. Squeeze him, like a tube of toothpaste, from the bottom – that is, behind the girth – and you will find he quickly starts to move forward, particularly if there is another older horse to follow.

Young horses will vary considerably in their first reaction to a lesson in straight-line riding. Some will be just like a piece of rubber and bend in all directions, not understanding anything. These probably need just to be taught more slowly and I have found great benefit from driving this type of horse in long reins, at the same time as hacking, to encourage him to go forward in a straight line, following his nose with his tail.

While I believe in lungeing a young horse to build up muscle strength and promote correct balance, long reins encourage the horse to use himself in the right manner for polo. The difference between a horse worked solely on the lunge and one worked in long reins is that the latter learns to go away from the outside rein down the side in a straight line, whereas the lunged horse bends around in a circle and, in fact, is very much more 'rubbery' to ride.

At this stage a snaffle bit encourages the horse to go forward into the bit and also to start going straight. Care must be taken to maintain the right contact on the reins – light but firm enough for the horse to feel the bit in his mouth and gain confidence from that. Just as a wayward child needs direction from which it gains the confidence to sort itself out, so does a young horse require firm but very kind and patient direction from the rider, with the use of the aids mentioned.

Once the horse is going confidently forward, start to increase his pace to a trot and do the basic transitions between walk and trot, making sure that he can do them smoothly before progressing into a canter. Remember that he has been hopping, skipping and cantering around a field, completely free, but suddenly you are asking him to start to do these movements with perhaps 12 stone on his back. Totally unaccustomed as he is to it, he needs time to balance his natural abilities with your weight.

The only way to get a horse going straight is to make him understand that he must go away from the leg. I always use spurs on a young horse and carry a whip – not to hurt the animal but to encourage him. I find the response from a young horse that has been ridden correctly with spurs to be much lighter and keener and he is therefore more enjoyable to ride. He also seems to progress so much more rapidly and, as he does so, he gains in confidence.

Confidence, in fact, is basically what we are aiming at because as a horse gains confidence, in the understanding both of his rider and of his surroundings, he is able to 'get it all together' and give you the correct responses to your requests. Always take care not to ask for something that the horse is not capable of giving, particularly during this period of his education. Encourage him to do the simple things well.

Depending on his learning threshold, a week of hacking should find the horse progressing smoothly from a walk through to a canter in a straight line and going away from the legs reasonably effectively. This means that, while he is walking along in a straight line, you should be able to bend him around your legs so that he moves forward slightly in a half-pass mode, with pressure from your legs, and can be driven confidently forward with your seat into a light hand. Use the hacking exercises on page 99 to build his confidence.

Repetition through the changes of pace is important at this stage, so the pony grasps what you are asking him to do. While out hacking, I like to set aside five to ten minutes to stop in a pleasant area and practise stopping, cantering, striking off on the correct leading leg and various other simple manoeuvres, stops, starts and turning in small, balanced circles.

Further exercise patterns.

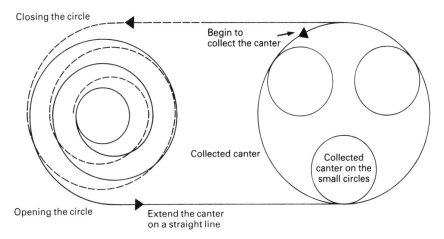

Closing the circle
Begin to collect the canter
Collected canter
Collected canter on the small circles
Opening the circle
Extend the canter on a straight line

Don't forget the importance of the voice aid with a young horse – few things are so rewarding as his response to your praise by giving you that little bit extra. Just as you can be very firm when a wayward animal won't do what you ask, so you must praise your horse when he does what you require – and be lavish with that praise – because he appreciates it, it builds his confidence much more rapidly and you will find the response to praise infinitely more rewarding than the response to chastisement.

You should encourage your young horse to develop a light mouth, a receptive mind and a positive attitude. Gain his compliance through confidence rather than domination. Use firm, kind patience at all times rather than fear; the only exception to this rule is when a young horse becomes wayward and just will not listen to your commands. All horses have some natural ability in a particular area and, by building on this, you can increase their confidence more rapidly. It is also a confidence boost for them to find something they do easily, which is what you want as well.

While I am training a young horse, I spend a considerable period of time at a sitting trot. I have found through dressage that this is a very good gait for producing the correct impulsion and response to the aids in a young animal. Many polo ponies hardly trot at all – and my aim is not necessarily to teach them to do so; it is, in fact, to teach them response to the aids, which is crucial to their ability at a later stage, with collection and impulsion – two of the vital elements of a polo pony's learning.

Introducing the Young Pony to the Polo Stick

Once the young horse is going confidently forward at the three main paces – walk, trot and canter – and the transitions are nice and smooth, it is time to think about introducing him to the game of polo by showing him the polo stick. His reaction will depend considerably on the history of his break-in treatment and the nature of his overall handling. Some horses will immediately shy away from the stick, while others seem not to worry about it at all. If you are lucky, you will have no problems in encouraging the horse to take no notice of the stick.

The initial introduction of the pony to a polo stick is very important. The more nervous the pony, the greater care you must take over this. You should be extremely careful never to hit a young pony with the stick by mistake, for it will alarm him and quickly make him nervous and he will try to avoid the ball at all costs. You then have a problem and must take trouble to rebuild his confidence by tapping the ball in a circle away from him, to the right, and pushing him to the ball each time with the outside leg. Firm kindness with loads of praise will work wonders in such a case. Always use the stick and ball exercise shown on page 114 as your first introduction to the ball each day.

I always take the stick for the first time while on top of the horse and have the groom pass it to me very slowly so that the horse understands that I am never going to hit him with it and he has no reason to fear it. I encourage a nervous horse to smell the stick, look at it and perhaps shy away a little. Then I use the outside leg to correct him so that he responds and stands while I gradually move the stick in the various positions around him slowly, smoothly and without upsetting him in any way – perhaps even using it to stroke him down each side of the neck. If the horse is nervous, I take him out and work him for a reasonable period before introducing him to the stick for the first time when he is tired rather than fresh.

In dealing with the extremely nervous pony, the basis remains the same but special care must be taken not to upset him or give him any reason to fear the stick. He will learn to distinguish between the whip and the polo stick provided you never, ever hit him with the polo stick.

Let us presume that the horse I am on has shied violently away from the stick as I've taken it, and has perhaps even pawed at it with a hoof to show his anger and fear. I have encouraged him to stand and smell the stick, and very cautiously he has looked at it, snorted, sniffed and is extremely nervous of the whole idea. I will now ride him forwards with the stick straight across the wither and encourage him to forget about it for a minute or two while we just work in the normal manner, walking with possibly a little jogging to relax him.

Once our forward progression is back to normal and settled, I will gradually take the stick down the offside of the horse, perhaps so that he can't see it at first, and then very slowly start swinging it parallel with his body so that he initially catches only glimpses of it. Immediately he starts to go away from the stick I will use the left leg firmly just behind the girth to encourage him to go straight and ignore the stick. This swinging exercise, which should be performed equally on both sides, is of vital importance and should be continued until the horse totally ignores it. This can take days, and is a gradual progression of confidence building.

The very rare horse that just does not seem to settle down with this method can be boxed on a low feed ration for a couple of weeks. If you hang three or four polo sticks in the box so that he has to walk through them all the time, he rapidly begins to accept the facts that they are there and they are not going to hurt him, so he learns to ignore them.

Care should be taken during the period of acclimatisation exercises to swing the stick only parallel with the horse. Do not try any fancy shots because your aim is to build the horse's confidence so that he understands he is not going to get hit with the mallet. Start to swing it around in a full circle, both forwards and backwards, on each side of the horse only when he is ready to accept an increase in the speed and motion of the stick. Don't forget that extra time taken at this stage of a horse's learning curve will be amply rewarded later on. It will take longer to cure a pony that is stick-shy than to develop one that is completely settled with the polo stick.

It is crucial to remember at this stage to do equal work on both sides of the pony. Hacking can play an important part in training the pony's mind to accept the swinging of the polo stick. Having already become confident in his acceptance of hacking and the aids, he rapidly associates one with the other and is able to transfer his confidence in hacking to his acceptance of the stick. In New Zealand we used to carry polo sticks around the farm and practise knocking the heads off the thistles. It was excellent for our hand/eye co-ordination as well as for the conditioning of the polo pony's mind.

An intensive course of stick swinging in an arena, using the fence to keep the horse straight while swinging the stick on the other side, can be beneficial to make the horse understand that you are not going to hurt him.

Not until he has accepted the stick parallel with his body in all your swings do you start to get him accustomed to the tricky under-the-neck and behind-the-tail shots. Just do these in a gradual manner and the horse will soon accept that the stick won't hurt him and therefore he won't object to any of the various things you do with it.

Introducing the Young Pony to the Ball

Introducing the young pony to the ball should not be attempted until he is totally relaxed with the swing of the stick. If he is still slightly alarmed by the stick, immediately you introduce the ball you are giving him something more to shy away from.

On first introducing the pony to the ball, take it on your stick side and tap it slowly away 20 degrees to the right. Gradually, at the walk, go towards the ball and tap it away again. Progress in 20-degree and increasingly large taps in a circle to the right to encourage the pony to go towards the ball from a distance. The circle to the right is the easiest way of driving him to the ball and it encourages him to go towards it when he knows it will be hit away from him. On the nearside the circle should be away from him to the left.

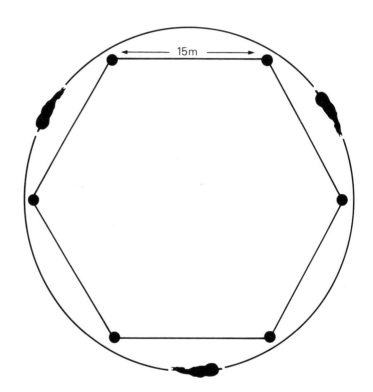

The stick and ball pattern *for the young pony. Tap the ball to each point consecutively. Complete a full circle if you miss the ball. Do not stop or turn quickly. Use the outside leg to maintain impulsion and the neck rein lightly on the neck to maintain direction.*

15m

Do this exercise at the walk on both sides of the horse before you progress to the next stage. Ensure that your approach to the ball is always correct – that is, 2–3 feet either to the left of the offside or to the right of the nearside shots. Never ask the pony to walk straight at the ball because this is the start of teaching him to 'run off' the ball. A bad habit like this is picked up very quickly and takes ages to break.

If the pony accepts the ball without a problem and has already accepted the stick, there is no reason not to progress straight into stick and balling, first at the walk doing half-shots and then building up the speed into a nice flowing canter. The speed should be collected but smooth, with steady impulsion. It may be easier to maintain half-shots at this stage to avoid upsetting the young pony unnecessarily. The important thing is smoothness – avoid upsetting the settled and calm attitude of the pony at all costs.

As always, equal work on each side of the horse is essential, and you should maintain the swing of the stick parallel to the horse at all times in his initial training with the ball.

Some horses have difficulty in understanding that they should keep either to the left or to the right of the ball and I have devised several exercises to ensure that a horse progresses properly to the ball. These exercises also help to teach the rider to maintain the correct distance from the ball.

Place four balls in a square about 30 yards apart. Canter your horse on the inside leading leg in a circle, using the four balls as inside markers and passing each one at a distance of exactly 2 feet. Once your horse is going correctly, start to swing your stick over the top of each ball, but don't hit it. This exercise, as you keep the horse going with a lovely flowing momentum around in a circle, rapidly settles him to the task of going to the ball properly because there is no alarm and no reason for him not to do precisely what you ask.

When the horse is going correctly on each leg, rearrange the four balls in a straight line – again, about 30 yards apart. Practise cantering up and down each side of the line, swinging your stick about 2 feet in front of each ball and encouraging the horse to go absolutely straight. This is excellent training for both horse and rider and, in a very short space of time, the horse understands the aids you are giving him for a correct approach to the ball.

Don't forget to praise the horse when he does these manoeuvres correctly. Make much of him, because it is of vital importance that he understands when he is doing the right thing in both the approach to the ball and the swinging of the stick. A little encouragement at the appropriate time saves a lot of work and is always worthwhile.

Once the pony is happy to go past the ball at the right distance and consistently takes you to where you can hit the ball without deviating, you can move on to the next exercise. Hit the ball away to the right, leave the line of the ball and then push the horse gently back towards it. After cutting the ball each time, you will maintain the circle in a similar action to the original circle where you were just going past the ball and not hitting it. Again, smoothness and precise control are essential.

Initially use half-shots because these will alarm the pony less when your stick makes contact with the ball. Start slowly and gradually build up to a lovely easy canter. It is important to establish a nice cruising speed for the young pony to stick and ball to. He should keep at that speed constantly and not go faster as you hit the ball. Try to squeeze him into the canter and, if he starts to increase his speed, go past the ball, canter round in a circle, without changing legs, and come back to hit the ball. Do not hit it until the pony is going precisely and correctly in his approach to the ball each time.

If the pony doesn't go right to the ball at this stage, don't lunge at it in an attempt to hit it, because this upsets the pony. Concentrate on a smooth, easy rhythm and your progress will be rapid. Practise the exercise on each side of your pony equally to the same stage each time before you take him a stage further in speed and in his ability to go to the ball.

When the horse shows no deviation or alarm at the ball or the stick, start your full swings. You must, as before, be smooth and methodical. Don't try to hit the ball too hard, but play for the horse rather than your stroke at this time.

The crucial error when stick and balling, for the pony, is to stop and start, again and again. The pony should be kept in lovely, smooth, flowing circles, preferably on the same leg so that he remains balanced at all times while you go to the ball.

At this point the importance of the leading leg should be mentioned. As explained on page 70, the pony leads with either front leg when cantering, depending on his balance and direction. He should be leading on the leg which is next to the ball at all times; if he is not, leave the ball, change the horse's leg, and come back to it on a nice, easy circle, maintaining the circle so that the horse does not change the leg as you hit the ball. It is essential to encourage the young pony to maintain the leading leg as you go to hit the ball. If he gets into the habit of changing his legs at that moment, your hitting will become inconsistent because of the unevenness of his approach to the ball.

Patience is essential and swinging parallel with the horse is of vital importance in the early stages. Don't ever swing across his nose or he will start to run off the ball. Nor should you try to progress too fast. Ten minutes spent at this stage is worth ten hours later on. Make sure that the horse does every exercise correctly before you progress to the next stage. If he starts to run off the ball, go back to the exercise with the balls in a square described on page 114. Then, when he is going kindly to the ball each time and you swing over the top of the ball, start to hit an occasional ball when he goes perfectly and then keep circling until you have hit all the balls away. If he still runs off the ball when you've hit it in a straight line, start again, and this time hit long cut shots so you can squeeze the horse to the ball with the outside leg, thus keeping him straight, in the big circle.

Remember that a horse starts to run off the ball because he feels that you are going to hit him – perhaps he feels he is too close to it, and becomes nervous. It is essential, therefore, that you ride him well off the line of the ball and squeeze him back towards it as you hit the ball, rather than riding him at the ball and then allowing him to fade away because you know he is going to run off. If you do the latter, you will rapidly teach him to run off the ball, a habit which is very difficult to cure.

Once you start the horse stick and balling, in the early days concentrate on that and don't mix schooling with it. The horse needs to have the repetition of stick and ball, to relax in a smooth, flowing gait, without the interruption of schooling to unsettle him. If at any time the horse gets excited during the stick and ball session, take time to settle him down away from the ball, let him relax completely and cool down. It is sometimes better to leave the session and go out hacking, where you know he will settle down, rather than have him jumping around the ground.

When the young horse is thoroughly accustomed to both stick and ball, he will benefit from playing a long chukka of polo. It should be slow, with not too much initial body contact, just enough meeting of other horses, easy riding off and very little galloping. These chukkas maintain his mental attitude to the game in the right plane, which is crucial to his progress. The Americans and Argentinians have a much better attitude to 'green pony' chukkas than do the English, who invariably want to play 'flat out' at every opportunity.

REMAKING THE PONY WITH A PROBLEM

I recently bought a number of ponies from a high-goal polo string dispersal sale and was surprised to find that one of the very good but highly sensitive horses in this string was in fact stick-shy. The pony had built up such a problem in her mind regarding the polo stick that she became almost impossible to mount and was very difficult in the stable. By the time we got the horse (I certainly couldn't get on her to try her out before we bought her) she was in a highly nervous and confused state. Juan, the head groom at the time, was able to climb on the horse, and gave me some consolation in reporting that she had terrific ability but obviously needed a long period of settling down.

Initially this process was done by hacking, at the same time carrying an Argentinian rebenque – a soft flapper strap, 2 feet long and 2 inches wide, fixed to a wooden handle – which encourages the horse to relax and ignore the movements of the rider. By regular and consistent flapping, gently down the neck and around the body, it acts like the horse's tail and seems to build confidence.

The next thing we taught her was education to a stockwhip. At the first sign of Juan flicking the stockwhip around the front of her, the horse went backwards 30 yards without stopping and stood there almost on her hind legs like a scared rabbit. I thought we were going to lose all the confidence we had worked so hard for. However, Juan wanted to continue, so I left him to it. Perhaps I was being educated in something as well as the horse! After about three weeks of either standing in front of or sitting on the horse and flicking his stockwhip, first on one side and then on the other, and around the horse's head, together with normal exercise, Juan succeeded in making her amazingly quiet and thus able to accept the whistling generated by the polo stick in a full swing.

Once the horse started to respond to this programme we gradually began to stick and ball her at the same time, and the use of the stockwhip was shown to be beneficial by her calmer attitude to this exercise. Over a period of about two months the horse really settled down and has since turned into one of our top polo ponies. Whereas before she would become alarmed and boil over at the slightest thing, she accepted anything we did with the polo stick after this – and I was also considerably wiser.

This horse was an Argentinian pony which had possibly been used too quickly and put under too much pressure by playing high-goal polo to an extreme level. So Argentinian methods proved to be very successful in her rehabilitation. The basic problem was changing the horse's mind. We had to give her confidence that she wouldn't be hurt by anything and get her re-accustomed to the firm kindness which is essential in the handling of the highly strung thoroughbred. The exercise had to repeated the following season, after the mare had been turned out, but this time it took only a day or two for her to relax again.

Indoor polo has played a major part in the rehabilitation of several difficult horses that I have had, and its features of close proximity to the swishing of sticks and the thumping of the big rubber ball, plus continual close contact with other horses, have resulted in their more rapid acceptance of the hustle and bustle of polo. If a horse gets rapidly excited and starts to pull, you can turn him into a wall without using too much hand or leg and this shows the difficult horse that he has to stop whenever he is asked to, by increasingly lighter aids, thus resulting in his becoming more relaxed.

5

BREEDING THE POLO PONY

THERE ARE MANY excellent books available on thoroughbred breeding and for detailed technical information on the subject the reader is advised to consult them. The discussion on polo-pony breeding in this book centres on whether it is better, although it is certainly not more economical, to breed polo ponies or to buy ponies which have been bred for other purposes initially and to make them into polo ponies.

One of the prime advantages of breeding your own ponies is that you can ensure that the dam has been proved on the polo field. In my view approximately 80 per cent of the mare's characteristics are passed on to the foal and approximately 20 per cent are given by the stallion. But, more important, I believe that the mare controls certain traits and leaves certain characteristics in the foal while the stallion dominates others. Certainly the foal's physique comes chiefly from the mare – its conformation, its robust constitution, its ability to survive and its future playing ability.

The stallion, on the other hand, controls the mentality of the foal, whose temperament basically follows the pattern of the stallion's. It is therefore vital that the stallion has the right temperament. He should, of course, also have excellent conformation, because you wouldn't want to breed from one that didn't. He should be the right size, because obviously that will have some bearing on the size of the foal, though it is not a dominant influence. And, most important, the stallion should have presence, dignity and style, which will all affect the foal's ability and temperament. If possible, before you use him to breed your polo ponies, a stallion should have already proved that he can produce foals of the right temperament or, better still, play polo himself. You can then expect the foal to respond directly to polo schooling and education.

In researching a stallion, therefore, look first for temperament, then for style, quality, conformation and presence – probably in that order. Size is less important, though you wouldn't want to breed from a

17-hand stallion or from a 15-hand one, unless everything else was perfect.

These days, when polo is of high quality at all levels, the ideal polo pony, whether purchased or bred by oneself, is a thoroughbred. The ideal thoroughbred is one with strong quarters, a short back, a reasonably long, slender neck, a lovely head and well-set, quite widely spaced ears. He should stand nicely over his legs and have a fine, strong shoulder. His hindquarters should not be too heavy and he should slope well up to a reasonably narrow wither, to hold the saddle in the correct place as you lean out for the shot – it is very difficult to keep the saddle in place on a pony with a rounded wither.

While it is true that some of the ugliest horses have played good polo, their ability possibly made up for their looks. So in attempting to breed or buy the ideal horse, it is of great importance to look initially for one which is well put together and pleasing to the eye. You can always sell a pretty horse, but a horse which is not so beautiful has to prove himself all the time!

Second – and crucially – the horse should go straight and move freely. A horse with a short action at the trot probably has no real scope in a gallop. The perfect polo pony has the ability to lengthen his stride without necessarily increasing the pace of that stride. Again, a short, choppy canter is much more difficult to hit the ball from than a smooth canter. But that canter stride must also be able to shorten quickly, so that the horse can handle well in tight play.

When looking for your polo pony, concern yourself more with how fast he stops, turns and goes the other way, and how smoothly he performs these actions, than how quickly he goes in general. It is not uncommon to hear a seller say, 'By Jove, this pony can run,' but what he might not tell you is that when you try to stop him at the other end, he doesn't handle quite so well.

If you decide to breed your own polo ponies, it is of vital importance to maintain the standard of the quality of your breeding herd – that is, your mares. Too many people are inclined to say, 'Oh, I've got a mare. I'd like to breed a foal,' and they find the nearest stallion, put the mare to him and wonder why three years later they haven't got what they really set out to produce. When selecting your brood mare, use the best you can find. She shouldn't just be average – too many average mares are bred from, certainly in England where the cost of keeping a horse is as high as if not higher than anywhere else in the world. As you must aim to produce a foal that is even better than the mare herself, you obviously should use the best stallion you can find too.

There is a belief that one shouldn't breed from a mare that has broken down because there is possibly a fault in her conformation. I don't entirely agree, for if the mare's conformation appears good, there are probably other reasons behind her breakdown. I believe that polo ponies break down in many cases because they are exceptionally brave,

High-goal potential.
Breeding, training and finally playing the perfect pony is a wonderfully rewarding element of polo.

and give everything they have to the player when under stress; the ground might have been in a bad state, the horse might have been hit in the leg or galloped on – there are many possible contributory factors. So provided the mare's conformation looks good, I believe her foal's percentage chance of staying sound is just as high as that of the foal of a mare which has never broken down, and that not to breed from her would be a disastrous loss of talent.

I had a brilliant English thoroughbred mare that injured herself while turning. She slipped and ruptured the tendon sheath on a hock. Two years later, after she had had a foal, we put her back into work when she didn't hold to the stallion and played her for a further three years. She is now back on the breeding programme because her first foal is playing and has shown exceptional talent.

After substantiating that the proposed brood mare's conformation and temperament are correct – and I believe temperament to be more important again than conformation – I would certainly breed from the mare that played good polo but broke down, particularly if I had played the mare and knew her well.

The size of the ideal pony is relative to the size of the rider and the level of polo which you intend to play. When breeding, obviously you must strive for the top and try to breed high-goal polo ponies. The ideal high-goal pony is between 15.0 and, at most, 16 hands. Aim at the range between 15.0 and 15.3 hands and, if he looks to be growing too big, possibly as a yearling or two-year-old, avoid over-feeding. You should also avoid the temptation to breed a pony that is just 15 hands, so that you then have to feed the foal like a king and struggle to get him to 14.3.

As already explained, it is the size of the mare rather than that of the stallion which controls the size of the foal, although obviously a 17-hand stallion will provide growing genes that give the foal the ability to outgrow the mare. Don't, therefore, attempt to breed from a mare and stallion of vastly differing heights: the mother's size must control the overall size of the foal because if she were 12 hands and she had a potential 16-hand foal inside her, she would probably not be able to foal down safely.

GENERAL CARE OF BROOD MARES

Brood mares can be run as a group on a farm. In fact, in Argentina some of the big ranches run mares in large numbers with stallions, and on the really large properties they are split up into bands of twenty to forty per stallion. They can be herded very effectively in this manner, and are brought in only when it is time to catch the two-year-olds to break them in and to 'cut' the colt foals. Nature plays an important part in ensuring that only the fit, alert foals actually make it to the polo field.

In the more practical world of small properties and proportionate numbers of horses, the mares can very easily be kept together in numbers of up to ten or fifteen, provided the paddocks are big enough. When they are foaling, however, they should be kept alone or with just one or two others and allowed to foal naturally out in the field. It is not essential to bring a mare into a loose box unless the weather is bad, and I believe that it encourages disease and infection. Foaling in bad weather should be avoided: to avoid this problem, put the mares with the stallion in late spring and the resulting foals are then born eleven months later in the late spring or early summer of the following year when the weather is good and grass is available. The foaling date of our mares bears no relevance to that of thoroughbred mares, which is always 1 January in England and 1 August in the southern hemisphere.

Our breeding herd is made up of thoroughbred English mares and proven polo mares, probably imported from Argentina, but we use a strong-boned New Zealand thoroughbred stallion who has the ideal temperament and runs out with the mares but is readily able to be handled at any time. Provided you respect him for the fact that he is a stallion and not necessarily going to take everything lying down, he is certainly very tractable; we ride him, and we could play polo on him. He is a bit old for that now but he would have been a polo pony in his younger days. He was a super jumping horse, with a lot of scope and an action which is perfect for polo or jumping – the ability to lengthen and shorten his stride without losing smoothness.

We run the stallion and the mares together at our own convenience, but we separate them late on in the autumn after he has served them at least twice. We can then look after him and keep his condition right during the winter, and then prepare him, by getting him fit, for covering the mares in late spring.

All of our field horses are checked daily. We inspect their feet on a fortnightly basis, obviously taking care to ensure they are trimmed and well shaped. We worm the mares regularly on a three-monthly programme and, when they are suckling, we ensure that they are kept in good condition. As soon as supplementary feed is necessary we feed them a special foaling mix, which is quite high in protein and contains a calcium additive. They will still be suckling but this coarse feed ration encourages the foals to start eating with their mothers from the same feed trough.

We run our mares and foals together in one paddock right through until the foals are weaned, and the only problem we have is that one of the mares is particularly dominant at feeding time, so care must be taken to spread the feeds well out and make sure that she is fed first. If her behaviour became a problem, we would separate her from the rest at feeding time.

There is always a dominant animal in any herd of horses and mares with foals are no exception. The dominant animal in polo being the one you want, it is essential to encourage this characteristic because of course he is the one that wins the ride-off and gets you to the ball first in the game. The more of this type of polo pony we can breed, the better, and this could cause a problem if there are several dominant mares in the same field.

It is useful to know that mares can be treated with hormones to bring them in season if they are not coming in regularly. We certainly treat some of the mares we put to the stallion later in the season, and it guarantees that they are going to come in and will probably get in foal.

A major breakthrough in horse breeding in recent years is the ability to fertilise by artificial insemination and thereby breed from the best stallions without necessarily having them available in the flesh. More recently in the USA egg transplantation and the use of surrogate mothers has been tried. Eggs from the best mares can be split and duplicate progeny produced. This gives the ability to breed more of the very top ponies than were ever conceived naturally on a one-to-one basis years ago. Of course, it is not a cheap technique, but it is hoped that progeny so produced will tend to be brilliant and that there will be very, very few failures among them. While the commercial herds will still be bred stallion-to-mare, some outstanding individual ponies may well be reproduced in the future by this highly scientific method.

SERVING THE MARE   The mare comes in season again between the seventh and the twelfth day after foaling and, if she has had an easy foaling and there is no vaginal damage, we always cover her with the stallion during that time. Her first cycle is a very regular one and most mares will hold to that mating successfully.

A mare on good feed in the spring and early summer should come in season approximately every twenty-one days. Signs to watch for are agitation in her behaviour, more frequent urination when around any other horses, and holding the tail to one side with the hind legs slightly apart. However, confusion can arise occasionally when a mare that is already in foal comes into a false 'season' and, although she appears ready, she will not take the stallion.

In a large breeding operation it is good husbandry to have the vet give the mares a pregnancy test at least forty-two days after their last covering. Thus you can ensure that they are in foal and can feed them accordingly; you can also decide on the appropriate course of action with mares that are not in foal for any particular reason. Just as heifers that don't get in calf or cows that calve irregularly are not regarded as commercial, so unless she is exceptionally brilliant, the mare that is difficult to get in foal is really not a commercial proposition either and should be taken out of the breeding herd.

Care should be taken in the covering of a mare that the stallion doesn't get hurt. Never cover a mare with hind shoes on, and if the mare is a maiden, take the precaution of making sure that in the teasing stage the stallion can't get kicked. The stallion who is used to running with his mares is able to look after himself in most circumstances but, if the mare is particularly prone to kicking, certain precautions should be taken such as fitting kicking boots or hobbles. It is too late to be wise after the event. If the stallion is unable to serve subsequent mares because of injury, it could prove very costly.

It is also important to remember that, prior to the covering season, the stallion should be prepared and got reasonably fit. We actually ride our stallion to get him fit. Regular exercise – not too long, but consistent – and high-quality feed are essential at this stage. The cleanliness of his penis should be checked, and it should be washed in soap and water if necessary. In thoroughbred studs the stallion is washed after each service, but this is not necessary when the stallion is run out with the mares.

Another problem which should be watched for is equine arteritis, a disease which causes the mare to abort a foal early. This is transmitted by the stallion, although he gets infected by contaminated mares. In an extensively run organisation with mares out in the field which are served by only one stallion, your horses are unlikely to contract the disease. However, if the stallion is also serving mares from other studs which have been served by other stallions, it is essential that each mare is tested before being served by the stallion. There is a simple veterinary swabbing test which can ensure that the mare is clean.

GENERAL CARE OF FOALS

A sensible veterinary programme is important for the foals. If there has been any problem in the foaling, it is advisable to give the foal a general antibiotic within twenty-four hours of birth to prevent infection, and the mare should have one too, particularly if she has torn the vagina or the afterbirth has not come away freely within the first few hours of foaling. At the first sign of scouring in the newborn foal, contact your vet immediately, otherwise essential body electrolytes and fluids will be lost and this could be the start of a fatal viral infection. Urgent action must be taken to save the foal before he becomes dehydrated. It is essential that the foal receives colostrum that is present in the mare's milk during the first three days after foaling, because this is the natural way in which he receives the mare's antibodies. If for any reason this colostrum is not available, extra care should be taken with the foal, which should be checked each day to ensure that there are no problems. A natural scour may take place after about ten days, when the mare comes into season – the milk changes – but this is nothing to worry about.

A worming programme must be established for the foal, preferably with the wormer that has the widest spectrum of worm kill. It should be administered every six weeks, and it is particularly important at weaning time to ensure that the worming programme is up to date. If in doubt, worm the foal just prior to weaning and again after ten days, being sure not to exceed the stated dose of the wormer. The foal also needs a course of vaccinations for tetanus and flu.

Feed gets shorter as winter approaches for mares with foals at foot that are out at grass. Supplementary feed will need to be given to the mares and the foals will eat this as required, but an additional creep feed system can be arranged for the foals to which the mares do not have access. It consists of a frame with a constant supply of feed inside, which is too small for the mares to enter.

One disadvantage of running mares and foals together in an extensive concern is that the individual handling of the foal tends to be left until the foal is bigger. If a foal is handled in the first few days of his life quite frequently for periods of time, possibly up to half an hour, he seems to accept people in the same way as he accepts his mother. Foals to which we have given this attention show increased intelligence and

The next generation.
Victoria Grace feeding the
babies.

learning capabilities and certainly have proved without doubt to be better able to take to the game of polo without the stresses that are often associated with the learning programme. They do not have quite the same respect for people sometimes, but this doesn't seem to pose a problem after they have been broken in, and their nature is wonderful.

If possible, in the first week after birth, foals should be handled all over, led around and generally played with. Their legs should be picked up and their bodies stroked. It is important to handle and stroke the foals while they are young, and they rapidly come to accept a human being as an essential part of their life. Any work done with the foals in the first three months of their life is very easy because they are not too strong. Time spent at this stage is amply rewarded later on, for breaking in and handling the foals becomes so much easier and no great stress to the animals.

While it is essential to show a horse at any stage of his career who is boss, the less one has to fight to dominate the animal, the easier it is for him to learn, and he seems to be far more rapid in his acceptance of your instructions. After the initial period of a week or ten days of handling – we try to do it every day – the foals should be left for about a month, after which it is advisable to try to handle them regularly every week, depending on the total work load.

By the time the foal is ready to wean, he should be leading without a problem and be able to be caught or come up to you for little attentions when you go into the field. The stress factor at weaning should then be virtually negligible.

Weaning is the first major stress for a foal. Foals should be weaned at five to seven months depending on the condition of the mare (i.e. whether she is in foal), the quality of the feed and the growth of the foal. There are several methods of weaning, and we have evolved what I consider to be the best, which seems to entail less stress than any other we've tried. Wean several foals at the same time and put them together with a quiet gelding to act as the 'daddy'. Their mothers should be taken right away. The foals have been playing with each other and therefore are used to being together; for perhaps two or three hours they are upset at being separated from the mares, but they quickly settle down, never miss feeding and seem to progress without any loss of condition.

Other weaning methods, such as putting the foal in a box by itself next to the mare, seem to prolong the agony and the foal suffers a lengthy period of considerable mental tension and stress.

After weaning, and when the resulting initial period of stress has been overcome, foals should be put out on the best feed available or, if winter is approaching, penned in a large enclosure together, possibly with a free run out to a convenient paddock. Care should be taken to maintain their feed intake at this stage, particularly if it is cold and wet, because it is crucial to their future growth pattern. We give them *ad lib* access to good-quality hay and feed at least twice a day. This basic management pattern carries on throughout the winter and in the spring, and we try to get them out on to the fresh grass as soon as the weather permits. The worming programme every six weeks to a maximum of two months should be strictly adhered to, and the handling programme possibly reduced to once every fortnight or even month, depending on the total work load of the staff.

We try to bring the yearlings in and carefully check them over physically at least every month, picking up their feet, checking their legs and grooming them, just to keep them aware of the fact that the human being is their guide and instructor. In the late autumn of the yearling stage we usually teach them to lunge, and of course, by this time, they have travelled quite frequently in the horse-box and are well accustomed to it.

In the spring and summer of the two-year-old's life a little lungeing, general handling and leading around, to remind him who is the boss, produces him in about September at the age of two and a half ready both mentally and physically for the increased stress of his breaking-in.

The first stage in the breaking-in of a polo pony, either Argentinian- or English-style, is to teach him to lead from another horse and to tie up, if he has not already had that instruction.

He is then gradually introduced to the saddle and, over a period of some days, the bridle, the bit or an Argentinian rawhide thong is put in his mouth and he is mounted and ridden away. Depending on the total handling the animal has received in his life so far, this can take from a week to a month. Care must be taken to ensure that the pony remains light in the mouth and readily able to accept the bit.

Driving in long reins teaches a young horse to go straight, and back up, perhaps more easily than riding. It also gets him more collected in reverse, and encourages him to reverse straight, which is of major importance in the training of a young polo pony.

The basic training and schooling as already outlined in Chapter 4 then begins, but great care must be taken not to give a pony too much in his first winter, from the age of two and a half to three years, and if at any time a horse starts to show stress, he should be turned out and left in the field for a while to relax.

At this age a pony should, after the initial breaking-in period, settle into a reasonably easy training programme. The normal programme would consist of being ridden two or three days a week from the field for periods of from half an hour to an hour. For the first month the best thing is to ride as often as possible, but not for too long. The basic work programme is done whenever it is convenient, to fit in with your overall farming schedule. Depending on the individual horse's abilities, he should be introduced to the stick and the ball during this winter or in the following summer, at about three years of age.

6

BUYING A POLO PONY

BUYING THE MADE POLO PONY

WHEN DECIDING TO buy a polo pony, analyse carefully what you require in the animal and then endeavour by a process of elimination to find the ideal pony to fit those requirements. The pony's capabilities should, of course, be related to those of the player: a beginner will not necessarily want the same qualities as a player who is two or three seasons into the game. It is more important for a beginner's horse to be well-seasoned, quiet and tractable than fast, and a pony that can be stick and balled (not all ponies can) is best for the novice player.

As a buyer it is important, if you are not an experienced rider, to seek the help of somebody who is well experienced in buying polo ponies. In this context you should never forget that the professional is in the game to stay and will take care to sell a player the right pony, whereas the average player who is selling a horse will, if the buyer thinks he likes the horse, be quite happy to sell it to him regardless of whether it is the right horse or not. In taking the advice of a professional you will usually get a form of guarantee which may not be otherwise obtainable from the average player. This would mean that, if subsequently the horse proved to be not quite what you thought and something that you weren't able to cope with, you would be able to take it back to the professional and ask him to change the horse for you without a problem. If in any doubt, always discuss this possibility fully before committing yourself to a deal.

Remember that a player who is selling a pony – unless he is giving up polo completely – has a reason to sell, probably because the horse is not playing polo well enough. Players frequently upgrade their strings by buying a better horse and selling their worst one. On the other hand, the player coming into the game is often able to pick up a nice, easy horse for his first pony which a more seasoned player is getting rid of only because it may not be quite fast enough to cope with the polo he is now playing. This is ideal for a player's first pony.

When buying a polo pony a vet certificate is, for the inexperienced purchaser, a basis on which he can start to evaluate the animal. The vet visits a pony and, in one to two hours, makes an assessment of that pony's abilities and his overall soundness on that day. If the vet sees anything that is not perfect, it is his job to establish the problem and, if possible, the reason for it, and to try to evaluate that in relation to the pony's future abilities in polo. A vet is very properly governed by his analysis of the examination on the day. It is difficult for him to differentiate on the vet form between a major problem, that might render the pony useless in the game, and a minor interim problem which, in the long term, would pose no great threat to the pony's future potential in polo.

I have a number of horses which have failed the vet test but have done me good service over a long period of time. I mention this with no disrespect to any vet – conversely I have had a horse pass the vet test and become chronically lame with navicular within three months. This was a young horse and I had no reason to suspect that anything might be wrong, but perhaps I should have had the pony X-rayed as a precaution at the time. It is not possible for any external examination to reveal the possibility of a navicular or pedalostitis problem. One has to weigh up the total cost of the horse in relation to polo-pony values and, if you are paying a high price, it is certainly worth having the pony fully X-rayed before the purchase. If you are paying a lower price and the pony appears to have a minor problem, there is a good case for discussing with the vendor the possibility of a guarantee to ensure that the problem comes right or is of no detriment to the pony's polo-playing ability.

It is, of course, critical to bear in mind your objectives in purchasing the pony in the first place and, if you are going to stress him to the limit, soundness must be a prerogative in the purchase. If a horse fails the vet test, it is essential to have a verbal discussion with the vet to establish what he feels he can't actually put on the vet certificate. He will qualify his opinion much better in a verbal discussion, which will enable you to make a better assessment of the potential value of the pony.

During my experience of mounting a large number of players in the game of polo, I have had a few surprises. Horses that I was sure would be ideal for certain players have in fact proved not to be so, and the horse I would have picked as being almost unplayable by a virtually inexperienced player has turned out to go very well for that particular person for reasons beyond description. Basically players fall into two categories – those who like a horse that runs immediately you drop the hand, and those who prefer a horse which has to be pushed into the game. You should define your preference and this will certainly make it easier to pick the ideal pony for you, and as you gain experience in the game, your preference may change.

It is essential that you feel 100 per cent comfortable on the horse during all of his work. Make sure that your first pony is nice and easy and does not have too much power for your particular level of polo. A tendency among many players is to buy a pony which demands too much from them during the early stage of their polo career. It is more important to have a pony which allows you to concentrate on the game and on hitting the ball, than one which is difficult and makes you concentrate on just the riding instead. For your second and third ponies, it is possible to choose a more challenging horse, but for your first you should concentrate on buying a horse that is going to be ideal to teach you and take you further in the game. The important consideration is the time you can spend, in a week, actually riding. This determines whether you buy either a younger horse and improve it with time, or a fully made pony and possibly have to pay more for it.

As soon as you are confident in the game, however, it is an important part of the learning process to challenge your abilities by taking a horse of a greater capacity than you may play to at the time, so that you are always endeavouring to improve your game, and are mounted to the level at which you are intending to play. Confidence is of paramount importance in the game of polo and your first horse is vital in the build-up of that confidence.

Before purchasing a made polo pony it is essential to spend a period of time riding him to ensure that he is compatible with your requirements and is in fact the ideal type of horse for you. Then stick and ball him to make sure that he goes properly to the ball and enables you to play all the shots to your best ability. Lastly, it is essential to play the horse in a chukka, because only then will he show you his true capabilities in the game and his temperament under pressure. Remember that it is not necessarily how fast he runs on the stick and ball field, but how fast he stops, turns and runs the other way, and the way he handles himself while stopping and turning, that are important.

If the horse performs very well but fails the vet test, you are faced with a difficult decision, and this could be the ideal time for you to ask the vendor to provide some form of guarantee on the soundness of the horse. While bearing in mind that it is useless to buy an animal which is going to be unsound and give you less-than-regular polo, it is often a shame to pass up the opportunity to own a very good playing pony for the sake of a possible minor problem. This is where a discussion with the vet, as advised earlier, can be a wise move.

If you can ride and stick and ball the pony, but it is completely impossible to play him in a chukka before you buy him, beware of the pony that doesn't stop straight, that fiddles about or gets excited, that shakes his head while stopping, or that won't run true to the ball when stick and balling. While most of these are curable in some horses, you don't necessarily want to buy somebody else's problem and I would suggest that money back or horse exchange be agreed should the pony turn out to be unsuitable for your requirements.

The Age of the Horse   Too much attention is paid to the age of a made polo pony. If the horse is sound aged fifteen, has played a lot of polo and you feel he is the right horse for you, I would always recommend buying him, particularly if he is your first horse. If he is sound at fifteen he is probably going to be sound at twenty-five: people don't realise these days just how long a polo pony can go on playing. In fact, I have several horses playing polo in my stable that are well over twenty. Originally they were high-goal ponies. They are sound, love the game and are loved by children, so it seems a shame to retire them just because they are older.

Provided the horse is looked after and always kept reasonably fit, he will play polo to a standard which he has achieved over a long period of time and be very, very happy doing it. Just like human beings, certain ponies unfortunately suffer from arthritis and various other problems but, given that these don't set in, a pony can last, I believe, ten years longer than is commonly supposed. The pony at fifteen has experience which cannot be found in a younger horse. That experience can save you ages in learning time. He has forgotten more about polo than you will learn in the first two years of your playing career, and he can show you where you should be and how you should get there.

In my early polo career I was given a horse which I was told would buck me off on the polo ground, but she would also serve to teach me. She did precisely that, and I have always remembered the benefit she was to me. She was a beautiful mare and, when she was about fifteen or sixteen years old, a seven-goal player asked me if she was for sale. It is interesting to note that Juan Carlos Harriott, when he played his last Open in Argentina – handicap ten goals and, at his peak, probably two goals better than any other player in the world – played on ponies that were all over fourteen years old. If they can play at that level of polo at fourteen they can play on and on at the lower levels at which we play in the rest of the world.

THE UNMADE POLO   If you are confident of your riding ability and follow closely the various
PONY   schooling instructions outlined in Chapter 4, adapting them to your own particular circumstances, there is no reason why you should not buy a pony that hasn't been schooled for polo and train him yourself, provided he is not your only one. If you are short of time, however, it is pointless to spend the time you do have fiddling around trying to make a pony for polo when, in actual fact, you want to play the game. It is better in that case to leave the making of ponies to somebody considerably more qualified than you who has more time. You will also enjoy your polo more and improve in the game far more rapidly. Schooling young horses is never the best thing for your own game.

In your assessment of these facts, remember the following: first, it is better initially to spend your money learning the game than maintaining your horse; and, second, once you have learnt the game, it is important for you to be able to play it, so at that point in time you possibly should buy your first *made* polo pony. Not until after that should you even consider buying a pony that is not completely made. Until you are playing polo regularly twice a week, it is probably more beneficial to rent ponies, if they are available, than to buy your own. Once that critical point has been reached, if you still wish to buy an unmade pony, you should evaluate the pros and cons very carefully and ensure you have the time to devote to the young horse before you buy him. As a string of ponies is built up, however, it is important for all good young players to remember that if they have to sell their best horses to enable them to play, they limit their ability to reach the top of the game.

The Low-goal Pony

There is considerable benefit in teaching a three-quarter thoroughbred horse to play low-goal polo, rather than the thoroughbred which is almost essential for the high-goal game. The speed requirement of a low-goal pony is not quite so great and the handling and bumping requirement is perhaps greater. It is often possible to get a smaller, more compact animal that is not quite thoroughbred which, because he is not so hot-blooded, accepts the game much more readily than some thoroughbreds.

A 15.1-hand horse which has been used as a woman's hack till the age of six or seven is an ideal candidate to train for polo. Although not easy to find, these horses learn very rapidly, prove mentally stable and, of course, have been educated in all the normal aspects of hacking and possibly jumping too. The wider a horse's overall experience, the easier he is to turn into a polo pony, given the fact that he has a naturally responsive mouth.

When selecting a horse to make into a polo pony, it is essential that he has a sensitive mouth, even in a snaffle bit. Most of his work will have been in a snaffle bit before you get him, and the pony that is responsive to a snaffle will adapt to a short-cheek pelham or a small ring gag and play polo very effectively as soon as the basic schooling programme has been completed. The main thing you will have to teach this type of horse is to respond properly to the neck-rein, because all of his riding prior to your finding him will have been with two hands on the reins. Thus his response to your neck-rein training is very significant; it will control how quickly you can bring him into polo.

In some countries polo cross ponies are brought into the game very swiftly because they are almost completely made for the job, and occasionally it is possible to pick up a pony club pony which is around 15 hands, or preferably a little bigger, that has gained experience in pony club and gymkhana work. In countries where stock horses are available and not necessarily thoroughbred, these too can prove very easy to make and certainly in most cases are fast enough for polo at six-to-eight-goal level. In England we find these days that more and more low-goal polo is being played by ponies which have been, and are sometimes still used in the high-goal game, with the result that the speed of low-goal polo seems to have increased considerably in recent years.

The player with anticipation who plays a slower pony which turns very quickly and is quick off the mark can still play a major part in a low-goal game of polo even if his horse is not the fastest in the chukka. It is very much more important to pick a horse with a calm temperament, which is sympathetic and responsive to your aids. You must choose a sound pony to make for polo, because it is pointless putting all the necessary work into a pony that is not 100 per cent sound if at the end of it he can't repay the effort you have put into him.

The Medium- or High-goal Pony

If your requirement is for a medium- or high-goal pony, a thoroughbred is almost essential, for he will have the natural ability to run fast enough to compete. He will also be not terribly expensive to buy and often reasonably easy to obtain, because throughbreds that are too small for racing are often the ideal size for polo. Rejects from the track are sold in most racing countries and, provided they are the right size and have the right type of conformation and temperament, they can make excellent polo ponies, after their minds have been educated into the 'polo mode' so that they can accept the training essential for the game.

The ideal conformation in a polo pony is discussed in Chapter 5, but there are a few more points to look for when buying a thoroughbred to train for the game. The thickness of the bone in the front leg between the knee and the fetlock is particularly important as it is a good indication of the overall 'strength' of the pony. The light thoroughbred with a fine bone should probably be avoided, because the horse needs to be strong enough to cope with the rigours of high-goal polo. However, if the bone is just a little light but the pony is ideal in other respects, I would try him.

As well as conformation, consider temperament. While you should expect to spend a fair amount of time in re-educating the horse's mind to the overall requirements of polo as opposed to racing, it is essential to begin with an animal of the right temperament, otherwise you double your work load and halve the possibility of success before you start.

If you are buying at an auction, take the precaution of ensuring that the horse's gait at the trot is correct, straight and reasonably extended, that he will trot next to you when led, that he will go backwards in the halter when asked and that he doesn't fight any of your requests. He should also be absolutely quiet for you to do anything with, such as picking up his legs or pulling his tail. Of course in a thoroughbred auction it is not possible for you to ride a horse before you buy him, and there is no guarantee from the vendor. You buy the horse as you see him on the day, and therefore you should usually get him more cheaply. If, after you have bought a horse at auction, he turns out to be a doubtful prospect, don't waste time trying to beat the odds and make him – he will probably take you four times as long and end up as half a horse. Get rid of him early by putting him back in the same auction two months later.

When it comes to training the thoroughbred for polo, he is already partly there. Given that he has been taught to gallop, the benefits of buying this type of horse are that he has already learnt to go straight and positively into the bit; he has been galloping with and next to other horses; and he is reasonably accustomed to groups of horses doing various things. The basic difference is that the pony will not respond to any form of neck-rein and will probably 'take hold' of the bit too firmly. 'Re-educating' his mouth could take considerable time, and he may still eventually let you down in this respect when he gets into fast polo. The competitiveness which the horse has been taught will make it difficult for him to come back behind the bit like the good polo pony should, and stop and turn – not necessarily when he wants to, but whenever you want him to.

The various exercises and schooling programmes outlined in Chapter 4 are ideal for retraining the thoroughbred for polo. After an initial turn-out period to settle the horse and relax his mind and body from the training he has already received, quite intensive schooling can begin – schooling that is aimed first at re-educating his brain and then his body to the special abilities essential to polo as opposed to racing.

Chesney, 8 years. *English thoroughbred owned by David Jamison and ridden by Carlos Gracida – winner of several Best Playing Pony awards and one of the top horses in English polo today.*

7
THE POLO STABLE

THE STABLE

IF YOU ARE lucky enough, the stable might be already there for you. On the other hand, you may be presented with a barn and have to subdivide it. A loose box for a polo pony should be a minimum of 10 × 10 feet; because of his nature, he is possibly the easiest of horses to cope with in a stable. (For a 16-hand showjumper it should be at least 12 × 12 feet, for a mare and foal 12–15 × 15 feet. A foaling box should be 20 × 20 feet.) It is possible to divide a barn very cheaply: with half-round poles and railway sleepers, for example, you can make it into adequate stabling. The use of four rails to separate horses, although not perfect, is certainly adequate in most cases – if you are making only temporary stabling this is all that is required and I have found it very serviceable.

If you are building a stable from scratch, wooden stabling is manufactured to a high standard and can be very attractive when the layout is well designed. We have found the use of concrete blocks to partition boxes very effective. They are highly durable, with very low maintenance costs, and look smart when painted in the club colours. High-quality doors and stable fittings help to make this form of stabling possibly the most effective in the long-term. Labour-saving devices such as swing-through feed tubs and automatic watering systems are reasonably easy to install during the erection of the stable complex, and can prove to be very labour-saving in your stable-management programme.

It is essential, when considering the construction of your stabling, to ensure that plenty of fresh air can circulate. Draughts, however, should be reduced to a minimum, because in cold weather horses can be adversely affected by a sudden cold draught or become chilled while standing still in a stable. Barn stabling in particular must be well ventilated, otherwise colds and runny noses can spread quickly, and it is wise to remove a horse with a runny nose from the barn before he infects the whole string.

Victorian-style boxes.
Ideal polo pony stabling
in a high barn.

In areas of limited space it is possible to have horses standing in stalls rather than in complete loose boxes. A stall should be approximately 8 feet deep and 6 feet wide. The horse is then tied with his head facing towards the back wall on a tethering rope which slides through a ring on the wall, about 3 feet from the floor. A weight attached to the end of the rope, sitting on the floor, will pull the tethering rope firm to within about 3 feet of the ring. The weight then hits the floor and the horse stands in the right place. If the horse wants to move about, he gets about 6 feet of lead rope on which to do so, and he will be quite comfortable if a deep bed is kept under him. While not ideal, this is a way of stabling a lot of horses on a smaller area.

In countries with a warmer climate, pipe pens built on sand have proved to be very effective in the keeping of large numbers of horses. At the Eldorado Polo Club in Indio, California – possibly the fastest-growing polo club in the world – this form of stabling has proved to be extremely efficient. The pens, made from galvanised scaffold pipe gate sections welded together, are approximately 18 feet square and some have a partial roof to give the horse shade in the heat of the day and some protection from the occasional tropical storm. When horses are stabled on sand, however, great care should be taken to watch for sand colic – an impaction of the bowel which can cause a blockage. In this sort of pen stabling it might be worth feeding the hay in a permanent hay rack and trough which might help to guard against the intake of sand and thus prevent the colic.

Tack Room and Feed Room

When you are building your stable, remember that both a tack room and a feed room should be established for every ten or so boxes. Each should measure about 10 × 6 feet, unless more space is needed in the feed room to store hay. Adequate facilities should be provided for the storage of hay and straw or some other form of bedding.

The ideal tack room contains a saddle rack for each saddle and a named bridle hook for each horse, a large cupboard to hold all the veterinary supplies and a large chest for covers and various other items. It is convenient to keep bandages rolled up in pairs on a large tray so that they can easily be carried to the horses. Open shelving on the wall is ideal for things like studs, blacksmithing equipment, large sponges, saddle soap, clippers and a various assortment of items essential for the maintenance of the horse, and helps to keep the tack room tidy. Another useful fitting in a large tack room is a bridle-cleaning ring – a large wheel with about ten hooks welded to the rim, standing on its

Tack room design. Try to obtain a sufficient area in which to work on a rainy day.

axle, which revolves as you clean each bridle. Two or three grooms can work around it at the same time if necessary.

The feed room should contain two or three large galvanised or plastic tubs of various sizes in which to tip the bags of feed. Too much feed stored in bags in the feed room encourages rats and the tubs should be fitted with lids to keep them out. To combine the feed and tack rooms is not necessarily a good idea, unless your stable is quite a small one, because dust from the feed tends to settle on the cleaned tack.

Bedding

A deep, soft bed is essential to prevent swelling and abrasions on the horses' hocks, knees and fetlocks. While most horses are still bedded on straw, wood shavings have also become popular because horses don't eat them, although they can be a little bit dusty at times. In recent years paper, which is completely dust- and germ-free, has proved very effective too, and it is, of course, more easily disposable by burning.

When planning a stable, consideration should be given to the disposal of the muck. With a large number of horses, it can become quite a problem and also fairly costly. The straw which we currently use is largely removed by mushroom growers. However, wood shavings have to be carried away which can prove expensive. A recent development in the USA is a soft rubber mat which covers the concrete floor and only needs hosing down twice a day. Although not cheap, it should prove cost-effective from the point of view of both labour and bedding expenses, and it is worth careful research.

Paddocks and Exercise and Schooling Areas

It is quite essential to have a paddocking area adjacent to the stables, separated into small paddocks for turning out fully stabled horses. A couple of hours in the paddock whenever he gets bored relaxes a horse and is essential to his mental well-being.

Of prime importance in a large stabling organisation is the exercise area. In a polo stable where a number of horses have to be exercised on a regular basis, an exercise area can rapidly become a quagmire in wet weather. The requirement is a large, well-drained, more or less circular area with a straight fence for schooling and, preferably, a hill in the field. Areas such as quite steep sand slides and slopes are very beneficial for the muscling-up of polo ponies, and these are particularly suitable for individual schooling. The exercise track has to cope on a daily basis with a large string of ponies being exercised by a minimum number of grooms in a safe manner.

An outdoor schooling arena is an essential part of a large polo establishment. An arena 100 × 60 feet would be adequate for the short schooling of the polo pony. While there are various all-weather surfaces on the market these days, possibly the best for polo-pony schooling is coarse sand, which can be compressed into a firm surface and, provided it is adequately drained and lets the water through, will be usable in most weathers. If salt is added to the sandy surface during the winter, it will prevent freezing at least until the weather becomes too cold to allow work outside.

A round pen with quite high sides, or possibly solid walls, about 20 yards across, can be useful for breaking in young horses and also for the really tight schooling necessary to make a polo pony. Work in such an arena in only a headcollar can prove beneficial to ponies that are inclined to pull, and I have found a hackamore to be a very good bit for the close schooling of some horses.

The Horse Walker

If used sensibly, the horse walker can be an invaluable addition to the facility. It is ideal in the stable to walk a number of horses quietly around in a circle to cool down and loosen up after exercise. It is also very effective in the mental relaxation of some horses. It should be used only for walking and should be equipped with a free-wheeling system so that, if a horse stops, the clutch will slip and prevent damage. While exercising on the horse walker, horses should be supervised at all times. The correct siting of the walker in close proximity to the stable for ease of management is therefore advisable.

For safety's sake it is essential for the horse walker to be firmly anchored in position and the horse tied so that, if he pulls back really hard, he can break away without injury. The walker should thus be situated in a large pen to prevent the escape of a horse if he does break free.

Staff Facilities

The importance of the groom in the well-organised polo yard cannot be over-estimated. The groom is essential to the organisation and his well-being should be given top priority in the planning of both the lay-out of the facilities and the management of the stable. Because they have to work irregular hours, grooms need good accommodation – preferably a room to themselves – and good bathing facilities, and a well-organised relaxation area with catering facilities.

STABLE MANAGEMENT

To manage a large stable successfully, a number of skills are required: the art of organising people, the knowledge of how to do it all yourself so that you can show the grooms what is required at any time and the ability to maintain a good atmosphere in a large organisation.

The stable manager's most important duty is to establish a workable routine in the stable, so that all of the horses under his care are looked after properly, exercised regularly, and turned out well and on time for matches with maximum efficiency and a minimum of fuss and bother.

He must ensure that all the transport arrangements are made, that the grooms are given the necessary information about what is planned and that everything is achieved with plenty of time to spare. He must have confidence in the ability of his staff, but he also needs to be able to show them what is required and help if things get behind.

It is imperative in the larger organisation to have a fully experienced head groom who can ensure that the basic daily stable routine continues while the stable manager is responsible for the overall organisation, i.e. the weekly/monthly planning, and the players get on with all the complex organisation that is essential to the successful management of a number of teams. Polo teams play in many different leagues, at different levels of ability, signified by different total team handicaps, hence the complex management involved in planning the movement of both players and horses.

For the individual player who does not have time to organise his own stable, a groom who has had previous experience of polo is a must. He will have the horses to look after, and in most cases will take care of their daily routine and maintenance alone. The groom may also have to do the majority of the schooling and therefore should be a reasonably experienced rider – preferably with previous polo schooling experience as well.

If the stable is large and complex, the stable manager should appoint people to take charge of the various groups of horses within the organisation. A stable works most efficiently if each groom can be given individual horses to look after, with one or perhaps two players to groom for, and although this is not always possible, it has proved the best basis for an efficient organisation.

The groom's regular duties also include checking on the supply of feed and bedding, keeping the yard tidy and inspecting all the horses after they have played – preferably on a regular day each week. A Monday morning is the most peaceful time in a polo stable because it is normally the day all the horses rest after a busy weekend.

For the long-term benefit of the sport, an organisation of this kind should always try to take on one or two junior staff and teach them the basics of polo grooming; the teaching programme should be administered by the stable manager. In the Rangitiki Polo School, at Ascot Park Polo Club, we invariably train a number of student grooms each season, and many have since made polo their vocation. With the worldwide increase in the popularity of the sport, the polo groom can make a very good and interesting living all over the world.

THE STABLE ROUTINE

It is important to establish an organised stable routine. This will vary from country to country, basically because of the climate, and of course because polo might be played at different times of day.

The stable routine outlined here may be modified to suit any particular circumstances. An ideal routine for the summer season in England is to feed the horses at 7.00 am, muck out between 7.45 and 8.30, breakfast from 8.30 to 9.00, tack up the first lot of horses straight after breakfast and ride them out to exercise by 9.30. When these have had an hour's exercise, the second lot of horses can be tacked up and out by 11.00 am so that you have two complete sets of horses exercised by midday. This means that tack can be tidied up and lunch can be taken from 12.30 to 2.00 pm on non-polo days, or 12.30 to 1.30 if horses have to be taken to polo to be ready to play at 3.00 pm. In England play is between 3.00 and 6.30 pm, after which the horses are returned to the stable, the tack is tidied up and they are given their evening feed.

On non-polo days, when the horses are exercised for a longer period – possibly an hour and a half – the first lot can be schooled in the morning and the second lot in the afternoon. On these days horses might be schooled individually, and this would be done after the group work. Having already warmed up in the exercise, they should be schooled for only short periods of time to sharpen them up.

On polo days horses need not necessarily be worked, although on match days all the match ponies should be taken out for at least half an hour in the morning. Match ponies will play considerably better having had half an hour to an hour of walk and jog in the morning, or perhaps a short gallop, if they are to play at 3.00 pm that day.

It is a very important part of the daily routine to leave the stable tidy, both at lunchtime and in the evening. Try to ensure that the yard is swept and clean after you finish work at the end of the day. There is nothing more demoralising than having to start work in the morning in a dirty yard. Tack should be given a quick clean each day following afternoon work and a thorough going over at least once a week, preferably on the horses' day off, which is normally Monday.

As already mentioned, it is beneficial in a large organisation if certain grooms can be assigned to certain horses. In my own establishment this is not always possible because we have numerous horses doing different things. We find that grooms tend to be assigned to players rather than to horses, and therefore will be responsible for whichever horses that player is riding on any given day. When we have a match team which mostly stays together, we then assign grooms to look after the player's particular match ponies.

Grooms who have their horses boxed should make a habit at mucking-out time, as they walk into the box, of feeling all the horses' legs. With experience it is possible rapidly to detect an oncoming problem in this way (see pages 150–154 for further information).

Whatever organisation is used, the daily stable routine remains the same. For horses kept in the field, however, it can be slightly different. First, it is not essential to exercise all of them every day. But it is important that on the days match ponies kept in the field are exercised it is for the same period of time as if they were in boxes because, after all, they must be equally as fit. The fact that they are walking around in a field day and night, though, means they needn't have quite the same total number of hours per week of exercise, and the benefit is that they remain considerably more relaxed.

The total amount of exercise given to the boxed pony is essential to dissipate the stored-up energy gained from hours of inactivity. At some of the top high-goal stables, ponies are exercised twice a day – once to condition them for fitness and the second time to dissipate that stored-up energy. So the second exercising might be a quiet walk or jog out, perhaps with a bit of feeding in a field or somewhere beside the track to relax them and take their mind off the polo field.

Polo days have their own special routine. Presuming that polo is to be played in the afternoon, as it is in England, these days will vary their routine after lunch. The routine of getting the ponies to the polo ground – whether they go tacked up or untacked – will depend on the location of the stable. It is equally satisfactory to take them tacked up or untacked, but either way it is essential to allow yourself the time to do the job in a professional manner. Horses should always be ready at least twenty minutes before the game tacked up and standing with a loose girth and surcingle in the pony lines. This enables the groom to relax and have time to make last-minute adjustments, or to rectify something which possibly has been forgotten, such as the studs. It is also important for the player to have time to stick and ball any horse that he needs to settle down, and to sit on the saddles before he actually plays so that the stirrups are adjusted to the proper length. The twenty-minute rule must be adhered to. The groom should ensure that all the stirrups are correctly adjusted and should measure the stirrup length by placing his fingers on the knob over the top of the stirrup bar and pulling the stirrups up under his armpit. If the saddles are the same, they should all be the same length.

DAILY CARE OF THE POLO PONY

Within the general stable routine already outlined on page 141, it is essential for the groom to establish a daily routine for the individual polo pony. While the horse is eating breakfast, he should be mucked out and, if you don't intend to ride him that day, groomed for ten to fifteen minutes before you go on to the next horse. If possible, a horse should be groomed for twenty minutes each day, so that a short grooming – of, say, ten minutes – could be given at the time mentioned, followed by a further grooming of about ten minutes in the afternoon, perhaps before the evening feed.

On polo days each horse should be brushed off after he comes back to the stable and is dried off. This will take approximately five minutes for each horse.

After exercise, if the horse is really sweaty, he should be hosed down and scraped to remove excess water. If the weather is warm, every horse should be hosed after exercise. In cooler weather horses should not be hosed but be groomed when they are dry after exercise. Take care not to put a wet horse into the loose box to stand and shiver. A jute or New Zealand rug upside down on a wet horse will enable him to dry, and the secret is to put straw between the horse's back and the rug to enable air to circulate – warm air that will stop him getting chilled.

If a horse is slightly low in condition, a lunchtime feed given before you go for your lunch is advantageous, but not if the horse is going to play polo that afternoon. One third to one half of the usual hay ration should be given in the morning after exercise, if not too late; or, if the pony is going to play polo in the afternoon, it should not be given with the morning feed. Hay is bulky and sits in the stomach, taking time to be digested and pass through, so none should be fed for at least five hours before a pony is to be played. A small feed of oats could be given up to three hours before the pony plays with no ill effect. Make sure that he does not drink for at least three hours before he plays, and remember that the faster the polo, the more important and extended these times should become.

Don't forget to feel each horse's legs every day. Get into this habit and you will rapidly notice any change in the temperature of a leg which might disclose a potential problem and should be brought to the notice of the stable manager or the player concerned.

The groom plays the major part in keeping a polo pony playing and it is crucial not to have horses laid up with problems which can be avoided. While you should never play a pony which is in pain, keeping the pony playing the game is essential to the long-term success of the team. In order to keep high-goal ponies on the road, or as a precaution for horses with minor leg problems, individual horses may require cooling lotion or cold-water bandages to cool the legs and brace the tendons after they have played hard. It is attention to details like these which distinguishes the good groom.

It is the stable manager's job to ensure that medication is administered correctly and regularly, and to keep a vet book in which it is recorded daily, though sometimes it is easier for the individual groom who looks after one player's ponies to keep this book.

The groom is responsible for the overall well-being of the horse, but certainly not for decisions on possible injury. He might not have the experience to foresee prior to a major injury that a horse might be running into a problem. It is essential therefore for the groom to discuss, either with the player or with the stable manager, any potential problem that he might suspect. Two heads are certainly better than one in such a case and an injury might well be prevented by remedial action taken earlier rather than later, when the horse has broken down. If there is any doubt, the vet should be telephoned; the problem can always be discussed with him on the phone and he will pay a visit if he thinks it necessary.

When faced with a problem of this kind, then, a groom should not panic but should refer it to someone with experience. In many cases time is needed to make the correct diagnosis and cure the problem. If you call in the vet immediately, he won't always be able to put his finger on what the trouble is and he may well say, 'Rest the pony for a couple of days, if necessary treating a local area, and see what happens with time.' However, the groom can rest in the knowledge that he has acquainted the vet with the fact that all is not right, and he is much better qualified to make the necessary decisions. The ideas expressed here are meant as a guide to the groom who doesn't have adequate veterinary care in constant close attendance on his horses, and therefore, when confronting a potential problem, has to make up his or her own mind as to the best course of action.

In the daily care of the horse, special attention should be paid to the 'difficult' parts: between the legs, under the chin, under the belly and behind the hind legs. A gelding's penis should be washed and kept clean, as should the area between the hind legs (particularly if the horse's motion is at all runny, in which case his health should be watched carefully). Particular care should be taken of the stabled horse's feet: they should be cleaned out regularly every day, and the slightest sign of any thrush (an infection that can creep in round the frog of the foot or in the crack in the middle of the frog running up into the heel) should be cleaned out with methylated spirits and/or a 5 per cent solution of formalin – excellent for curing this problem and for hardening the sole of the hoof. A deep-seated thrush can be the cause of apparent lameness in the horse and certain horses seem more prone to the problem. In these cases regular treatment – say, twice a week – with hoof oil around the sole of the foot and in all the cracks keeps the thrush infection at bay and the horse's frogs and heels moist and supple. Use methylated spirit first if the frog is at all smelly.

Remember that it is the action of the frog pressing on the ground which pumps the blood around the horse's lower leg and it is essential, therefore, to keep the frogs and heels pliable so that they move in the correct manner when a horse moves about the box. Their action is similar to that of a percussion pump, and works by direct ground pressure expanding and contracting the hoof.

An adequate supply of water should always be available to the polo pony except for the period before he is due to play a game. A big drink of water just before he plays is certain to stop the horse from performing properly and also can be dangerous, possibly causing a ruptured stomach, if the pony is played hard.

It is most important that the horse's daily routine follows a consistent pattern and thus contributes to his overall contentment and general well-being. This is really the essence of the animal's ability to play to his maximum performance level, and to continue doing so throughout the season. These days, to win tournaments of any size, the team needs to win at least five consecutive games, and therefore the ponies have to be trained to 95 per cent maximum and hold that capacity – 'bubbling' just under the maximum for quite extended periods. The good trainer is very careful not to over-train his string so they go 'over the top' and fall away, becoming 'dead' and incapable of playing to their true form. This often happens to horses imported shortly before being launched into a busy season: they need special care when they first arrive to avoid succumbing to the problem about six weeks after they start to play matches here. Acclimatisation and an extra six weeks of easy work would help the horse to cope with this added stress factor.

Keeping Records

In a well-organised stable, records kept up to date can give an accurate picture of a particular horse in the event of a problem – a sprain or twist, a bad bruise, or regular treatment such as worming.

If a card file is kept on each pony, a change of staff can find out important details – the correct bridle, a special saddle, a 'level' of feed, i.e. the ratio of oats to nuts and hay – which together have a dramatic effect on the way a horse will play, and any particular habits a pony will have. Records should also include blacksmithing details and dates, any medication, and the quantity of work per week the horse is currently doing. This provides a year-on-year comparison of the work programme and the capabilities of each horse as well as his overall health.

GENERAL VETERINARY CARE

A polo pony should be shod regularly – approximately every four to six weeks, depending on the amount of road work he has to do. Stud holes should be put in the hind shoes to enable studs to be screwed in prior to polo. These are removed after every game, and great care should be taken that studs are never left in when horses are turned out together in the field.

In some countries ponies run together out in the field are shod with permanent corkins, which are formed by the blacksmith by bending over the ends of the hind shoes during shoeing. These horses should not be fed in close proximity to each other because of the danger of kicking, which can occur as they naturally try to dominate each other, resulting in unfortunate cuts which could have devastating consequences in the preparation of your match string. As ponies get fitter, so they become more dominant, and it is therefore particularly important not to put horses which are strangers together in a small paddock. Although being outside is better for the really fit young horse from the point of view of his mental state, it is more risky than being in a box, and this must be taken into consideration in the daily routine.

Standing still on hard concrete in a box causes 'big leg' swelling problems in some horses and a horse that comes out of the stable every morning with swollen legs should be turned out every night in the field if possible, because walking around will prevent it. If you have to treat this problem in the box, use cooling lotion, cold-water bandages, or other forms of slight pressure bandage to try to reduce the swelling in the legs. Sheepskin pads, lightly bandaged on to the legs, prove very beneficial in these cases, maintaining warmth and therefore blood circulation, and cold hosing after work, for about twenty minutes, is also very effective.

A horse's coat is a good indication of his overall well-being. If it becomes dull and lack-lustre, re-examine the overall feed, paying special attention to vitamin/mineral supplements and in particular his intake of salt. Salt is of vital importance to the polo pony because of his salt loss through sweat every time he plays, particularly in hot weather.

The horse's droppings should automatically be noted every day, and if they become hard, he should immediately be given a bran mash to loosen the droppings. If the droppings are runny, again bran mash is the best feed to re-establish the correct balance in the horse's digestive system. Care should be taken not to change a sensitive horse's feed mixture too quickly back from bran mash to straight oats or high-protein feed mix, and if a horse stops regular work his ration of protein should be reduced immediately to avoid an excess of protein in the system.

All the horses in the stable should receive a regular bran mash feed every week, if on a normal grain and mixed feed ration. Bran mash is made by mixing two dippers of bran plus a handful of Epsom salts with enough warm water to make it damp but not runny. A handful of molasses meal will make it more palatable. Linseed has a very beneficial effect on a horse's coat and can be added to the night feed either in pure oil form or, better still, as boiled linseed. Remember that boiling a cupful of linseed in a gallon pot full of water gives quite a large volume – it expands dramatically when cooked on very low heat overnight, and is likely to flow over the top of the container if care is not taken. Add roughly a quarter of a dipper to the evening feed.

These days a specially mixed nut or cube, with all the requirements for a healthy horse, is prepared by most feed manufacturers. We have fed this to our horses in recent years and they have never looked better. It is also much easier to run a big stable if a standard feed is used – all you need to do is vary the quantity to suit each horse, and make up the bulk with extra hay.

Check the horse's teeth at regular intervals. His teeth should be done at the beginning of every season, and every two months they need to be looked over to ensure that they have not developed sharp edges or points and corners – particularly at the back of the back teeth – which would make eating painful. The front of the back molars of a horse that plays in a gag bit should be well rounded and sloping back so that the cheeks cannot be cut if jammed between the bit and the teeth with the action of the gag. If the horse's mouth becomes cut on the inside, change the bit to one which is going to take pressure off the damaged area for about ten days or a fortnight to enable it to heal. A horse with a sore mouth is a potential problem and will not play up to his capability, if he plays at all. A sore mouth will frequently cause a young horse to 'pull through the bridle', making him difficult to stop. In this case, a complete break from riding for two weeks is essential to allow the problem to mend. The horse can be exercised on the lead to keep him fit.

The regular worming of horses is essential and, depending on the programme decided in consultation with your vet, it is usually done every six weeks to three months. The annual flu 'vac' and tetanus injection, which should be given before the horse starts to play polo at the beginning of the season, have already been mentioned.

The Veterinary Chest

It is important, if a vet is not readily available, to have a fairly comprehensive veterinary chest to hand. This should be kept in a locked cupboard in the tack room, so that it cannot be used by anybody unqualified. It should contain antibiotics, a general antiseptic and disinfectant, de-wormers, liniments, bandages, syringes and a thermometer – or whatever you might require, depending on your own personal ability to diagnose and treat your horse's veterinary problems. People who don't have the experience which is essential for diagnosis should carry only the bare minimum and call in the vet whenever in doubt.

In close cooperation with your vet, you should gradually put together the regular requirements of your veterinary kit. You will need tranquillisers or sedatives; pain killers – a muscle relaxant, for instance, for colic; mineral supplements, vitamin B12 and other general vitamins that can be given by injection; medication which helps to cure disease, such as antibiotics, de-wormers, and a good curative such as tincture of iodine or sulphathiazol cream. Purple spray is also an essential for the stable veterinary chest: this contains an antiobiotic plus gentian violet (which is a very good disinfectant) and is ideal for most cuts and abrasions. Hydrogen peroxide is a very useful wound cleanser, and used neat it is an excellent treatment for any foot problem. Formalin solution diluted to 10 per cent or even 5 per cent can be highly effective, particularly for anything in the sole of the hoof, but take care not to get it on your hands. Not widely considered in horse care, formalin is perhaps better known as the basis of a solution used for the treatment of foot-rot in sheep. Provided care is taken not to dry out the wound before it has healed, and thus seal in the infection, formalin proves an excellent medication in the treatment of puncture wounds in the sole, or for thrush and heel infections, and subsequent treatments with 10 per cent formalin will also harden the sole. In an emergency any spirit – whisky, for example – is a good cleanser of infection, particularly in the hoof to sterilise a puncture wound or a cut.

Other medicines useful to have in the vet chest are cough linctus (we use Benylin), eye drops and anti-inflammatory drugs such as Equipalazone. Kaolin poultice (sometimes called antiphlogistine) and a poultice of Epsom salts spread on gamgee (a combination gauze and cotton wool padding) and mixed with vinegar will certainly prove invaluable. As mentioned earlier, Epsom salts are also a vital ingredient of a bran mash, and act as the drawing agent when 'tubbing' a horse's foot – add a good handful to two pints of hot water.

Sulphanylamide powder is very beneficial, as are Stockholm tar, a zinc oxide ointment and green oils, which are general healing creams. A mixture of one-third zinc oxide ointment, one-third sulphanylamide powder and one-third Stockholm tar is most useful for spreading on wounds which seem to take ages to heal. If proud flesh is involved, a small quantity of copper sulphate crystals can be added to this cream which will gently form scabs and remove the proud flesh. Treatment three or four times a week while the horse is turned out should prove effective.

A green cream called Dermobian is very beneficial and possibly the best healing cream available in England. Cornucrescine is a very good hoof-growing cream which, rubbed in regularly round the top of the coronet, can promote the more rapid growth of hoof horn. It also encourages the regrowth of hair.

The vet chest should also contain various wound-care and bandaging materials, alcohol for cleaning wounds, distilled water, cotton wool, gamgee for protective bandaging or poultices, stretch sticking plaster and hospital tape. A good curved needle and some sterile thread can sometimes save a visit from the vet to stitch up a minor wound and often a stitch in time saves nine!

Possibly the best initial treatment for an open wound which may have been stitched is glycerine gauze. This promotes rapid growth of healing tissue. Take care not to use it for too long because it can encourage the growth of proud flesh, which can then take considerable time to heal.

It is important to store drugs locked in a cool, dark cupboard, so ensure that your tack room is furnished appropriately. Drugs should be used before the expiry date on the packaging. Before administering any drug, you should be sure to read the instructions supplied and understand the recommended dose. Safely dispose of any unlabelled bottles if the contents are unknown. If in doubt about how to dispose of waste medicines, discuss it with your vet or local chemist.

When treating veterinary problems, ensure absolute cleanliness at all times, use plenty of disinfectant and plenty of water and, unless you are certain as to the correct treatment of an ailment, always consult your vet.

The Twitch

An invaluable aid to the care of the horse, a twitch can be made from a piece of wood 12 to 18 inches long, with a hole bored through it about an inch from the end. A piece of plaited string is threaded through the hole, and tied in a circle about 6 inches in diameter.

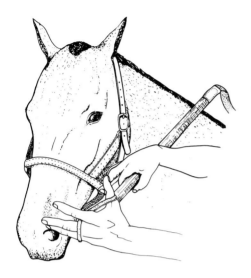

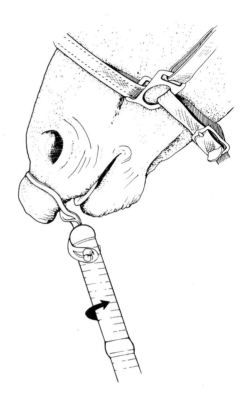

The thong of the rebenque makes an excellent twitch. When twisted around the nose it releases a natural anaesthetic, which can be extremely useful when performing some veterinary activities or clipping a difficult horse.

As in the diagrams the fingers are put through the twitch and the horse's nose is pulled through the circle of string, held by the left hand, while the right hand twists the handle gently but firmly in a clockwise direction until it tightens on the nose. The action of squeezing the nose of a horse releases a tranquillity drug in the horse's body, and is not unkind if used for not more than 10 minutes at a time. If used properly, it will distract the horse's attention from essential handling and other slightly uncomfortable but routine treatment. Longer use causes him to go numb, and will prevent him from feeling the benefit of the twitch. It should be removed for a few minutes to allow the blood to circulate normally before using it again.

Colic

Colic in a horse is similar to an acute stomach ache in a human being and may be just a passing problem which is sometimes accentuated because a horse cannot burp. Signs of colic are general agitation, getting up and lying down rather more often than usual, looking round at the belly and possibly licking the flank. The horse will also probably begin to sweat. To start the cure administer 10–20 cc of a muscle relaxant if available, and a large bottle of beer – a widely used remedy in New Zealand – can help too. If the colic is prolonged, you must call the vet. It is essential to prevent the horse from rolling, which can twist the gut.

The horse should then be quietly walked until he shows signs of relaxing as the pain eases. It is important to keep a careful watch on him to check for any relapse. If it happens again soon afterwards, however, the vet should be consulted immediately to ascertain if the cause is serious, such as a renal blockage. It is wise not to stress the horse too soon after a bad bout of colic: he needs a few days of relaxing exercise to get his metabolism back together again, and as a precaution in case of minor internal damage.

Strained Tendons and Ligaments

A strained tendon sometimes occurs if a pony slips while turning sharply or, occasionally, in wet weather or on a rough ground, puts his foot in a hole and twists it, or overstretches the tendons with uneven pressure. The pony will normally go lame immediately and have to be taken off the field. The more difficult lameness to diagnose is where the pony has been fine going back to the lines, but the leg swells later, and you notice it as the horse is being taken away from the pony lines. To check, lift the leg, and feel the tendon between the finger and thumb. If it is strained it will vary in its feel – softer and squashy where the blood has leaked into the tissues.

If a tendon strain occurs on the polo field, immediately bandage with a tight, cold-water bandage to prevent initial swelling while transporting the pony back to the yard. On arrival inspect the leg again to ensure that your diagnosis is correct, place a thin support bandage on the leg to maintain pressure from the outside and stand the horse in an ice pack for as long as you think necessary to prevent or minimise the internal bleeding which causes swelling.

I have stood a horse with this problem in ice for two days without any detriment, while making a significant improvement to the swelling, and thus probably halving his total recuperation time. The ice pack I use is about 18 inches of rubber tubing cut from a car tyre. It passes over the horse's foot and is secured under the fetlock with a piece of string. It runs up above the knee and stays there by its own rigidity. Packed out with ice, it is the ideal form of ice pack. If it slips down, it can be held up by a piece of string over the top of the pony's wither and back under the neck. The pony is then free to wander around the box.

If swelling is discovered in a pony's leg the day after polo and a sprain is suspected, try the ice pack for from two to four hours to see if it immediately reduces the swelling. If it has no effect, poultice with Epsom salts or kaolin – warm but not too hot, otherwise it can burn the skin – until the swelling is reduced, which may take one to two weeks. The horse, of course, must be kept in the box if a leg sprain is suspected, and not allowed to walk out in the field.

Care should be taken not to start the horse back in work too soon after a strained tendon or ligament has occurred. Treatment with a working blister, an astringent lotion which is painted on to the leg, once the filling has gone out of the leg and it is cold, followed by an adequate rest period turned out, will usually rectify most sprains, but support bandages should be used when the horse is brought back into work. Always support both legs of the pair (front or back) if one is injured, as a horse will instinctively tend to over-stress the good leg by favouring the bad one a little.

Time is the best healer of all strains, but correct treatment is essential to help time to do its work. The original severe blister was a poisonous mercuric oxide – red blister – which had to be used with a neck cradle to prevent the horse from rubbing the blistered leg with his muzzle, and badly burning it with the blister or, worse, poisoning himself. Blistering has the effect of dramatically forcing a surge of blood and healing fluids through the system into the injured tissues, thus speeding up the healing process. I have had marvellous results from a blister which, I believe, incorporates some form of rapidly absorbed healing stimulant and does not blister in the old accepted manner – it is an individual vet's proprietary recipe. Together with at least six months' rest, it has enabled me to bring back to the game horses which I thought would never play polo again.

Other Leg/Foot Injuries

Swelling in the leg is not always the result of a sprain, and the correct diagnosis is, of course, essential to the success of the treatment. Bruising from an over-reach or a hit with a stick may be the cause, and this can be discovered only by careful feeling for tenderness, sometimes over a period of days. If in doubt, start with the sole of the foot and work up. Foot squeezers – a giant pair of tongs with square ends – enable you to put pressure on individual areas in the horse's foot, and if the horse flinches it is an indication that possibly all is not well. Experience in responding to the flinching of a horse will enable you to ascertain the probable reason for the lameness in the leg. Foot problems can sometimes cause swelling higher up the leg, just to confuse the diagnosis.

If a foot injury is suspected – often a puncture wound – and the vet is not available, call the blacksmith. Pressure resulting from a build-up of puss or fluid in a horse's foot will rapidly cause him to become dramatically lame and put only his toe on the ground. Such a build-up of fluid must be let go through the sole of the foot, preferably through the injury site so that it is opened up and cleaned out. The hole must be made big enough to let the injury drain properly: a tiny little one will rapidly seal and the problem could recur. It is essential for your medication to be able to get into the problem area and for collected fluid to keep draining out. This type of injury should always be poulticed – hot, moist bran and a handful of Epsom salts in a plastic bag around the foot are very effective. The foot should be 'tubbed' twice a day – the horse is stood with the injured foot in half a bucket of hot water to which a double handful of Epsom salts has been added. Once the horse is sound in the hoof, the blacksmith can always put a pad under the shoe to protect the hole in the sole. A daily injection of antibiotics for at least three days – and usually five – should be given to the horse once an infection has been diagnosed.

In cases where the skin has been broken by cuts or kicks and there is a possibility of infection, it is usually beneficial to administer an antibiotic as a precaution while externally treating the problem. Cuts must be cleaned immediately and, if necessary, stitched. Kicks, on the other hand, cause internal bruising as well as the visible external damage and therefore need some form of bruise treatment such as poulticing to reduce the inflammation or hosing for half an hour at a time to reduce the heat in the affected area. If stitching is required, it must be done within hours of the wound, and if there is a delay the wound must be kept moist. If it dries, the stitches will probably fail.

If a corn is suspected, remove the shoe and examine the area of the sole formerly covered by the shoe to see if any red tissue is present. This is the sign of a corn and should be carefully cut out with a hoof parer to remove the pressure that is applied by the shoe. The shoe can often be replaced but sometimes will have to have a pad underneath it to spread the pressure evenly over the sole of the foot and away from the painful area. Two or three days' poulticing, without the shoe in bad cases, will speed recovery.

Ringworm

Ringworm, an easily transmitted skin complaint, can be a major problem in polo because of the presence of a large number of horses which frequently make close physical contact while riding off in the game. As soon as a case is suspected, the horse should be isolated while steps are taken to ascertain whether it is in fact ringworm. If it is, establish a treatment programme in conjunction with your vet which will avoid cross-contamination between horses in your stable. Give the infected animal time to recover completely before bringing him back into your stable and into the sport.

Bear in mind that ringworm is a very difficult thing to kill. A fungus that lives in woodwork, on fenceposts and in loose boxes for years, it 'breaks out' occasionally, especially in hot, muggy weather. Care should be taken to keep horses clean and dry and to wash their saddle blankets and girths very regularly in a special bacterial disinfectant to lessen the chance of cross-infection between them. In Britain a very good disinfectant, Imavarol, is available which will kill ringworm; immediately a case is suspected a programme for the use of this product should be established in the stable.

A powder called Fulsan is a beneficial back-up to ringworm treatment – it is added to the feed of horses which may have become infected but are not yet showing any signs of the disease and it will prevent an outbreak.

It is important to remember that the incubation period for ringworm is three weeks, and one of the problems is that a horse can become re-infected after he has been cured. Horses with ringworm or any skin infection should remain isolated until there is absolutely no possibility of their contaminating others. The groom should be alert to early signs of skin infections like ringworm – slightly raised, roughly circular areas of balding skin form grey lesions with tiny bits of skin coming away in the broken hair. The first signs are normally seen around the girth area or the head. The groom should be instructed to report immediately to the stable manager should any possibility of such an infection be suspected.

There is an associated fungus called Canadian pox which is not nearly so virulent as ringworm, although it too requires isolation of the horse and individual treatment of the sores with an appropriate fungicidal preparation.

TACKING UP THE PONY BEFORE A GAME

First of all, sort out the tack that you are going to require for each pony and put it near the horse as he stands in the pony lines.

The first job is to bandage the pony, starting with the left front leg. While kneeling to the side of this leg, take the firmly rolled bandage in your right hand and pass the end between the pony's front legs. Position the first level of bandage about 2 inches below the left knee and pass your left hand, holding the end of the bandage, back between your body and the pony's leg, to a distance of about a foot behind the leg. Pass your hand holding the rolled bandage from below and up over the top of the bandage held in your left hand, leaving the foot of bandage to be folded down the back of the leg to protect the tendon. Then pass the rolled bandage in your right hand over the top of the bandage held flat on the leg by the left hand and pull firmly so that it doesn't slip.

From there proceed to bandage down the leg, overlapping the bandage by half its width with each revolution of the leg. On each leg go down just below the little knob on the back of the fetlock; this should be covered in each case, but particularly on the back legs, because some horses sit on their hind fetlocks as they stop. Bring the bandage back up the leg, again overlapping it by half its width with each turn, and fasten it with the Velcro fastener just under the knee – *not* half-way up the leg. It should be fastened at the top because that part of the tendon doesn't move in the extension of the leg, and so the fastening can be kept tight there. In the old-fashioned bandages fastened with tape, the tape must be tied around the top of the bandage just below the knee. The right leg is done in the same way, and most people bandage in the same direction for each leg.

The tension on the bandage should be quite firm and, as you pass it from hand to hand, you should pull each turn with the right hand holding the horse's leg. Some people bandage in the foot of support bandage which hangs down and protects the tendon as they start to come up the leg from the bottom. I prefer, however, to bandage it in from the top going down, after the first turn, so that it sits smoothly behind the tendon and the bandage goes over the top of it, both on the way down and on the way back up to the top, thus giving maximum support and even pressure to the tendon.

Occasionally horses wear support bandages on their front legs. These are special extra-stretch bandages and should be put on carefully, pulled out to half their total tension. They are otherwise put on in basically the same way as ordinary bandages, but should go down below the fetlocks if their purpose is primarily to protect and support the suspensory ligaments and the main tendon at the back of the leg.

If you have trouble with the fetlock on a horse, the support bandage can be taken around the bottom of the fetlock and used specifically to support the fetlock joint and the low suspensories down the side of the fetlock. In that case, the playing bandage should drop just below the fetlock to cover part of the support bandage as well.

Exactly the same method of bandaging is used on the hind legs except that the protective foot of bandage which is saved is brought down the outside and slightly towards the front of the hind leg to protect the horse from a hit in the leg with a mallet on a backhand shot. Take the bandage a little lower on the hind leg under the fetlock in case the horse has a habit of sitting down on his hind fetlocks when turning. In such a case the hind fetlocks can rub on the ground and wearing can occur on the back and inside of the fetlock joint.

A recent development, now used in many high-goal strings, is 'skid boots'. These go over the back bandages and are made from a thin, flexible rubber compound. They give excellent protection to the horse which scrapes his heels when he sits down in a quick stop and turn.

Having bandaged the horse, check that the studs are inserted in the hind shoes and then proceed to put on the bridle and saddle. After placing the reins and neck strap over the horse's head, slip off the halter. While holding the bridle put the right hand between the ears of the horse and pull the head-piece of the bridle on while guiding the bit into the mouth with the left hand. Do up the chin-strap, checking that the bit is adjusted properly and the bit rubbers are on each side of the horse's mouth. When sitting properly, the bit should just start to wrinkle the skin at the corner of the mouth.

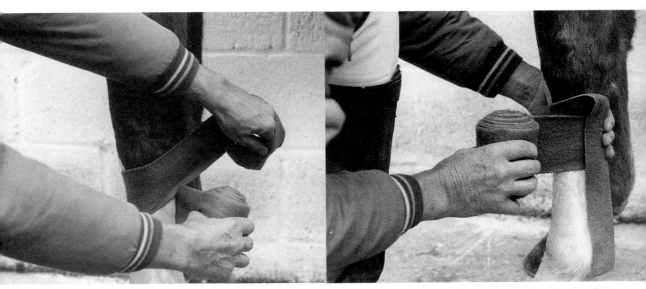

a Bandaging the pony. *To put the protective playing bandage on correctly it should be tightly rolled and held as shown, with the rolled section in the right hand.*

b *A piece is left to hang down the back of the foreleg to protect the tendon and the bandage is pulled tightly forward and up to provide support.*

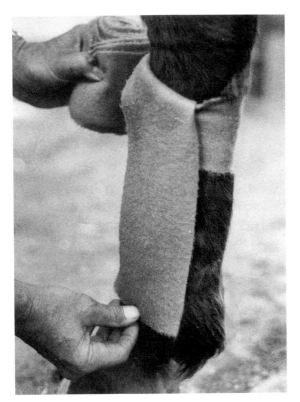

e *The hind leg*. *When bandaging the back leg the extra piece of bandage should hang down the outside of the leg to provide added protection from the stick.*

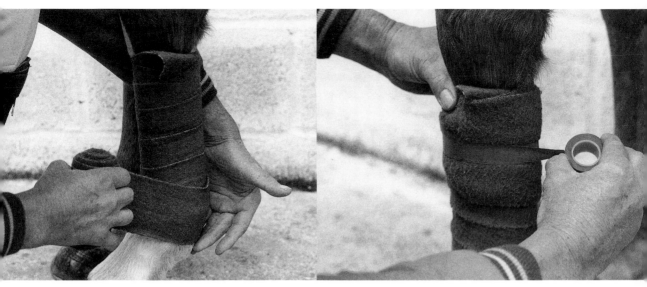

c *The bandage is wound down the leg half a width at a time as far as the point at the bottom of the fetlock, which you will be able to feel with your fingers.*

d *After winding it back up to the top, again pulling it tight each time, secure it with a velcro or ribbon tie. For extra security this should be reinforced with electrical tape, which looks very smart when co-ordinated with the tail. It is very important to stress the care that should be taken with bandaging since a loose bandage can cause a bad accident.*

The polo bridle for each horse should be kept complete at all times and taken apart only for cleaning. It should hang on the horse's named peg in the tack room, with his name on the cheek-piece. This is because individual horses go in individual bridles and the properly organised team has a bridle for every horse. The bridle includes the standing martingale which will have been adjusted for length to suit that particular horse.

It is normal for most horses which play in gag bits to have a drop noseband underneath the bit. This is not fastened at this stage of tacking up; the pony is left in the lines with it undone and the halter is put on over the top of the bridle. The drop noseband is done up only when the pony is taken out of the pony lines to play.

After the bridle you put on the breast-plate and the saddle, with the girth done up two holes from tight. (The breast-plate can move with the saddle from horse to horse.) Remember to check that the pommel is high enough over the wither – some thoroughbred high-withered horses will need an extra saddle cloth to ensure that the saddle is lifted well off the top of the wither.

The tail is attended to last. There are three ways to tie the tail up for polo, the first and probably the most common being with plastic tape. The tail is three-plaited right down to the end of the hair, the hair is then turned hard up at the bottom of the dock and the plait, being longer than the tail, is turned down inside and bound with three rows of plastic insulation tape to hold it. The tape is quite fun because it can be in the team's colours and looks very smart if all the horses are turned out in the same manner.

The second and also very popular way of tying up the tail is with long, elastic tail bandages. These are used to bandage the tail, after it has been plaited, from top to bottom and then folded back up to the top again, leaving a little bit of the tail sticking out at the bottom of the bandage and a small loop of the plait to hold the bandage up about three-quarters of the way to the top. Again, care should be taken to bind the tail tightly so that the bandage does not slip off.

The third method of tying up the tail, which we always use for chukkas, is the Argentinian tail knot. This avoids the mess of plastic tape littering the pony lines after a game of polo, for it involves plaiting the tail and tying it up without using anything other than a piece of the

a Tying up the tail. *The tail must always be tied back for polo to prevent it from hooking the player's stick. To plait the tail divide it into three equal segments.*

b *It is plaited to the end and secured with electrical tape which is perfect for this job and can be colour co-ordinated. It is then folded on to the bone of the tail from the base of the tail bone.*

pony's own hair, wound tightly round the end of the plait. Proceed to plait the tail down to within a foot of the end, but leave hanging out of the plait a long thin piece of hair. After plaiting the tail to two-thirds of its length, turn the plaited end half-way up the dock of the tail, as far up as you possibly can. Split it in two and pass half around each side of the tail, taking a piece in either hand and pulling it very firmly around the tail returning to the front. Then twist the two pieces of hair very tightly around each other. After three or four twists, take the piece of hair that you have left hanging down unplaited beside the tail and insert the end into the twisting hair. Continue twisting until you reach the end of the hair, which should be about 6 inches long, and again keep twisting until it doubles over and starts to twist around itself. You then have a little knob of the twisted hair and a loop in your hand from the hair that has been twisted in. Start to wind that piece of hair in the same direction around the twisted knob, which should now be quite firm, and just continue until the ring of hair comes tight around the knob of the plait in your hand. The last twist or two around the knob will hold the whole thing very firmly, and if it is put in properly the tail should stay up all afternoon.

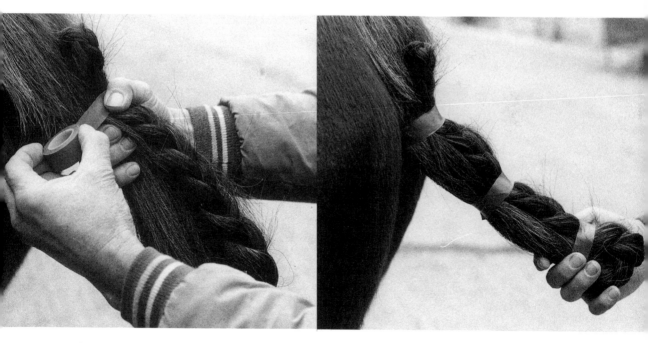

c *Secure the plait with tape at the top to ensure it is sufficiently tight and as short as possible.*

d *Then secure it twice more, making sure the tape is evenly spaced.*

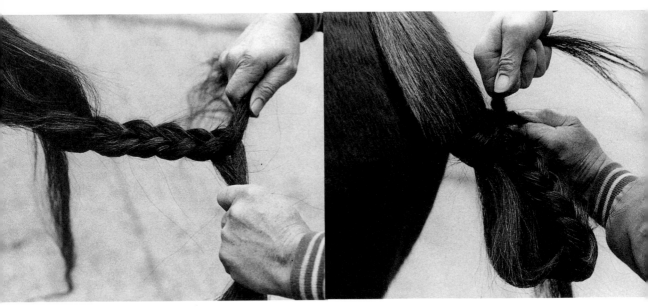

a The Argentine tail knot. *As with plaiting, start by dividing into three but leave a single long piece separate from the three bunches. The tail is plaited half-way down and then the three bunches are blended into two evenly-sized sections.*

b *The two sections are folded up the front of the tail, twisted around the back and brought to the front. They are then twisted together.*

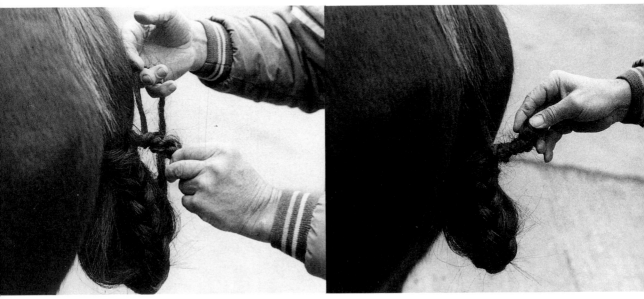

e *Keep twisting this loop and a second loop forms. This is secured tightly by twisting the remainder of the larger loop around the base of the secondary loop until . . .*

f *. . . there is no more hair to twist. The knot will hold the tail tightly together, but takes practice to accomplish successfully.*

c *At this point the extra piece is wound into the two pieces and all three are twisted together very tightly until . . .*

d *. . . a loop is formed.*

The most important thing about tying up the tail – particularly for matches – is to fold it up as tight to the end of the dock as you can, so that it is as short as possible when completed. There is nothing more devastating than to be hooked by your own pony in the execution of an offside forehand shot which could have scored a goal, and a long floppy tail is very effective at doing just that. Some horses can time it to perfection!

Your horse is now standing in the pony lines ready to play polo. After a last-minute check of everything, you move on to your next horse. If you tack up the horses in the order in which you expect them to be played, you will always have the first horse ready to play polo should there be an emergency and you get held up with the last one.

The good groom can operate with two saddles and, exchanging saddles from one horse to the other, he will mount a player through a match of polo with no problem at all. In England we tend to have a saddle for each horse in the match but in chukkas a groom will mount me with two saddles without any difficulty. The benefit of having a saddle for each horse means that you can change the order at the last minute should circumstances change and the team against which you are playing be mounted in a different way from that which you had assumed. It is also important to have a spare horse saddled in case of emergency, so I always have a miminim of three saddles for each player.

Tacking up in stages before a match. Note the use of rugs. Always make sure that your first horse is tacked up first.

The order of mounting your team is discussed in team tactics on page 176, but it is very important to bear in mind that playing the right pony at the right time may win you the game, while playing the wrong pony may lose it, particularly where the strongest player in your team is concerned. The number 1 and number 2 should never play their weakest ponies in the same chukka. Neither should the 2 and 3, or the 3 and 4. If one is playing an easy horse, the other can play a fast and more difficult one.

PRESENTATION OF THE HORSE FOR A GAME

As the groom brings the pony out from the pony lines, he tightens the girth and puts a surcingle over the top of the saddle, doing it up through the martingale strap over the top of the girth (in the USA and certain other countries it may be called an over-girth). It is essential to put this over everything as a last safety precaution to hold the saddle firmly in place, should the girth or girth straps break in the game. As the player goes to mount the horse, the groom, having checked and tightened the girth, should hold the horse on its right side, with his right hand on the end of the martingale where it connects to the cavesson noseband under the chin, and possibly the right rein just next to the bit, and with his left hand push down the stirrup on the offside of the saddle. This holds the saddle firmly in place while the player mounts from the nearside. The groom should hold the horse until the player is happy with the length of the stirrups and everything appears to be ready for him to proceed. An Argentinian groom's trick is to put his left foot in the stirrup instead of pushing down with his left hand – it is easier!

If the game is progressing some distance away from the pony lines, the groom should take each pony up to the edge of the field ready for when the player comes off to change his horse. As soon as possible after the next chukka begins, a good groom will have his next pony standing ready in case of a problem.

After a pony has completed his chukka, the groom loosens the girth two holes and takes him back to the pony lines. If the pony doesn't have to play again, the groom strips the tack off him quickly, washes him down and scrapes him off so that the pony dries with a clean skin. If the pony has to play another chukka, the groom leaves the saddle on and, after loosening the girth, sponges the pony's neck just to get the main sweat off and lets him stand in the pony lines until he is needed again.

The groom's attitude should be one of quick, quiet firmness towards the pony. Once the game is in progress, speed is essential in producing each pony ready to play. The groom should take the pony to the same place each time so that the player knows where to come if he needs to change his pony in a hurry for any reason.

After the end of the game all horses should be untacked completely and washed off. The groom should wash each pony's mouth out and ensure that everything is 100 per cent right with each one before starting on the next. Any problems should be attended to or noted for attention back at the yard. Tack should be sorted out and loaded up, and the horses should be prepared for their return to the stables.

The groom should check each pony's legs individually while still in the pony lines to ensure that there is no swelling resulting from the game; if he is in any doubt, he should take the pony out of the lines and trot him to check for lameness. If a pony is lame after play, certain important procedures should be followed to ensure that whatever damage may have been done is minimised. For instance, a major cut should be stitched before a pony leaves the lines, if at all possible. A thorough examination to try to ascertain the point of lameness will probably be easier at this point than later when the leg may have swollen more. If lameness is due to a sprain of any kind, a tight, wet and cold bandage should be applied to the injured leg, and preferably to the other leg as well, particularly if they are front legs, while the pony travels home. In such a case the pony should never walk, but be boxed home. Always seek veterinary care if in any doubt.

Occasionally a pony may stiffen up after the game and come out of the pony lines looking sore, but with a few minutes of walking the muscles will relax and the pony should become sound. It is beneficial to walk such ponies out in a pen on returning to the stable rather than just putting them back into their boxes. Take care that the really stiff pony does not have azoturia, in which case he should be treated with a muscle-relaxing drug and not be walked but rested for a day or two at least until the lactic acid is excreted from the muscles.

In the days when ponies always used to be ridden to the polo ground, sometimes over long distances, they were always very sound, possibly more than is the case now when most are boxed to polo. The walk back to the stable was ideal to relax the muscles and gradually cleanse the body systems by gentle exercise and it was also very beneficial to the overall well-being of the horse. Unless a pony has dicey legs, I prefer to walk him back to the stables rather than box him. Unfortunately problems of time and distance these days require that most horses are boxed to polo.

8

TRANSPORTING THE POLO PONY

BECAUSE OF THE ever-changing laws governing movement of horses and, in fact, livestock in general between countries, this book will not attempt to list in detail the current restrictions which control the shipment of polo ponies, The shipping agent you employ to handle the shipment will advise you of all the necessary steps to take, and information is available in England from the Ministry of Agriculture, Fisheries and Food, which has a section that controls the import and export of livestock. The aim here is merely to put intending purchasers of polo ponies into the general picture regarding problems that are likely to be faced and the sensible ways to make preparations for overcoming them.

There are various illnesses and diseases of the horse which are fatal in many cases, but fortunately are not widespread throughout the world. Therefore a system of very strict quarantine and veterinary health certificates is essential to transport horses between countries. It is virtually impossible to move horses from countries in which African horse sickness is prevalent and, as the horse is a potential carrier of rabies, any country with rabies is involved in specific quarantine restrictions for horses. Blood disorders like equine infectious anaemia and equine viral arteritis can prevent horses from being shipped, and piroplasmosis – a disease borne by ticks – prevents horses from being moved, for instance, from tropical countries like Santo Domingo into the USA and Europe. However, horses from the more temperate climates of Argentina, New Zealand, North America, Australia and the majority of European nations can be transported among the various countries of these regions with reasonable freedom, given that individual restrictions are adhered to. Normally you should expect about one month's quarantine before leaving and after arriving in some countries.

In the international transportation of horses, it is essential to have an agent who understands and is up to date with the restrictions operating between the country of origin and the country of destination. He must be aware, too, of the restrictions that may be involved if the horse has to pass through a third country. There are also quite strict rules and regulations concerning the transport of animals by road: for instance, the number of hours of travelling that they can adequately cope with before they should be off-loaded and rested for a period of time.

All of this makes the international transport of polo ponies quite a difficult operation, but certainly not impossible. Given that the rules and regulations are adhered to very closely and the specific paperwork is carried out to perfection, horses can be moved successfully and the benefits certainly outweigh the disadvantages in most cases.

For years until the Falklands War, Argentina had been the main source of polo ponies imported into England. Horses were then imported from Australia, New Zealand and the USA to fill the gap which was created. In recent years a very large trade in horses has developed from New Zealand to England and has provided an economical source of partly trained ponies which have done very well in English polo. With the current relaxation in the trade barriers between Argentina and England, however, contacts for the export of horses are being renewed, and it is anticipated that substantial numbers will be shipped into England from Argentina over the next few years.

When debating whether to import a pony for yourself from one of these countries, certain guidelines should be followed in trying to evaluate the benefits against the disadvantages. The biggest disadvantage of importing a horse from another country is the fact that, when you have gone to all the trouble of bringing him over, he may not be quite what you expected when you first made the arrangement. Ponies do change, sometimes quite dramatically, as a result of the stresses of international travel, particularly if they are young. It is really best for a player to ride a polo pony himself in a chukka of polo to establish that the horse is ideal for him. There is no other way for him to get the best pony for himself. A third party is unable to predict with absolute certainty that a pony is going to be exactly right for another player.

However, the polo professional is capable of making an excellent assessment of a purchaser's requirements and, if not able to provide the perfect horse, his selections will certainly prove highly capable and his services have, over the years, been the method by which many players have imported ponies successfully from other countries. If possible, travel over to the country in question and ride a selection of horses before you actually choose the ones that you intend to import. This is by far the best and most successful method of selection, and also the most enjoyable – wherever you might travel to try horses, you will be given a great reception and have a wonderful time.

When importing a pony from another country, it is wise to compare your own local climate with that of the country from which the pony will come. The more similar these are, the more readily the pony will acclimatise to his new environment. You should also be aware that a horse, in changing not only countries but sometimes hemispheres too, will suffer mental stresses which may confuse him and render him incapable of playing to his maximum capacity for quite a long time. Substantial adjustments have to made by the animal – even the drinking water is different form one country to another. The complete acclimatisation of the horse in his new country may take a period of a year rather than three months.

In fact a number of polo ponies – some of them very good – take ages to play with quite the same capabilities that they showed in their country of origin. Occasionally I have been asked to sort out horses so badly affected mentally by the stresses of international transport that they have been unable to play polo on arrival and have taken a full year, and a considerable amount of work, before they have settled and gradually been re-introduced to the game.

As a basic guide to estimating acclimatisation time, for every day of international travel at least a day should be allowed before any further stress whatsoever is placed on the animal. The travel time should be calculated from the moment the horse leaves his old home until the moment he arrives at his new one, so it will be considerably longer than just the air or boat trip. A horse that is shipped by air from Argentina, for instance, will need at least a week of very quiet handling, box rest and time turned out in a field with not too much grass to recover from the physical and mental stresses of the journey. A considerably longer period, of course, will be required for him fully to get used to his new conditions, but the horse is quite capable of playing polo to a reasonably high standard while he completes his acclimatisation adjustments so long as care is taken not to push him too hard or for too long.

A horse that has spent weeks on a boat in travel from, say, New Zealand will need at least a month of acclimatisation and relaxation – first in a darkened box to stabilise his mind and body after the continuous movement of the ship, and then turned out in a field during the day, when the weather is good, to get his muscles co-ordinated, and finally gradually being brought into slow work. His demeanour in the paddock will tell you when he is ready to work; and remember that an extra week of easy preparation will pay dividends towards the end of the season.

Transport by air has proved to be the most efficient way of moving horses from A to B with the least stress because, of course, the trip is done in days rather than weeks. However, cost-effectiveness is still of importance to the purchaser and, in many cases, the boat is considerably cheaper than the plane, particularly for the purchaser who is shipping more than just one or two animals.

In working out your overall budget, bear in mind that it costs just as much to transport and keep a bad horse as it does a good one. It is far better to pay the extra for a better-quality horse to begin with, particularly if you do not have the time or the organisation to improve the young animal to the standard which you require. Remember that the horse imported from a country like Argentina or New Zealand is, in most cases, only half- or three-quarters made: after all, the country is in the business of producing polo ponies, not finishing them, and the longer it keeps the animal, the more expensive it will obviously be for the buyer.

Considerable strides have been made recently in the preparation of horse protectors for travelling. Head and poll protectors, sheepskin leg protectors, and tail protectors which are held on with a strap up to a roller, are very effective in minimising the possibility of injury to a horse while in transit. It is advisable to insure the horse for mortality, but all-risks insurance is not economically viable. Remember that most superficial injuries will have time to mend during the horse's acclimatisation period after arrival.

It is essential to ensure that the horse you intend to import passes a very strict veterinary test before he leaves his country of origin. In recent years there has been a considerable improvement in the standard of veterinary practice overseas. However, in England the standard is still very much higher than in other parts of the world, and you should bear in mind the possibility that you might want to sell an imported horse which has proved not absolutely ideal for you and he would need to pass a local veterinary examination prior to his sale in that country.

It is important to notify your own vet of the potential arrival of horses from abroad. He and your stable manager can then organise the ideal plan for their immediate care on arrival and their future programme of exercise and work to bring them into polo in the best condition.

The main benefit in buying horses abroad is that there is a considerably wider choice from which to select the ideal animal for your particular requirements. A number of very well-qualified players bring horses to England every year, which play excellently for their new owners. We have had great success in bringing over a number of superb Argentine ponies in the last couple of years and, with the current growth in the sport, we will keep importing, breeding and making our own ponies. I hope soon to play my first match on ponies that we have bred, broken and trained completely ourselves – there is no more thrilling reward in polo than to achieve this and then win the match as well!

TRANSPORTING HORSES TO POLO

Depending on the total distance involved, horses can be transported without partitions, boxed nose to tail. Provided they are tied short so that they cannot bite each other's rump, they travel very well and, once they have established a travelling routine, are very settled. In this country the government, at the instigation of the RSPCA, has intro-

The 'highwayman's' knot.
Just pull the end firmly, and the horse is free on the lead. Essential in the horse box, this knot is ideal for tying up horses.

(top left) *A loop of the lead rein is passed through a loop of string (baling twine) for safety, since the string will break more easily than the lead rope if the horse pulls back.*

(top right) *The left hand reaches inside the loop to take hold of the end of the rope nearest the pony.*

(middle left) *This piece is then pulled through the first loop. The right hand holds on to the horse so the knot does not tighten before it is completed.*

(middle right) *The left hand reaches inside the second loop to take hold of the free end of the rope.*

(bottom left) *This third loop is pulled through and held by the left hand.*

(bottom right) *The right hand pulls on the horse end of the rope to tighten the knot in the same way the horse will when he tries to walk away.*

duced laws restricting the transport of livestock in compartments with partitions further than 12 feet apart, to try to prevent cruelty in travel between the UK and the Continent. Now most boxes have partitions between each horse. For a number of years, until the laws changed, I transported up to twelve horses in my box without a partition and, in my view, they travelled better, the horses moved with the flow of the box much more easily, and the safety record was excellent. I have had problems only in transporting horses in a box which had two partitions between nine horses.

It is, of course, important not to pack horses too tightly into a box – provided they have room, they stand nice and easy. Occasionally a horse will panic or seem to kick repeatedly, and then you should go in and check what the problem is. It may be that the next-door horse is biting him in the rump, and it is a good idea to carry muzzles in the box, particularly on a long trip, in case of biting. When strange horses are to be carried together without partitions, muzzle all of them as a precaution. Kicking is most often started with biting, and I stand no such nonsense from horses in my box. I am very firm with them and take whatever action I believe is essential to make them behave. It is possible to walk through a quite tightly packed box of horses, going under the front of each one and down the side between them. They will step aside to allow you the space necessary to walk between them.

In the very rare case of a horse panicking and starting to flounder in the box and struggle for his feet, you may have to take a horse or two off the back to loosen them up and give the excited one time to calm down. It is also advisable, having loosened them, to change the position of the excited horse: his immediate neighbours were probably leaning in and therefore sandwiching the pony, causing him to become nervous and upset.

Very occasionally the horse right at the front panics – because he has the hard wall of the box to stand against, and all the other horses seem to squash him towards it. If this happens, I recommend changing the first and the second horses around.

With the number of horses we transport, we have occasionally had minor problems and the worst have always involved horses in individual partitions which go right to the floor. We now build our partitions down to 18 inches above the floor, with a rubber skirt to the floor, which enables the horses to spread their legs better and seems to prevent most of the major upsets.

If we are travelling with match ponies for long periods in the box, we always bandage their legs as a protection against small kicking problems, although it is not essential to bandage them before they travel on a short trip to polo. Bandages put on for travelling should be considerably looser than those worn for the game. If the journey to the ground is short, it may be convenient to take the horses already bandaged to play.

Because of the number of horses we transport, we often have to take more than one load, in which case the first load will go up completely untacked and the second may go up bandaged or even completely tacked up ready to play. Horses completely tacked up in the box should not be loaded too tightly as the saddles take up quite a lot of room. Horses, as a rule, should not wear covers while travelling in a box because they are very inclined to sweat.

PART
TWO

La Espadaña 40-goal team: *Carlos Gracida (10), Alphonso Pieres (10), Gonzalo Pieres (10) and Errestro Trotz (10) holding aloft the Palermo Open Trophy.*

1

THE GAME

THE ORIGINS OF polo are so deeply embedded in the mists of time that it is impossible to trace when men and horses first came together in what has evolved into the most thrilling game ever devised: a man with a horse and a polo stick is an elemental partnership. Polo is believed to have originated as a game between villages in Persia and the Mongol Empire in which any number of players could join to defend the honour of their tribe with no holds barred. Gradually, over the centuries, rules have been laid down for the safety of both horse and rider so that nowadays, with the game played at probably three times the speed of those first little mountain ponies, high-goal polo is a contest between top athletes and some of the finest horse flesh in the world outside the race track.

Polo as we know it today evolved from the form of the game discovered in India during the days of the Raj. British Army personnel brought it back to England with them, and it was first played here in about 1862. The Hurlingham Polo Association (HPA) devised the first set of rules shortly after that, and still remains the world's guiding body in the sport. All the playing countries have now established their own rules based on the HPA rules and have set up their own polo associations, most of which are affiliated to the HPA.

Modern polo is played on a ground 300 yards long and 200 yards wide or 160 yards if the field is edged with 10-inch boards down each side and surrounded by a safety zone.

Each game is divided into chukkas which last up to seven and a half minutes. It is played between two teams who do battle for the designated number of chukkas, normally played to a conclusion. A bell is rung after seven minutes and if in the next half-minute the ball runs out of play, or play is stopped for any reason, the chukka ends. If play continues until seven and a half minutes with no stoppage, a second bell is rung, at which time the ball becomes dead and the chukka ends. A sudden death, extra-time chukka is played if the last chukka ends with a tied score, and the first to score wins. Sometimes the goal posts are widened when playing the extra time.

The number of chukkas per game varies between four and eight, depending on the standard of polo being played. In England in polo up to fifteen goals, four or sometimes five chukkas are played in each game; in the USA six chukkas of polo are played in almost every game; and in Argentina in the open tournament, they play eight chukkas in each game.

There are four players on each team. Number 1 is the attacking player, number 2 the midfield attacker, number 3 the pivot man and number 4 the back – the most conservative player on the field, whose job is basically to try to prevent the other team from scoring and to turn the play to his team's advantage.

Each player is given a handicap by a committee in his club, which is then ratified by the HPA and recognised worldwide, depending on his contribution to the team game, and his individual ability. The addition of the handicaps of the four players in a team constitutes the team handicap, and it is this which decides what level of tournament the team shall enter. In England the handicap ranges of the main tournaments are 0 to 6 and 4 to 8 (low goal), 8 to 12 (intermediate), 12 to 15 (medium), and 17 to 22 (high), with an increasing number of −2 to 2- or 4-goal tournaments reflecting the growing number of players coming into the game.

However, spectators in the International Tournament played every year in England can see games up to perhaps 33 goals, while high-goal polo in the USA is 25 or 30 goals. Open polo in the USA sometimes gets as high as 36 or 37 goals, and in Argentina it can reach 40 goals – the maximum for any team.

In England the handicap of each player begins at −2 and, although the first handicap varies in different countries, occasionally being as low as −4, while others begin at 0, all countries have the same maximum rating of 10 goals. At the time of writing there are only twelve players in the world rated at the magical 10 goals – nine Argentinians, two Mexicans and the first 10-goal arena player for many years in the USA.

Originally the polo pony was, as his name indicates, actually a small pony, standing no more than 12.0 hands. Later the height was raised to 13.3 and in 1899 it was increased to 14.2 hands, which is still the regulation pony height in other equestrian competitions. The height restriction was removed altogether by the USA in 1916 and by England in 1919. Now ponies up to approximately 16 hands are played, though the ideal height is 15.0 to 15.3.

Polo differs in concept from most other games in that the 'line of play' is up and down the ground from end to end rather than across from side to side. Most team sports pass the ball across the field seeking an opening, whereas in polo the ball is passed up and down the ground and players ride into position to receive passes from behind them. There is no offside in polo and only during certain set plays are there limitations on the positions to which a player may ride on the ground at any time.

With the pony achieving speeds of up to 40 miles an hour and the ball being hit at up to 100 miles an hour, the athletic ability of both horse and rider is taxed to the maximum; and because of the speed and the physical demands on both, polo is arguably the most exciting sport in the world. The physical contact essential in a ride-off, the precise timing required when hooking another player's stick while he is in the act of swinging at the ball, the cut and thrust of trying to win a particular ball or play in the rapid changes of direction in the game, and the thrill of racing down the ground and hitting the ball distances of up to 150 yards give polo an image not enjoyed by any other sport. Rightly known as the 'king of games', it has an attraction for competitive sportsmen the world over and is rapidly increasing in popularity. Currently polo is played in some fifty-five countries, with inaugural games being played in Japan and the USSR, a growing number of clubs in most of the countries in Europe, an excess of two hundred clubs currently registered in the USA and growing numbers in Canada and South America. As it spreads rapidly through the Middle East, Africa, Asia and the Pacific, polo is becoming more popular than ever before.

2

PLAYERS' POSITIONS

THE BRIEF OUTLINE of the four individual positions of the players given below is followed by a more detailed discussion of these positions during the game, chiefly from the point of view of mental attitude and physical attributes. The positions of the individual players in the various pieces of set play are discussed in Chapters 3 and 4.

The number 1, or attacker, runs in anticipation of a forward pass. He is responsible in defence for preventing the opposition *number 4*'s goal shot. He should be light and quick-thinking and his anticipation should be that of the eternal optimist, believing that every shot made by his team is going to be better than average and every shot made by the opposition is going to be muffed, with the possibility that the play might turn in his team's favour.

The number 2, the midfield attacker, is the hardest-working player in any team. He must, at the same time as trying to challenge and beat the opposing *number 3* at all times, win the ball, fight and make holes in the opposition's play for his number 3 to push through. Generally thinking positively on attack, he should be strong, hard-riding and very quick to defend should the play turn against his team. The better the standard of polo, the quicker he needs to be, both in attack and in defence. The importance of the quick-thinking number 2 in a well-balanced team cannot be over-emphasised.

The number 3, the attacking defender, is the pivot man. He should, while controlling his opposition *number 2*, set up the play and generally control the game. He should have instinctive knowledge of the natural movements of his own team-mates and therefore be rapidly able to assess where they are most likely to be at all times. His ability to control the ball in tight play and to place his passes with accurate precision becomes paramount in the better games of polo. The quicker he can turn defence into attack, the more opportunity will be given to his team to win the game.

The number 4, the back, entails the ultimate in defence. He should always think the very worst is going to happen from his team's point of view, and try to anticipate a situation so that he can control the opposition's *number 1*. Out-thinking his opponent, he must ride him out of the play and back the ball to a position where his team can gain possession. He must combine rapidly with his number 3, and between them, going for passes from one another, they must turn the play and feed their forwards with the ball.

In the basic concept of team play, the forwards should interchange if necessary, while the two defensive players should swap positions freely to encourage passing between team-mates. If the number 1 finds himself back at number 4 as a result of a rapid change of situation, he should play the number 4 position until the first opportunity arises for him to resume his position at number 1. Remember, however, that a team with players out of position is not as effective as a team with all its players in the correct positions, and therefore while the number 1 is at number 4 his team will be operating at less than maximum efficiency.

One of the successful ingredients of a winning team is having the right player in the right position on the field. Most players in polo play a certain position more easily and naturally than any of the others. In order to clarify this, the main mental and physical requirements of each position are outlined below.

Finally, remember that, when organising a team, it is not necessarily correct to pick the best four players that are available. This way you might well end up without a number 1 at all and the team would suffer because of the bad positional play which would then result. In winning polo the team comes first and the individual second.

POSITION NUMBER 1: THE ATTACKER

The number 1 is charged with four distinct duties. He acts as the link between his team and the goal; he must mark the opposing *number 4*; he should endeavour to keep the ball in play at all times; and he should maintain the correct position relative to the speed and flow of play in the game.

Many players go out for their first chukka and are put at number 1. This is in some ways unfortunate because, while the player is thus kept in the front of the game and possibly therefore out of the way, he is less able to watch the game evolve behind him, and often finds it difficult to anticipate his position. It is arguably more beneficial for the novice player to play first at number 4, where he can more readily see the game unfold before him, thus gaining a better appreciation of its overall flow and increasing his ability to anticipate that flow. It is also better for a learner who is not such a good rider to play at number 4 while he builds up his confidence in the game. It is in my opinion easier for a player to move from number 4 to number 1 than *vice versa*, and it is

*The world's best number 1 players – **Pepe Heguy – 10 goals** about to hit, closely watched by **Carlos Gracida – 10 goals**, careful not to foul.*

often better to have your slowest player at back so he does not slow down your attack; but he must be taught to avoid fouling at all costs.

The good number 1 will take an opportunist's look at the game and, in many situations, will take a chance. This means anticipating that the ball is going to come out further and faster on his side of the play, and he will then get into a position where he can reach the ball first and thus possibly give his team a goal-scoring opportunity.

In good polo it is important that the number 1 should be well-mounted on fast ponies. In the better polo the position is a very specialist one, and the good, quick-thinking number 1 is crucial to his team's success. He needs to be able to hit the ball accurately and consistently and to out-ride the opposing *number 4* in speed and in anticipation of the ball. The number 1 position is ideally suited to the slight player who can turn his pony very fast and move quickly into top gear, thus possibly leaving the slower and heavier *number 4* in his wake.

In defence, as he comes over the half-way line, he should be in a position to ride off the *number 4* and cover him, particularly as he gets closer to the goal, to ensure that his opponent always hits his goal shot under maximum pressure. At the first sign of play turning in his favour, he must anticipate and turn inside the *number 4*, getting into a position to receive a pass free of his opposition and thus giving his team the chance to attack.

Number 1 can be the most frustrating position to play because you are always turning in anticipation of the ball, which may or may not come depending on the dominance of your midfield players. No matter how frustrating it is, you should not go back into the game to try to win the ball unless your position is then taken by your number 2. A team without a number 1 is a team that plays ineffectively in attack, and every time the opposite *number 4* backs the ball it is an opportunity lost for your team.

Remember that a team wins a game of polo only by scoring goals in attack. A team that wins the ball in defence doesn't necessarily win the game. The number 1, by staying out in his position of anticipation, can often take *the back* further away from the play, therefore spreading out the game to the benefit of his team. It is essential that the number 1 flows up and down the ground at the same speed as the game, so that he maintains a reasonably consistent position relative to his number 2 and retains contact with the game.

There are occasions when the correct move for the number 1 is to drop back into the number 2 position and fight for the ball. In this case his number 2 must be very quick to see the change and move out rapidly to the number 1 position in anticipation of winning the ball. The ability to switch positions decisively and quickly often presents a goal-scoring opportunity. It is the player without the ball that creates the 'opportunity' in the game.

If, in the switching of play, the number 1 finds himself at back, or any other position, he should play out the sequence of that particular play wherever he finds himself, but should remember that as quickly as possible he must resume his position of number 1. This is possibly more important for the number 1 than for any other player on the ground.

When riding off the *number 4* as he is going for his back shot, the number 1 should never check up in anticipation. He should always pressurise the *number 4* to his utmost and make him hit all his back shots under maximum pressure. It is essential from a mental point of view that he try to dominate the *number 4* and thus put him into a mental state where he is worried about the number 1 all the time. The number 1 will then be able to concentrate more on his play than on the *number 4*'s anticipation of what might happen next.

The number 1 plays a vital part in the line-out and he must break quickly and go forward in anticipation of his team winning the ball: one swing at the ball and through past the *number 4*, riding forwards and looking backwards. In all of the set plays he should achieve his position early – he should take the trouble to know his correct position for all of the set plays at any time.

In hit-outs and penalties the number 1 should apply pressure on *the back* to make him hit the ball away. He should prevent *the back* from dribbling past him by positioning himself in the correct place. At the start of *the back's* approach to the ball, the number 1 should begin to apply pressure to his hitting by positioning himself wide and to the left as he faces into the *number 4*. The number 1 often has time to choose between one side or the other while preparing to ride off his opponent. He should always opt to ride on the stick side of *the back*, to make him hit all his shots – backwards and forwards – on the nearside. The resulting position gives the number 1 the stick side, and a definite advantage in a ride-off – his horse always pushes harder to the left, because his instinct is to go to the left of the ball. The instinct of the *number 4's* pony is also to go to the left of the ball, so he never pushes quite so hard to the right. While less essential in the middle of the game, this is quite a good general policy to follow if the choice can be made, because most players will hit a shot of less distance and possibly less accuracy on the nearside than on the offside of their horse, particularly when hitting under pressure.

If, as number 1, you make a break and find yourself running to the ball, and hitting it towards the goal, run as fast as you can early and steady fractionally, well before you get to the ball, and then hit a firm stroke with an almost full swing. Don't play a half-shot, particularly an under-the-neck or cut shot at goal. These shots are timed to perfection only when you play the full shot. The time to play a half-shot, with a firm wrist, is if the ball is bouncing in front of the goal and you can play a straight shot at goal: then you must remember to swing right down the line of the ball.

Everyone has been guilty at some time of missing the last shot to the goal. Perhaps it was mistimed because of taking a tap shot, but probably the player lifted his head to look at the goal rather than sighting the goal when he was at least 10 yards from the ball and then concentrating solely on the ball while making the shot. This problem is more common in low-goal polo – the last shot at goal is often taken more quickly than is customary for the player. Therefore, he must start his swing earlier than normal and concentrate very carefully on striking the ball early.

POSITION NUMBER 2: THE MIDFIELD ATTACKER

This is the defending attacker position, defender of the two attacking players, numbers 1 and 2, and attacker of the two midfield players, numbers 2 and 3. The number 2 should be the quickest and most aggressive man in the team. His job is to endeavour to out-play and out-think the opposing *number 3*, whom he must mark constantly and whose every move he must try to foil, not foul. By taking out the opposing *number 3*, he makes the hole for his own number 3 to go through. He should be at least as well-mounted as the opposing

Alphonso Pieres – 10 goals showing *beautiful balance and ball control at top speed. Arguably the best number 2 in the world.*

number 3 – preferably better – and at all times he should combine effectively with his number 3 in the setting-up of play. In most cases it is the combination of the 2 and 3 and their ability to win in the middle which will ensure the success of the team.

The number 2 has to turn in anticipation of an attack immediately he sees that his number 3 is dominating and will win the next play. He must be quick to anticipate a change of direction and must move like lightning to capitalise on the slightest error of the opposing team. This speed of anticipation and enterprise by the number 2 is an essential part of the success of any team.

He must concentrate on being able to carry the ball and on placing it to the advantage of his number 1. While it is essential for the number 2 to anticipate if he is hopelessly beaten in any play, it is also (and possibly more) important for him to make the opposing *number 3* play under pressure; to do so, remembering that he has two players between him and his goal, the number 2 should ride out the *number 3* and make him play his shots under maximum pressure at all times. If the number 2 anticipates and checks up for the backhand, therefore leaving the *number 3* to play the ball without any pressure, he has lost the initiative and given his opponent a very easy shot at the ball.

The number 2 must dominate the *number 3* at least as much as he is dominated in return, and not spend his time ineffectively chasing the *number 3*. If the *number 3* appears to be beating the number 2, the latter will have to concentrate on his anticipation to outwit his opponent's next move. It is critical that he is able to think and switch rapidly from attack to defence, and it is of vital importance for him to think of defence if he sees that his number 3 is moving on to attack past him.

It is essential for the number 2 to try to prevent his opposing *number 3* from turning on the ball and thus getting a clear shot. Because most good players will hit their offside forehand more accurately and with more distance than most of the other shots they play, the number 2 should try constantly to prevent the opposing defensive players from turning the ball, and force them to hit their back shots quickly and under pressure.

The number 2 should be involved in every play. While endeavouring to avoid fouling, he will possibly be penalised more than any other player, because it is essential that he is aggressive and tries to work at all times. His strokes should be quick and accurate and not necessarily of the greatest distance. In the game he will invariably be hitting under pressure and therefore he will seldom get an easy, clean shot. If he can't make a clean shot, it is more important for him to ensure that the opposing *number 3* does not win the ride-off than to hit the ball up to the number 1. If he can control the ball as well, this is a bonus, and often the mark of a player who has a natural instinct to do the right thing and one who will go a long way in the game. If he consistently beats his opposing *number 3*, his own number 3 will be able to make a good, clean shot, having anticipated his number 2's dominance. The number 2 is thus creating the holes which his number 3 can go through.

It is essential for the number 2 to be mounted on fast, reasonably handy, strong ponies that have a very good endurance. He must not let up during the whole chukka, so his horse must be able to keep up the pressure underneath him. The number 2 could be aptly described as the 'hatchet man' of the team but, as such, must always ride with consideration for the safety of both his pony and the opposing players. Too often in professional polo these days the number 2 becomes the 'hit man' rather than the 'hatchet man'. While arguably the spoilsports of polo, the best specialists in this position combine speed and agility with the ability to carry the ball to the goal – through, around or, in some way, past the opposition.

There are two main types of number 2 – the player who flies through the game and dominates it with his brilliant stick work and ability to control the ball, and the player who is able to control the opposing *number 3* by dint of having really good horses and often therefore taking him out of the play.

The older concept of the number 2 being primarily an attacking man and not really responsible for defence doesn't seem to operate quite so effectively in today's polo. When a team controls the possession of the ball, defence is of secondary importance. The anticipation of a good number 2 with his ability to change quickly from defence to attack is of prime importance to the overall success of the team.

POSITION NUMBER 3: THE PIVOT MAN

The number 3 position is appropriately played by the most experienced player in the team, and he has to be thoroughly versatile in his approach to the game. His ability to out-think the hard-riding opposing *number 2* and out-play the *number 2* who bases his game on anticipation, is essential to the success of his team. He should depend on quick thinking and immediate reaction to any given situation, and it is vital that his reaction is instinctively correct so that he can set up his team for a play.

He must be able to control the ball in any given situation and, at the same time, control his horse and the line so that he can win the ball and set it up to enable him to pass to one of his team who has moved in anticipation of his ability to control the play.

Without doubt the most complex of the four positions, the number 3 is constantly alternating between attack and defence. The rules essential to his position are not easy to define and his style of play may vary from game to game. Depending on the ability of his number 2 to switch positions, and of his number 4 to turn the play under pressure, he must be prepared to attack, and carry that attack on if the opportunity presents itself, rapidly turning in defence if he is beaten for the ball or ridden off by the opposing player. If, however, the rest of his team are not as strong or as quick to interchange with him, he must play more conservatively.

The number 3, being in the position to set up the team, must pass the ball very accurately. The secret in accurate passing is to pass it at the right moment. He must encourage the other members of his team to think that, when they are the players off the ball going to positions to receive the pass, they create the situation for the next play, thus enabling the number 3 to release the ball at the right moment for the successful culmination of that play.

The number 3 needs an instinctive game sense and a cool head to accomplish his play under pressure. It is essential for him to have an attacking attitude to the game. If at any time he is playing more back-hands than forehands, regardless of the score, he will be losing the game.

His horses, though perhaps not needing to have quite so much power as those of the number 2, should be the handiest in the game and, while he must cope with the power of a hard-riding *number 2*, he has to be able to out-manoeuvre his opponent and come up with the ball under pressure. His horses must enable him to make the play regardless of the pressure that is exerted on him.

Memo Gracida – 10 goals. The perfect number 3 performing a near-side backhand. Winner of a record number of US and British Opens, Memo displays a wonderful team spirit to lift his team to victory.

In many cases the number 3 will be the captain of the team and, as such, his role of responsibility starts well before the game. It is up to him to ensure that all the horses are ridden in the correct order and that his team is playing the correct tactical game. During the game he must plan ahead and work out what his team can do to win.

Anticipation must remain the key to the number 3's play. He must have the ability to anticipate the next play and, if he is ridden out or beaten for one play, he must always be able to win the next one to regain possession for his team. He needs to strike a balance between attack and defence and, while he needs to be aggressive, he must be certain that he can basically achieve what he sets out to do, particularly as he goes forward with the ball. His ability to pass the ball is vital in the overall flow of the game, but the positioning of his back shots is very important in the switch from defence to attack.

The number 3 must have the natural ability to judge whether he should make a safe and correct shot or possibly take a chance and try something unusual. He must take care or he could hit the shot in the wrong direction, which could be disastrous for his team. He is aptly known as the pivot man, for he must dominate the opposing *number 2* while remaining the essential link between his back and his number 2, with whom he must combine in a very effective manner. If he is going back, possibly the back will ride into a position to accept his pass or, if the number 2 is close to him, he will turn up to receive the number 3's pass, thus achieving the essential continuity to turn defence into attack.

POSITION NUMBER 4: THE BACK

The back is the primary defensive player and therefore thinks very conservatively in any given situation. While it is incorrect to say that he should never meet the ball, only in very exceptional circumstances should he take the risk, and then only if he is being covered by his number 3 coming back.

His is the prime responsibility for defence in the team and therefore he must ensure that he is not out-manoeuvred by his opposing *number 1*. He must cover his opponent, particularly in his own half, as well as anticipating the direction in which the ball is going to be hit, so that he can position himself to control the man and make the opportunity to win the ball. He must remember to control the ground at all times, which is important to his team, otherwise he is out of position.

Playing in the anchor position in the game, he must be utterly dominant in his control of the 'back door' and his ability to turn the ball, or to play the back shot in the right direction to set up an attacking momentum for his team. It is vital that both he and the number 3 'think anti-clockwise' around the ground – always tailing the offside backhand to retain possession. I have seen many goals – and often games – given away because players fail to realise the importance of this directional play, and the better the polo, the more important this becomes.

The better the opposing *number 1*, the more defensively the back has to play. When the *number 1* is not so good, the back can take more chances and possibly play more of an attacking role. He must add stability and control to the team. If he plays a basic defensive position and avoids the possibility of dangerous shots, he will give his team – and particularly the number 3 – the stability and confidence they need to mount the attacks which will result from the correct placement of his clearing shots.

The position of the back in the line-out is crucial. If the opposing *number 1* meets the ball, the back must be ready to pounce on him as soon as he breaks from the line-out. If he takes up a position at the rear of the line-out, he gives his opponent ample opportunity to get away and possibly score. He must pick up the first man who breaks through the line-out, ride him off without fouling and back the ball, if possible, in an anti-clockwise direction.

The back's ability to hit the ball confidently is crucial in his hit-outs

Howard Hipwood – 9 goals. *The perfect back completing a nearside backhand. The power of 'Big H' has terrified many but inspires all who play with him. Note the beautiful body twist to generate maximum power.*

from the back line – clever placement of his shot will result in the ball being carried well down the field. If he hits the ball in the wrong direction, however, he lays it open to interception from the other team, and his goal is immediately under pressure. Furthermore, with all his players in front of him, there is nobody who can back him up and rescue the situation. Before he hits the ball he must always look to see where the strong man in the other team is standing, and plan accordingly. When hitting the ball across the goal, he must ensure that all of his team-mates know the strategy.

It is essential for the back to control the area of ground around his own goal. He must never let the opposing *number 1* beat him and so get into a position where he can score should he receive a pass.

3

CRITICAL POSITIONS

T HE GAME OF polo – like chess – involves a series of moves. These moves are interspersed with set plays in which the positions of the individual players are critical to the way in which the team plays and its resulting success.

As in most other games, the law of averages works in polo, and if the team lines up in the most probable way to achieve its objectives, the law of averages will work in its favour. The better the standard of polo, the higher that probability will be. The players are more equal in their abilities and everybody can hit the ball to a reasonable standard. Therefore the elements of chance are reduced and, in most cases, the team that plays the best tactical game with the most precision will win. However, the brilliance of the individual or an excellent piece of team play can, of course, be decisive in a very close game.

In low-goal polo things are not quite the same. Occasionally a very good player on one side can dominate the other team because nobody can ride him off or control him satisfactorily. Also, because the standard of hitting is considerably lower, the element of chance plays a much greater part in the outcome of the individual movements in the game. On a bad ground the opportunist who plays for a miss is often successful but, when pitted against a team who play team polo regardless of how far they hit the ball, but who stay in their correct positions, the team usually comes out on top and certainly the game is infinitely better to watch.

The game of polo proceeds in lines up and down the ground. A player who rides beside his own team-mates is out of position and it is essential for him to get back on the line by anticipating where the ball will be – either by running along a line from the ball to the goal if his team is attacking, or following the previous players along the line of play. To ride beside the line, even 2 yards off it, is pointless, particularly if you ride too closely behind the players in front of you. Depending on the forward speed, you should be from 5 to 15 yards away to allow yourself time to hit the ball, should the players in front leave it for you.

When moving in anticipation, your primary move is to a position just left of the line, between the ball and the goal, either in defence or in attack, and remembering that you should already have taken care of your opposite number, you will then be in a position to pick up the ball should it come through on the anticipated line.

Passing to the right place. *In the **A** positions the black team have won control, and black 1 will get an easy goal shot if 2 puts the ball 10 yards from the goal. Note black 4 should hit the ball to A, not B, if his 3 is hard ridden or black may lose possession at B. In the **B** positions the white team have won possession and 3 will be able to back the ball. White 4 has ridden his opponent too wide – he should be just wide of the line between the ball and the right goal post.*

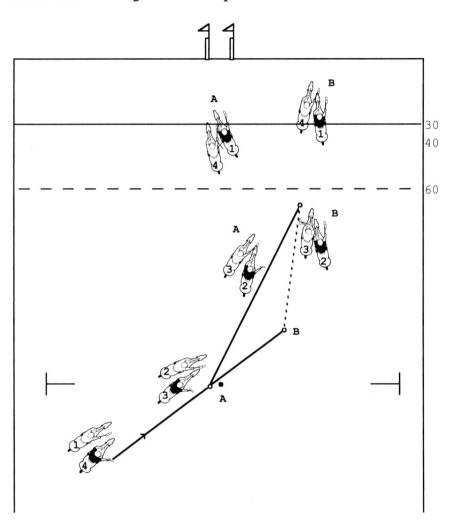

It is critical to control the ground which is important to your team at all times. If every individual in the team did that, the other team would never have a chance. There are times when a player, by clever positioning, must get one shot, and sometimes two, but in most cases he should never get the third, if his opponent is riding positively and hard. Thus it is of vital importance for the team to play as a team, passing to one another, and making the play for the next pass possible by clever anticipation of the players without the ball. If you control the area of the ground which is of importance to you, and then your team basically hits towards the goal, you will be creating goal-scoring opportunities.

While going in defence and particularly inside your own 60–yard line, it is important to clear the ball towards the side line as quickly as possible. Immediately you attack over the half-way line, you should be centring the ball towards the opposing goal as soon as possible. The earlier the ball is centred, the easier it is to score, particularly if your team have already controlled the area of ground surrounding the goal that you are attacking.

A play that passes over the 60-yard line in the middle of the ground has possibly a 90 per cent greater chance of achieving a goal than a play that goes over the 60-yard line 10 yards from the side line. Often the difference between the two plays is only the direction of one shot as the ball travels over the half-way line. At the same time, you must bear

Scoring goals. *Control the ball to the goal as soon as possible without losing possession. The line A-D to E is obviously the better line, and the shot A-B is the most important because it opens up the approach to goal. The shot C-D should go within the arc Y-Z, depending on the position of the defending players and whether the player hits more accurately while cutting or pulling the ball under the neck. The shots H-I and I-J risk hitting the ball behind, and give the defending team a good chance of clearing the ball anti-clockwise. When the horses are positioned as on the left, a shot into sector Y will almost certainly lose possession and a shot into Z will almost certainly give a goal-scoring opportunity. The optimum shot is to V for either black 1 or 2 to pick up.*

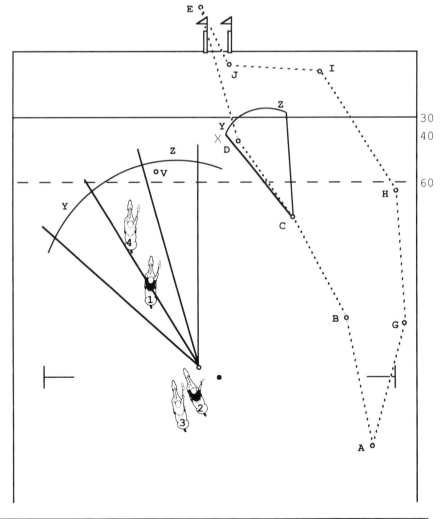

in mind that there is no point in hitting the ball to the other team, so your team must anticipate your shot towards the middle of the ground very early in the attack, thus enabling you to pass the ball 10 yards in front of them, and possibly 3 or 4 yards to their stick side, to ensure that they get the next shot at the ball.

Remember at all times that the correct pass to a player goes past him at least 10 yards and on his free side – his opponent should be controlled in the ride-off on the other side. If he is free, the ball should travel to the side which gives him the easiest shot to hit towards or through the goal.

Depending on the individual player's capabilities, between 50 and 80 per cent of all his shots will be offside forehands. Therefore, on average, that will be his best shot, particularly if hitting under pressure. If the player is being hard-ridden, the ball must be hit at least 2 or 3 yards wide on his free side to enable him to run to the ball and hit it without giving his opponent the opportunity of riding him off and possibly hitting the ball as well. Often one careless shot such as this will lose a goal opportunity at one end and result in a chance, perhaps even a goal, at the other end.

Also remember that the pass which goes 10–20 yards in front of your player in the right place when he is being hard-ridden is, in many cases, better than the pass which goes 50–60 yards past him. In that time he may lose the ride-off, and possession of the ball.

When approaching the goal from well away, it is always better to leave the ball 10 yards in front of the goal than to hit it wide from well out, particularly if you think you can get another shot at the ball before you are caught by the defending player. Even if you are caught, it is better to leave the ball 10 yards in front of the opposition's goal than to hit it over the back line and give them automatic possession with a hit in.

The secret of success in polo is to retain possession of the ball. No matter which member of your team has possession, the player without the ball makes the opportunity for the next pass. Therefore, prior to the game, your players must establish a team strategy for the various plays which are likely to happen in the game, and then automatically ride into those positions to allow the player with the ball the opportunity to make a pass instinctively to the right place.

THE LINE OF THE BALL

A clear interpretation of the line of the ball and of the various controversies and conditions that govern that line are given in the HPA rules reproduced in Appendix 1. This section, however, concentrates on explaining how the line of the ball controls the pattern of play, and what a player may do in given circumstances to prevent his opponent from hitting the ball, or to take the line himself in the correct manner and therefore win possession of the ball. It is essential for every player

Right of way. *A White 3 has equal right to back the ball on the nearside while black 2 is flying down the line for an offside forehand.* **B** *White must not meet two players coming down the line.* **C** *White 4 can meet the ball after his 3 has ridden off black 1. White 2 must immediately check and turn in anticipation. If white 4 changes the line across black 2 he must allow anyone coming fast behind black 2 to follow down the old line as well, unless they check up before he follows the ball.* **D** *White 4 may tap the ball towards z as long as he does not put his horse's head across the line. He must be under perfect control.* **E** *White 3 in defence may try to cut the ball towards x. This is incorrect because he will foul black 2 if he follows the ball. The offside tail shot past T is essential, because it sets up the anti-clockwise play.* **F** *The square shot or the flick sideways can change the line in front of black 2, particularly if he is flying. White 3 is parallel to the line as he hits the ball, and can often check up and follow the new line as the other players check and turn for the next play.*

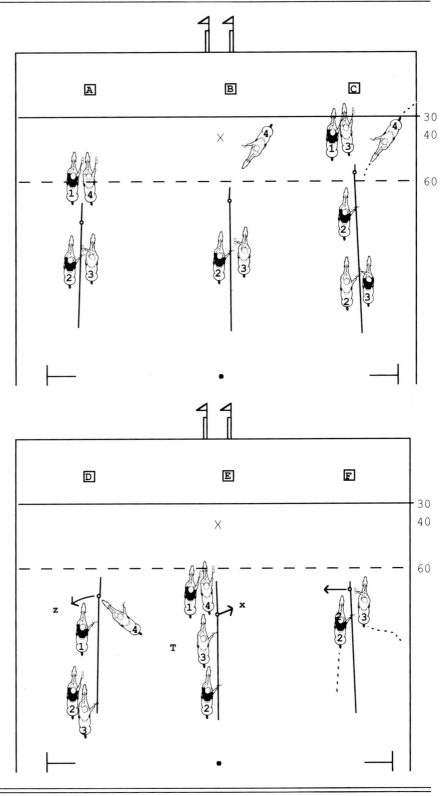

coming into the game to read the rules, and if there is anything he doesn't understand he should ask a more experienced player for help.

The line of the ball controls the basic line of play. Once the ball leaves the umpire's hand in the throw-in, it establishes a line. Players have the right to come up and down that line almost equally, provided they remain on the left side of it, with the ball on their right-hand or stick side. No one may cross in front of another player to get on to the line without fouling.

The rules of polo are similar to the rules of the road: the line of the ball could be likened to the white line down the middle of the road. Players in any country in the world where they drive on the left-hand side have an automatic and instinctive knowledge of what they can do on the polo field. Take care in those countries where they drive on the right – in polo, the wrong side! Players from these countries tend to think that if they start on the right of the line, they should not cross it because they will foul; however, because they have no right of way on the right side in polo, they will foul if an opponent is clever enough to meet the ball or ride for a hook and catch them on the wrong side.

Two players riding each other down the line of the ball, following the ball, have the right of way over every other player on the ground. They cannot be impeded or interfered with, apart from by a player who may come in from behind and well wide to hook the stick of his opponent who is attempting to hit the ball. However, they should never be joined in this way by a third player if there is any danger of a 'sandwich' developing: this is a foul sometimes called two on one and results from dangerously aggressive riding. A player may come up the line to meet the ball, provided he is on the correct side, which is always with the ball on his right-hand side at the start of his approach to the ball. He may not come across the line on to the correct side and then meet the ball without fouling. He must never meet the ball with two players coming down the line following the ball. Two players riding up the line to meet the ball have no right of way if one player is riding down the line, following the ball.

A player approaching from the side to meet the ball or to try to obtain possession may approach only from the left side of the ball, provided only one player is coming to hit it. He may not cross the line but, if he arrives before the other player, he may tap the ball across the front of the other player's horse, provided he does not cross the line, and must not pick up the new line until the other player has passed him, along the old line. Although he has changed the line, he has no right to it until all danger of possible collision is passed. Any players galloping down the old line have the right of way to pass, but they do not have the right to swing on to the new line and take the ball. This is always a foul and must be penalised by the umpire if he sees it.

The two most common ways of gaining possession of the ball are by riding off the player on the line and thus assuming the line, and by

The sandwich. *Always be clear who is riding with which man. A sandwich has formed here with Tony Nagle and William Lucas both riding off the player in the middle.*

hooking the player's stick as he comes in to hit the ball, if you are closer to the ball than he is. After he has missed the ball because you have hooked him, provided there is no other player coming down the line following him, you have the right to assume possession of the ball and the line. If you have the ball on your left-hand side, provided you play a shot on the nearside, you may immediately play a shot at the ball if only one player is coming down the stick side of the ball; but you may only do so if you do not infringe his line and therefore cross his right of way.

When you consider that players could be coming down that right of way at up to 40 miles an hour – the maximum speed of a galloping horse – you will understand that to infringe the line in any way could be exceedingly dangerous. This is why the line of the ball is the basis of the rules created to control the safety of polo.

It is essential, as your game gets better, to understand that you should first mark your man and then worry about the ball. Too many players coming into the game initially start to chase the ball all the time.

As you mark the good player, his anticipation will take you to the ball, and if you try to control him, he will take you correctly along the line in the right way and you will avoid fouling. You will also hope to make him hit the ball under pressure and therefore not quite so far or as well controlled as he might otherwise have done.

It is essential to meet the ball only in the correct manner. Often an inexperienced number 1 endeavours to meet the ball, possibly from a hit-out or a penalty 5 or 5(b), when an experienced back has tapped it so that it is approaching him slightly towards his left hand rather than towards his right. If he has to move any distance to the left before he starts to come down the line, he will foul the approaching player and should be penalised. He must turn away, let the other player make his shot, and ride him off as they go down the line together.

THE LINE-OUT   Both teams arrange themselves behind a line marked at the centre of the ground. The umpire throws the ball underhand and hard between the two teams to start the game. From the throw-in the game starts to

THROW-IN

The ball is thrown in under-hand and hard. Always be in position early and try to obtain possession quickly. Note that the number 3s should turn outward.

proceed up and down the ground. In the initial moves from the line-out the first pairing-off of the players takes place: the number 1s mark the number 4s, and the number 2s mark the number 3s. It is essential that, as you break from the line-out, you try to pair off with the player you are marking. Sometimes, because the ball is met at the number 1 position in the line-out, the number 1 will be tempted to go back, trying to ride his opposing *number 1* off, and therefore be forced out of position. Having made this move, he must either stop immediately or go hard to ensure he beats the opposing *number 1* in his first ride-off, because in all probability his number 4 will drop in behind him, anticipating his winning the ride-off after the second shot at least, and will then back the ball. The number 1 must not, having gone back 30 or 40 yards endeavouring to get to the opposing *number 1*, realise that he has then gone into the wrong position and pull out, because his team – particularly the back – will have anticipated that he will get the man. If he then pulls out, the opposing *number 1* will have a free run to the goal.

Pairing Off

Pairing off in the game is the essential part of the defensive strategy of the team. At any time this pairing may switch in the run of play, and the important thing is always to count your heads. If two players in one

Count your heads in defence. *If the other team switches positions you must always know which player you should mark. White 2 must race back to mark black 4. White 1 must steady a little, and pick up black 3.*

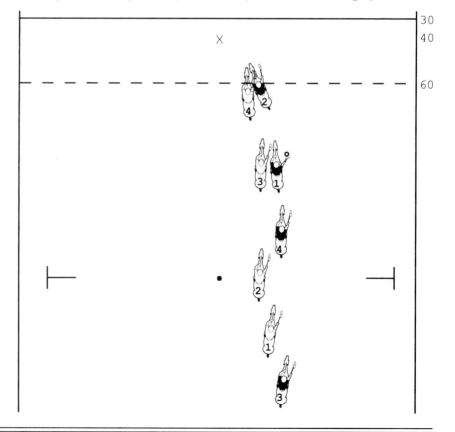

team are riding close together, and one is riding loose in the other team behind the two players, one of the two must immediately drop back and ride off the player coming up behind them. If he doesn't do this, the players behind him will be incorrectly paired off. The team which is attacking will then have an unmarked man who can run on to the ball and make the opportunity for a goal shot.

Count your heads at all times in the game and be aware of who and where your correct man is. If he is in front of you, you must go fast to pick him up. If he is behind you, check up so that you pick him up and ride him off properly. In pairing off, remember that the important thing is to control the area of ground which is vital to your team. Therefore you are not necessarily just riding alongside the player – you may be riding him to the left or to the right of the anticipated direction of play.

The Line and the Flow of Play

You should flow through the game at the same speed as the game. The player on the ball controls the speed of any play, and players both in front and behind should rapidly pick up the flow and move accordingly from 10 to 15 yards in front or behind, to ensure that the line of play is maintained. Assessing your correct distance from the player with the ball is of crucial importance to the speed of the game. The faster you play the game, the higher the standard of polo, and therefore the further apart the players will go and still be in their correct relative positions in the game.

This is something that is learnt with experience. However, when you understand the flow of play it is considerably easier to gain that experience. Once you can hit confidently and reasonably consistently, you can learn the game only by playing it. Having learnt the rules, and understood the areas of fouls which can occur, you are then ready to go out and start playing the game.

Try to understand the line of the ball which controls who has the right to the ball at any time. When you are learning, it is essential that you first try to understand the line of the ball and the changes of the line in the game. Once you understand this vital part of the game, be confident and pick up the line, and take the ball as you get to it. Seasoned players understand that a new player coming into the game is bound to make mistakes while learning the line of the ball and the run of play, and allowances are made for this. However, if you feel you have the line, don't hesitate, because only by making mistakes will you start to understand how the play flows in a match, and whether you actually do have the line. On the other hand, if in doubt, it is better to stay out and try to ride the man, because the foul that you may give away could result in the goal which costs your team the game. The main thing to remember is that crossing the line is a foul if somebody is coming down that line, and if you have to do it, leave your opponent to hit the ball unimpeded and go for the next play.

The difference between **the line of the ball** *and* **the right of way**. *Black 3 has correctly tapped the ball across the right of way on to a new line. He must not cross this right of way until after white 1 has passed, and white 1 cannot turn on to the new line and hit the ball. The dotted lines show the anticipated turns of the players; the solid line shows that the ideal shot is a pass to black 2 who quickly hits the shot to set up his 1.*

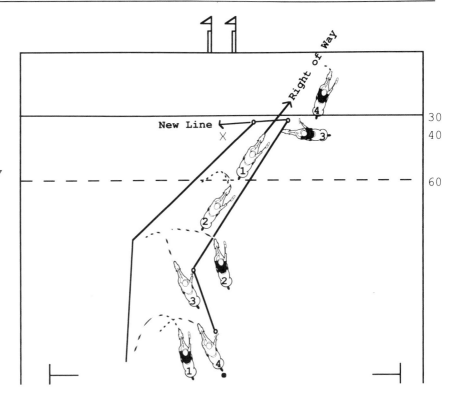

A player on the left- or right-hand side of that line, following the line and not being pursued closely by another player, has the right to take the ball on either side of his pony and should naturally ride for the easiest shot. If he is being hotly pursued by an opponent, he should remain on the same side of the ball on which he starts. He therefore will not cross the line and shouldn't foul, provided he entered the line safely.

If someone is following the ball which has come past him on the nearside, he may stay on the right, provided no other player is coming to meet the ball. If a player is coming correctly to meet the ball on his right or offside and you are caught on the same side of the line going to meet him head on, you must immediately switch to the left of the line, or if someone is already coming down the left, following the ball, you must immediately pull out and leave the line clear. Remember that one of those players will be in your own team and you must decide which of you will go for the ball – you can't both do it, so the one more likely to gain possession without fouling must push through while the other pulls out and moves in anticipation or support. Only playing experience will give you the correct instinctive reaction.

Courtesy and Sportsmanship on the Field

Some players who understand the line knowingly foul in the game to pick up the ball. This creates ill feeling, particularly if it is done cleverly by the better players and not spotted by the umpires, and is not fair gamesmanship. You should always observe the rules to the best of your ability and, if you foul, you should acknowledge the fact and leave the ball for the other team. You must never foul deliberately in a game of polo, particularly in order to avoid a goal. If the player in possession of the ball has played himself into a position where he has a legal goal shot, you can only place yourself between the ball and the goal. He has to hit a rolling ball and anything can happen, but never foul just to prevent him from making the goal – you may cause an accident, which is never worth the risk at any time.

It is essential in the competitive sport of polo to remain courteous at all times on the ground and, if you foul in error, two seconds of apologising takes the heat out of the situation completely. On the other hand, if you start to argue with the umpire, believing that the foul was incorrectly called, you may simply create ill feeling in the other team and certainly between yourself and the umpires. Only the captains of each team have the right to ask the umpire what the foul was for or who fouled. They have no right to any other discussion, and the umpires should not have discussions with the players during a chukka. Occasionally the interpretation of the rules confuses even the good players, and normally umpires are happy to explain fouls afterwards.

Because polo is a highly competitive sport, players can become very emotional. However, good sportsmanship should control your attitude to the game and to any given situation within it. You must accept the umpire's ruling, regardless of whether you believe it is incorrect or not – he is only endeavouring to do the best job he can. If you remember that he would probably much rather be playing in your position than umpiring in his, and if you can imagine yourself in his position at any controversial moment, you will more easily understand the task he faces and give him the respect to which he is entitled. Remember that the game is harder to umpire well than it is to play well.

It is very unfortunate that umpires in polo sometimes have to put up with unpleasantness from the players. They deserve our support rather than our castigation, and I hope that all the players who read these words will remember them when that whistle blows – or doesn't blow – just before they say something which is hurtful, totally unnecessary and probably wrong. We are all guilty of transgression in this respect at some time or other because of the intense, competitive nature of the game. However, umpires have various penalties available to deal with the problem and must not be frightened to use them for the good of the sport.

Dangerous riding and rough play should be avoided at all times on the field, particularly if, in trying to prevent or change a play, you have to come in at a difficult angle or are forced to try to 'bulldoze' the opposition. The best player goes smoothly through the game and, if he can't make one play, he will anticipate and go for the next. This is the best attitude to cultivate and makes for far better polo and certainly a greater appreciation of the game from everybody's point of view, particularly the spectators'. As sportsmanship deteriorates in any game, so the play becomes more and more dangerous and tempers start to fray. As soon as there is any such sign the umpire must immediately step in to put a stop to it.

HOOKING

A three-way hook. Never hook from the opposite side of a player to the ball. Both a legitimate hook by Jonathan Ingram and a foul hook by Peter Few-ster can be seen being made against the striker.

The correct hooking of another player's stick is a very important part of the game. However, foul hooking done on purpose is a gross mistake and causes not only intense irritation, but can also damage the other player's arm, particularly if he is not expecting such a move. In the down-swing of a polo stick, when the muscles are not tense and a foul hook occurs, considerable strain can be placed on the shoulder joints and the ligaments in the upper arm. In the polo school I always make a point of stressing the severity of a foul hook, because of the very real danger of an injury. On the other hand, a foul hook can occur by mistake if a player loses control of his stick when riding off. This should always be acknowledged and a penalty awarded on the spot. It is also a foul to endeavour to hook when not on the same side of the

Always try for a hook and never give up. This hook by Pippa Grace was just made against Major Ferguson and saved a certain goal.

other player's pony as the ball, though it is legal to hook from directly behind a pony as the player makes his swing at the ball. In the latter case, if possible, try to be more on the stick side than straight behind, and be careful to watch that your pony's head does not get hit by the other player's stick. His stick head travels in a bigger arc than you sometimes think, and could be very dangerous for your pony.

It is entirely correct to hook a backhand or forehand on either side, provided you are in the correct position to do so. Players tend to forget that this is very good play, and the quick hook can often win crucial possession in the game. It is important to perfect your hooking by practice on the stick-and-ball field with a friend, to speed up your reactions in match play.

4

SET-PLAY TACTICS

BECAUSE THE THROW-IN is the first opportunity for head-to-head conflict with the other team, and thus your first chance to exert your superiority over them, the line-out is possibly the most important of all the set plays to win. The team that wins major possession in the line-outs more often than not will win the game. As you ride out on to the ground for the throw-in to begin any game, you should have already done your warm-up procedure and stick-and-ball practice to 'get your eye in', and the last minute or two should be set aside for preparing your mind for the coming contest.

It is essential for you to have the confidence of knowing your position in all the set plays. You must ride quickly to your position and be 100 per cent sure that you know exactly whom you are marking in the other team at all times. Always try to be the first member of your team into position so that the others can be sure you know where you are going; this means they do not have to worry about your position and so can concentrate on their own.

It is the responsibility of the captain of the team to ensure that all his players are in position for every set play. If there are two good players and two not-so-experienced players in the team, the good ones should each pick a man and help him to get into position in all of the set plays, which should have been discussed before the game. Should you be helping a team-mate in this way, encourage him as you ride into position and make him aware of his particular job and of the man he should mark in the play that is about to begin.

PREPARATION FOR THE MATCH

It is vital that every player in the team goes out on to the ground with the correct mental attitude to win. Every player should arrive at the ground in plenty of time so that he can relax and adjust mentally before the match begins. He should, first of all, make sure that his horses are all in order and check the playing order with his groom. He should then check all the saddles to ensure that the stirrups are of the correct length, and finally put on his playing gear and get ready to do his warm-up stick and ball. If he has a difficult pony that needs more work before playing, he should arrange for it to be done by the groom, or he should school that pony first, and do whatever is essential so that when he starts the game he can expect all his ponies to play to their maximum potential. He should allow himself at least five minutes to stick and ball, plus a little time to warm up his first pony and sharpen him up before the commencement of the game.

If possible, the team should meet at least half an hour before each player begins his final preparation for the game to discuss and confirm the positions of the players during the set plays. Each player should be quite clear of the person he will mark in the opposition, and his responsibilities during the game. Because of the many combinations of tactics which are available to a team in their efforts to win a game of polo, these should have been discussed prior to the game in a special team theory session so that everybody is 100 per cent clear in their mind what may happen in any given situation. If you are unclear on any point during the game, ask your captain to clarify what is bothering you. If at any time during the game you are unclear as to your position or the person you should be marking, ask your captain immediately. Don't hesitate, because he will not be aware of your indecision and it could be critical. Take the opportunity as soon as possible or during the next break in the play to clarify your problem.

The captain of the team should be prepared at any time during the game to switch his tactics to achieve a winning position. It is essential that he retain a flexible attitude to cope with a change of circumstances not previously anticipated. After the first chukka, or at half-time, if a team appears not to be playing well, they should take the few minutes to discuss a possible change of tactics or positions.

The line-out for the first throw-in is a crucial part of the game, as has already been mentioned, and the number 1 who is really sharp will go into the line-out with every endeavour to win the first ball. The umpire will have already tossed and if your team has won the choice of ends, remember that at the throw-in one team will have the advantage of the stick side towards the ball. Unless there is a definite advantage to be gained from playing one way or the other, either because of the sun or the wind, the stick-side advantage should be a major consideration when choosing ends.

You may also need to decide whether to play uphill or downhill on a sloping field, and you can do this when stick and balling before the game. Unless you know the field, it is advisable to check the area in front of each goal to find out if it is evenly worn. One goal might be considerably more worn and damaged on the ground surface than the other, so it will be easier for you to play towards the smoother one to score your first goal at that end. The pattern of wear may show that, for some reason, more of the play is at one end, so consider the pros and cons carefully.

Playing the Game

Having decided which way the teams will play, you line up for the throw-in. Often there is a 'T' marked on the ground and the number 1s should stand behind this until the umpire commences his throw-in. The number 2s line up and the number 3s should always face outwards in the line-out. The number 4s should not stand at the end of the line-out. They should be 5–10 yards behind it and opposite the number 1 or 2 positions, ready to pick up the first player who breaks through the line-out, ride him off firmly and back the ball.

The number 1 should be ready to swing at the start of the movement of the umpire's hand. If the umpire throws in as he should – under-hand and hard – it may well be easier to pick up the ball at the number 1's position than if he throws in the ball – as is often the case these days – in the Argentinian manner, from over the top of his shoulder and down on to the ground just in front of the number 1.

The number 1's primary aim is one swing at the ball and through past the *number 4*, riding forwards and looking backwards. The job of the number 2 in the line-out is to try to block the opposition from coming through, and to win the ball, but certainly to frustrate the opposition if they win it and to prevent them from breaking completely through the line-out.

The line-out should be tight with no gaps, and the number 3 should turn outwards so that if the ball is thrown in under-hand and hard, it will go through the line-out approximately 30 per cent of the time and this will put him in the ideal position to pick up the ball. He will then be able to choose whether to back the ball past the opposing *number 4* to his number 1 who has ridden into an attacking position or whether he will take the ball around under the neck or with a cut shot and then pass it up to his number 1 somewhere in the vicinity of the 60-yard line.

Remember that you should never take a full swing in the line-out, and always be ready to hook your opponent's stick and work hard for the ball with a strong, stiff arm. The back should not be tempted to come through the line-out, or across the back end of it, and cross the line which has been formed in the original throw-in. If the number 3 stands pointing outwards from the line-out, the necessity for the number 4 to go for that ball is eliminated. If the opposing *number 3* turns into the line and the ball is not being thrown in very hard, the number 3 should be very careful that he is not always beaten for the ball – he will have to adjust his position and stand much closer to the number 2.

The throw-in from the side line to recommence play, when the ball has been hit out of play, differs from the throw-in from the centre only in that the umpire should get the players to stand 10 yards away from him inside the side line (from the centre, he will be just 5 yards away). It is therefore possibly easier for the number 1 to meet the ball in a throw-in from the side line.

Various line-out positions. A *and* **B** *from the centre. Much depends on how hard the umpire throws in the ball. In A, dotted lines show which way the players should go – the 2s go along the line of the ball. Black 4 is placed to pick up white 1 as he comes off the line-out. In* **B***, if the ball is thrown in hard, black 3 is in the best position, if softly then white is in a better position.* **C** *from the sideline. When attacking, the best player at controlling the ball should place himself at the end of the line-out, and his players should ensure the ball reaches him by hitting at the sticks of their opponents.* **D** *and* **E** *positions in the field. In* **D** *white 4 is in a good position to defend the goal and meet the ball but he must not meet two players. In* **E** *black 1 and 2 are dominating and white 3 has won the best position. Black 4 is ready for white 1.*

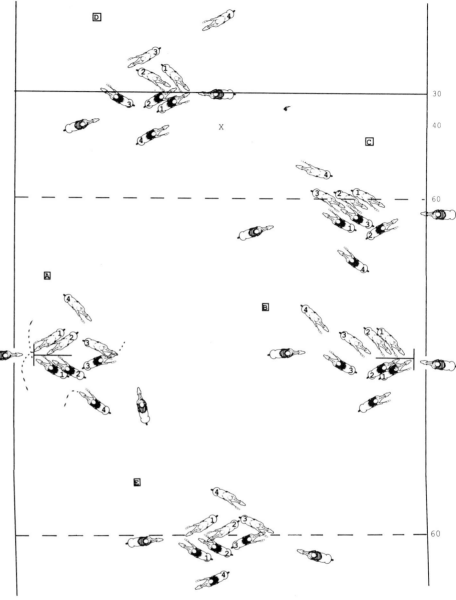

Care should be taken not to hit the ball back out again, because that is wasted possession. In the line-out inside the 60-yard line, if you are attacking and if your number 1 is quickest and best at dribbling the ball, you should consider putting him in the position of the number 3, turning outwards, and try to ensure, by blocking the other player's stick, that the ball goes right through the line-out to him. He will then be able to break quickly towards the goal.

In a line-out close to the goal, if you are attacking, it is essential to try to meet that ball at the number 1 position, so the player who is best at meeting any ball should be put at number 1 for that thrown-in. Conversely, if you are defending, it is essential that the ball goes through the line-out, because the umpire will be throwing it away from the goal. Therefore you should hit your opponent's stick to prevent him from meeting the ball and do everything to ensure that the ball goes right through the line-out and that your number 3 is positioned ready to take it away from the other end. The number 4 should position himself at least 10 yards from the line-out in the direction of the goal so that he can try to meet a goal shot, or turn in defence if he has room.

THE HIT-IN: DEFENSIVE POSITIONS

When the ball is hit over the back line by the attacking team, it should be placed by the goal judge just inside the back line, opposite where it crossed, or at least 4 yards wide of the goal posts, to be hit in by a defending player. If it is hit over by a defender, the umpire blows his whistle and places the ball on the 60-yard line opposite where it went over the back line, and a penalty 6 is executed – a free hit for the attacking team.

For the purposes of this discussion, it is presumed that the number 4 of the defending team takes the hit-ins; if the number 3 decided to take them, the two players would just switch positions for the duration of that play. His number 1 will stand straight out from the ball, roughly on the 60-yard line. His number 2 will stand wide towards the side line on whatever side the hit-out is to be taken, and the number 3 will stand in towards the goal about 25 yards away from the back line and in a position to protect the goal should the number 4 mishit or the ball be met by the attacking team.

If the number 4 is hitting out with the goal posts on his right-hand side, the number 3 should be about 25 yards from the ball, between the goal and the attacker on the extreme right, facing the attacking team. This will give his number 4 the option to hit past him. If the number 4 hits to the left-hand side line, he should ensure that the ball is hit well wide to his number 2. He must not hit too straight or he will risk the attacking team meeting the ball easily and give them a very good goal-scoring opportunity.

Frequently the number 4 should consider taking the ball across his own goal past his number 3, putting him on the line and giving his own

The Hit-in from the left.
1 *Black 4 carries the ball.
By prior arrangement
either his 3 plays the 4
position and 2 runs on
the line B or he drops
back to cover – A – and
the 3, who is better
placed, runs in
anticipation of a pass, as
shown.*

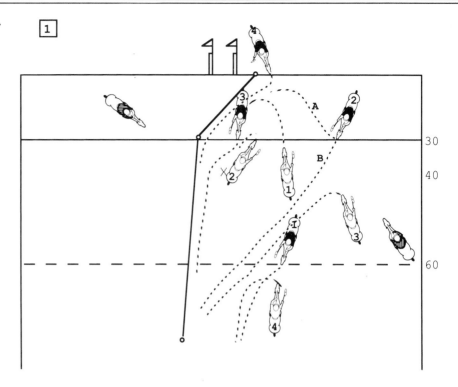

2 *Black 4 carries the ball
at top speed, followed by
his 3, while before he has
hit the ball at all, black 2
is running into a position
to control white 3 and
possibly receive a pass if
he is quick enough. Black
1 goes up the line in
anticipation.*

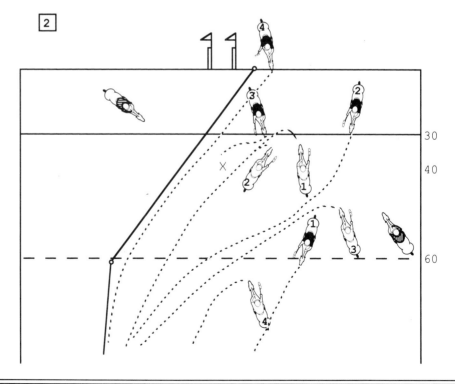

3 *The Hipwood play. By making this play, the whole ground is opened up to the black team instead of just the right half. It is essential to have a big hitter at 4.*

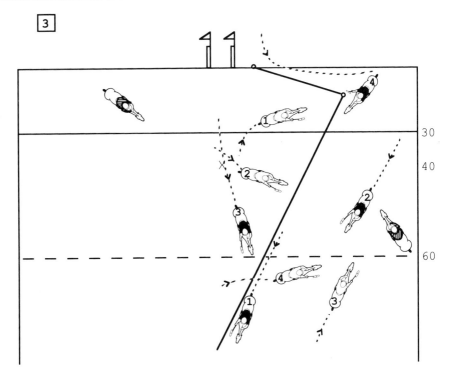

4 *Black 4 looks to be hitting across the goal, but plays an accurate pass to his 1 who has not gone as far up as usual. His position prevents white 3 from interfering, but allows black 2 to run for the pass. Black 3 must prevent white 2 from reaching black 1 before his pass.*

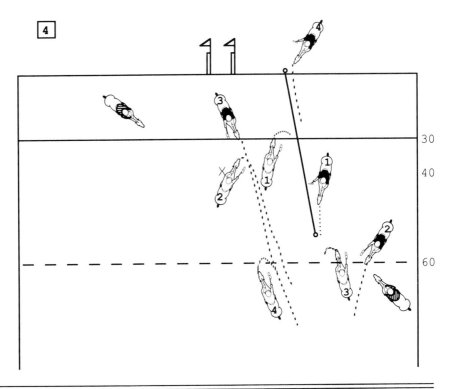

players the advantage of the stick side down the ground. This makes it considerably more difficult for the attacking team to take possession of the ball. If the number 4 goes fast with the ball, and the number 2 drops behind and plays the back position, the number 3 can go up for a pass or drop in right behind the line. The number 1 should then move up the right centre of the ground for a long pass.

I recently noticed Howard Hipwood, when hitting out on the left-hand side of the goal, carry the ball about 10 yards out from the back line, straight towards the left side line, in one or two taps, thus drawing the *number 1* towards him. He was very much in control of the ball and, as the *number 1* came forward to try to take the ball, he changed the line back towards the goal and placed the long shot right up the centre, thus giving his team the whole of the field on their stick side rather than just half of it. The attacking team must ride their opposition across the ground to gain possession in such a play.

It is essential to vary your play from the back line if you seem to be doing most of the hitting out. If you do not, the attacking team can anticipate where you are going to hit the ball. You must always hit away from the attacking team's strong player, thus making it harder for them to win the ball. It is essential that the team hitting out know precisely what the hitter is going to do with the ball. It is quite a good idea to have a series of signals so that everybody in your team knows where the ball is going to go.

THE HIT-IN: ATTACKING POSITIONS

The number 1 in the attacking team should stand wide and left of *the striker* on the 30-yard line. There are two different positions which can be adopted by the number 2. I used to think that he ought always to stand wide and mark the opposing *number 2* should the ball be hit wide towards him. However, more recently I have preferred to have the number 2 standing just over the 30-yard line opposite the *number 3* and prepared to meet the ball if it should be tapped straight towards him or to turn and pick up the *number 3* as he moves into a position to take the *number 4*'s pass, if the ball is hit right across the goal.

Years ago it was the exception rather than the rule for the player hitting out from the back line to tap the ball. Most often he hit the ball wide to the side line and, by having the number 2 standing wide, with the number 3 behind him, the attacking team had two players ready to prevent the ball from getting away from the back line. It is essential to think positively in this situation and, although you do not have possession of the ball, do everything you can to achieve it. Recently it seems to have been the habit of most of the players hitting the ball out from the back line to tap it and then hit it away; and when the ball is tapped, it is more frequently tapped on the stick side to the right than on the left-hand side of the ground or the attacking team's right-hand side, thus giving the defending team in possession the opportunity to carry the ball around the ground anti-clockwise and so make it difficult for the attacking team to get on to the line and take possession.

It is an essential part of forward thinking in the hit-out for the attacking team to endeavour to place a player in the right position to take a pass which is going up on the stick side of the defending team. If the number 2 stands in the middle opposite the defending *number 3*, the attacking number 3 should stand wide about 40–50 yards out, opposite the *number 2*, because that is his instinctive anticipation of where *the back* will hit the ball. The attacking back will stand approximately half-way between the number 1 and the number 3 in a diamond-type formation to give added depth to both of those areas of the ground. He should be prepared to take the stick side of the opposing *number 1* or he should control the *number 1* as he comes over the 60-yard line.

The better the polo, the more essential it is for the back to control the *number 1* before he anticipates where the ball is going to travel next. Once he has control he is free to go to where he anticipates the ball will be and get himself into a position where he might change the play. However, he should remember that if the *number 1* slips past him and the pass comes through because the rest of his team have been unable to achieve possession, he lays himself open to major problems if he has failed to anticipate correctly. The attacking back must evaluate the strength of his team and their ability to obtain possession. If in doubt, he must cover the *number 1*, depending on that player's individual ability to carry the ball down the ground.

The main variations in the hit-out taken from the right-hand side of the goal posts are, first of all, that the team hitting out will reverse its position, with the *number 2* again standing wide and the *number 3* defending the goal; the *number 1* will be in exactly the same place relative to the ball, and the attacking team will be in their positions as before.

Should the attacking team decide to have their number 2 wide, opposite the defending *number 2*, then the number 3 drops back to about 50 or 60 yards, the number 2 is just about on the 30-yard line opposite the *number 2* standing wide, and the 2 and 3 must be prepared to inter-change should either of them get the opportunity to meet the ball. It is important that the number 2 picks up the opposing *number 2* as he comes over the 30-yard line so that his number 3 can pick up the line of the long ball without fouling, and turn on it or back the ball to his number 2 or, better still, place a short pass to his back, who has run past him, on the new line up the centre to the right of the goal.

When the defending team is taking the ball down their right-hand side of the ground, they have the ball on their stick side as they start. This is an important benefit, and if the defending team regularly carry the ball over the half-way line from this side of the ground, the

Hit-in from the right.
Never hit to the other team. **1** *Black 4 taps the ball to X, then depending on who has the best position, he has two main directional options, Y or Z: Y for a pass in front of black 1, with a risk of him being hooked by white 3, and Z, where the risk of black 2 being ridden off by white 3 exists, so the ball should be hit short of Z to make that impossible, and black 2 should assume the line much more quickly than shown.*

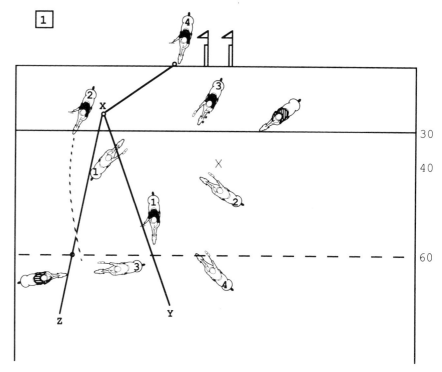

2 *The long hit-in should be hit well in front of black 1 to Y when he is running, or just in front of his 2 towards Z. Black 2 must hit quickly up to his 1 past X while immediately riding off the white 3, and trying to gain control. In both 1 and 2 black 3 follows along the line and black 4 stays 15 to 20 yards behind him. The white team should try to control the ground at every hit-in, and cover their men immediately, before they are allowed to break away.*

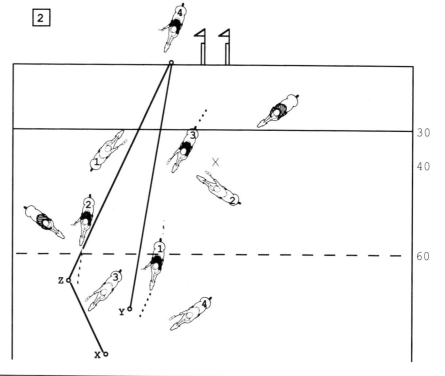

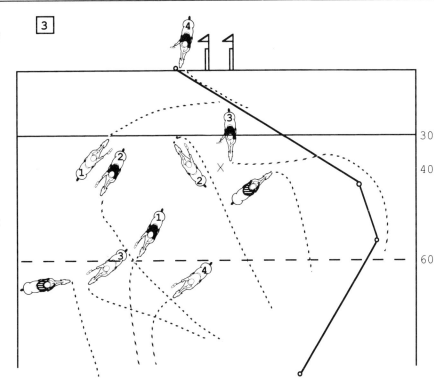

3 *It is essential to hit hard and wide, inside the 60-yard line so that black 3 can swing fast on to the line and hit very quickly. Note that his second shot should be short – about 20 yards – so he does not risk hitting the ball over the sideline. If black 4 follows his 3 very fast, black 2 should swing back to play the 4 position until the play breaks down, and then each player must resume his position as soon as possible.*

attacking team should place their team slightly wider than the defending team to pick those players up on the stick side as they come out with the ball. It is crucial for the attacking team to gain possession of the ball as soon as possible, from the hit-in.

I remember losing the final of a major tournament when my back hit the ball from the right-hand side of our goal, straight across the goal to the left-hand boards. A six-goal player on the other team picked up the ball as it changed its line down the boards, and he was able to score against us because he then had the ball on his stick side and we were unable to get on to his changing line. Had I known, and been galloping down the line, I would have hit the ball before he met it. That ingrained in my mind forever the essential part that communication plays within the team at all times.

PENALTIES

Penalties are given for infringements of the rules, or fouls, during the game. Fouls – such as crossing the line, possibly the most common in polo – increase in severity, depending on the nature of the foul, its position on the field, and the direction in which the game is proceeding at the time it is committed. Penalties are awarded by two umpires, one on each side of the ground, who control the game and blow a whistle

Defending desperately. It is important to be in the correct position to try and defend a penalty. Nicky Evans is perfectly placed to defend what looks like a lofted 60-yard penalty.

when a foul has occurred. A third man – the referee – sits on the stand to arbitrate if at any time the umpires cannot agree.

It is important to realise that the rules referred to are the HPA rules in England. Most polo-playing countries use the same ones – the HPA rules have been generally accepted as the basis on which most polo association rules are founded. However, players must also read the rules of their own local polo association very carefully and understand the differences, and possibly their interpretation. Although, in these days of international polo, umpires try to interpret the rules on an international basis, there are still certain variations from country to country, and the international player must take care to make himself aware of these differences.

For instance, when taking a penalty in England, the striker is allowed only a few seconds to tee up the ball and then he must canter round and approach the ball just once. If he doesn't take the swing at the ball on that first approach, the defending team has the right to attack the ball. The umpire should blow the whistle and throw the ball in if he considers the attacking team are wasting time. In most other countries, however, the player can take as long as he likes to tee up the ball – it is much easier to loft the ball over the top if it sits on a 2-inch-high divot of earth – and then circle two or three times if necessary to balance his horse on the correct leg, making the penalty shot only when everything is perfect. The English interpretation has evolved because, like the players, the spectators want to see the game continue, and some players were taking far too long to tee up.

The main penalties are numbered from 1 to 6, for infringements of decreasing severity. They are explained in detail below.

Penalty 1

This, penalty 1, is the severest in the game and is awarded for a dangerous or deliberate foul in order to stop a goal. It is the only goal in polo where ends are not changed and the umpire throws the ball into a line-out from 10 yards in front of the goal towards the side where the

Penalty 1. *A goal is awarded and the umpire throws the ball in 10 yards from the centre of the goal. The players do not change ends.*

10 yds

20 yds

30 yds

X   40 yds

50 yds

— — — — — — — — — — · 60 yds

foul occurred. The defending *back* should stand more or less in the middle of the goal, and the person who can meet the ball best should stand in the number 1 position for the attacking team, in the hope of hitting the ball through the goal in one hit and thus scoring two goals for one foul. If this happens, the players change ends and play resumes as normal from the centre.

Penalty 2

A penalty 2 is awarded for an infringement against the attacking team inside the 30-yard line or in the vicinity of 30–40 yards from the goal. Its award depends on the severity of the foul – if it is just a technical foul, a penalty 5 might be given. In most such cases, however, a penalty 2 would usually be awarded, and the umpire gives the captain of the attacking team the choice of taking the penalty from the spot where the foul occurred, or from the 30-yard mark in front of the goal, whichever is preferred.

Penalty 2 and 3. The umpire awards a penalty 2 on the spot or a 30 – the attacking captain has the option. In a penalty 3 the defending players take up the same positions and the ball is placed on the 40-yard spot marked X. Attacking players are in the same positions relative to the ball as in the penalty 2.

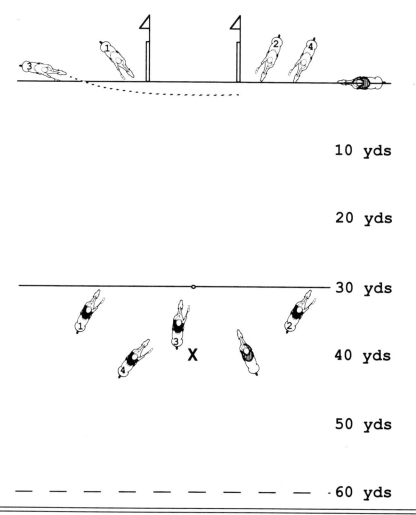

10 yds

20 yds

30 yds

40 yds

50 yds

60 yds

The attacking team must all stand behind the striker, while the defending team must stand behind the goal line and/or at least 30 yards from the ball if it is placed inside the 30-yard line. They must not come out over the goal line or get closer than 30 yards before the ball is hit or hit at, and they must not come out through the goal posts at any time while the penalty 2 is taken. It can be defended in the same way as a penalty 3.

Penalty 3

A penalty 3 is a 40-yard hit at goal taken from a cross marked 40 yards from the centre of the goal. This is for a foul committed inside the 60-yard line and possibly out wide around the 30-yard line, but again it depends on the severity of the foul. In both penalties 2 and 3 it is the accepted practice for the best person at meeting the ball to gallop across from behind the back line after the ball has been hit at goal, and try to meet the ball as it comes towards the goal in an attempt to clear it away, although this is technically a foul. If the attacking striker hits the ball at half-speed and gallops in, it would be impossible to do this without fouling. However it is the accepted practice when the ball is struck firmly, and it has resulted in some brilliant shots being saved by the defending team.

I once saw a seven-goal player come galloping across, meet a 30-yard penalty when it was hit about waist high, and in one hit it sailed out about 60 yards in front of him. Then, in two more shots, he scored at the other end of the ground, at least 50 yards ahead of his nearest rival who had raced back in defence.

The same rules apply for a penalty 2 and a penalty 3. The attacking players should be behind the striker and the defending players must be behind the goal line and must not come out through the goal posts at any time. Nobody must cross the goal line in the defending team until the ball has been hit or hit at.

In each of these penalties one umpire should stand behind the striker and the other to the side on the back line to ensure that the defending team do not infringe by crossing the back line too soon. If they do, and the ball is running through the goal but is saved, the goal should be awarded. If the ball is running wide, another hit should be awarded from the same spot. If the attacking team fail to carry out the penalties correctly, the defending team should hit out from the centre of the goal.

Penalty 4

The penalty 4 is a 60-yard hit at a goal, taken from a spot on the 60-yard line in the middle of the goal posts. The attacking team may stand where they like in front of the striker, and the defending team may stand wherever they like in front of the goal, provided they are behind the 30-yard line.

Penalty 4. *The players move as illustrated just as the ball is hit or is hit at.*

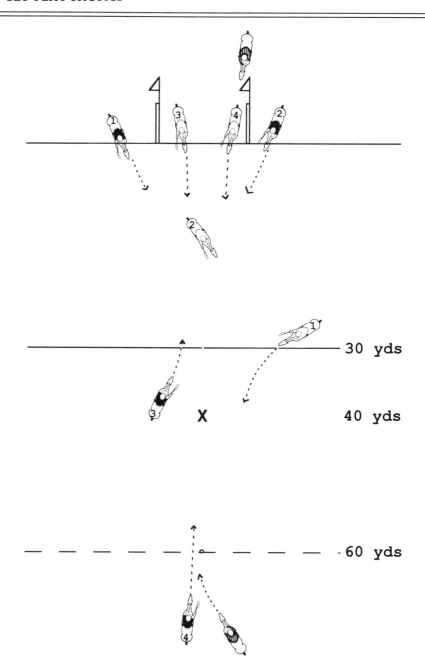

In the attacking team the number 1 and number 2 should come out from behind the goal line, about 5 yards wide of the posts, as the ball is hit, moving slightly towards the goal to meet the ball on its line should it be hit wide. The number 3 should stand about 25 yards from the striker with the line between the ball and the left-hand goal post on his offside, ready to follow down the line of the shot, firmly and with control, to claim the line of the penalty shot in case it is met by a defending player. Also, he should be quick to get on the line in case a player coming from the wrong side of that line meets the ball. He will then be able to gain a foul.

The defending team should stand with their *number 1* quite wide to the left to try to prevent the striker from tapping the ball towards or just wide of the right-hand goal post and then hitting an under-the-neck shot at goal from 30 or 40 yards out. The *number 2* should stand about 40 yards from the ball and more or less in the centre, with his stick down, prepared to meet the ball, and his horse at a slight angle to the line of the ball. The *numbers 3* and *4* should stand just inside each goal post and be prepared to call the defending team to leave the ball if it is hit wide.

Penalty 5(a)

Penalty 5(a) is awarded on the spot for an infringement by the attacking team while moving forward towards the defenders' goal. It can also be awarded anywhere on the field for a technical foul if the attacking team is fouled.

Positions for both the attacking and the defending team are similar in relation to the ball to those of a penalty 5(b), and similar tactics apply in both cases. (See pages 218 and 219.)

As the penalty gets closer to the back line, the positions of the defending team who are taking the penalty become similar to those of a hit-in.

Penalty 5(b)

Penalty 5(b) is awarded in two different situations:

1 When play has turned about the 60-yard line and is moving up towards the half-way line, and the team then going in defence fouls in trying to regain possession. If the foul is dangerous the umpire should carry the balls over the half-way line and up to the 60-yard spot, awarding a penalty 4.
2 When a dangerous foul is committed by the attacking team, between the half-way line and the goal they are attacking.

In deciding where the penalty should be awarded, the umpires should consider where the shot would have finished had it been made, and perhaps give the penalty from the nearest penalty spot in that area, having first given thought to the advantage of possession and which way the game was flowing at the time the penalty was awarded.

Positions for the 5(b)

The attacking team will have its number 3 about 25 yards away from the ball facing forward with the goal posts on his right-hand side. The number 2 will be a little bit wide on the other side, ready to gallop on to the pass, about 30–45 yards from the ball. The number 1 will be up

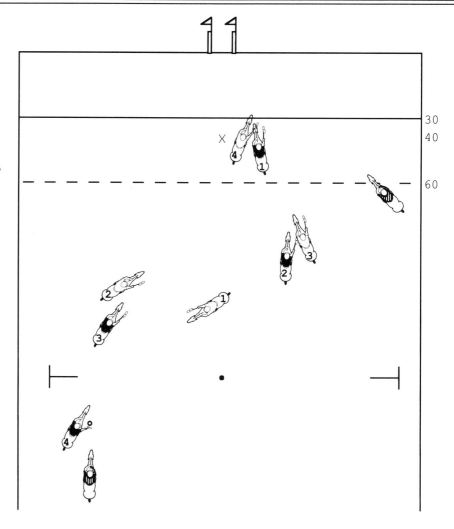

Penalty 5(a) – *On the Spot. These two penalties from the same spot show how important the positions of the players are as the penalty is hit.* **1** *The white team dominate, though white 2 should be on the other side of black 3.*

close to the 60-yard line, more or less in the middle of the ground, but prepared to take the stick side of the *number 4* and to control the goal area.

The defending team's *number 1* will be 30 yards wide, facing the hitter, well to the left of the line between the goal and the ball. The *number 2* will be about 40–50 yards from the ball, offering his stick side to the hitter, and more or less on the line between the ball and the goal. The *number 3* will be 55–60 yards away, facing away from the hitter with the line of the ball on his left controlling the number 2, and *the back* on about the 30-yard line facing the goal, almost directly in the line of the ball, covering the number 1.

The *number 1* must keep pressure on the hitter and make him hit away as soon as possible, and the hitter must endeavour to get the ball up to his team within 60 yards of the goal to give them a goal-scoring opportunity.

The attacking team should all know whether the hitter is going to tap the ball first or whether he is going to hit the big shot straight away. It is very important because they must time their runs so that they have maximum impulsion in whatever direction they are going, as the ball comes past them. Otherwise the defending team, who have the advantage of position, will ride them off the line and be able to play the back shot.

2 The black team could score through passes from 4 to 3 to 2 or 1 at the 40-yard mark or a big hit to the right of the same area.

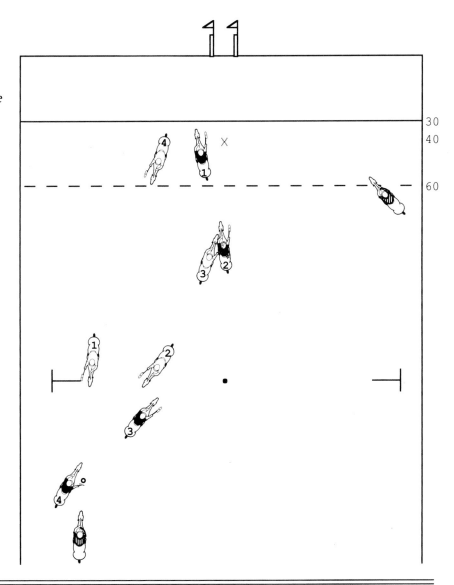

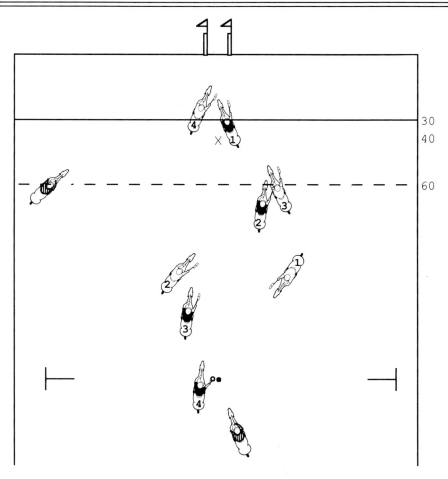

Penalty 5(b). *The team awarded the penalty should get themselves close to the black positions and then try to dominate the defending team. Black 2 should try to get on the other side of white 3. The defending team should mark their opposition and must try to protect the area around their goal. White 1 should always stand wide to prevent black 4 from tapping and dribbling the ball.*

The longest hitter in the team will normally take the 5(b) penalty and every effort should be made to produce it some 30 yards in front of the goal and, if possible, through the goal. The defending team must weigh up the length of the hitter's capabilities, be positioned to anticipate the place where the shot will land and be able to clear it accordingly.

Penalty 6

A penalty 6 is awarded when the defensive team hits the ball behind their own back line in order to prevent a goal. The penalty is taken from the 60-yard line by the attacking team, opposite the position where the ball went over the back line.

Both attacking and defensive positions will be similar to those of a penalty 4 and, if the ball is wide on the 60, in all probability the penalty taker will tap the ball to endeavour to get it closer to the goal before he takes the goal shot. The defending team should be well aware of this and position themselves accordingly, remembering that the defending team must not only be 30 yards from the ball, but must also be behind the 30-yard line.

Penalties 7–10

Penalty 7 outlines the rules for 'taking another hit', if the teams do not carry out the penalty correctly, while penalties 8–10 involve the retiring of players or ponies from the game for various reasons. These are spelt out in the HPA rules in the Appendix.

**CALLING
IN THE GAME
'Take the Man'**

As its name implies, this means that you should first ride the man and then hit the ball if you can.

'Leave it and take the man'. This action photograph shows a clear piece of team play. Peter Grace and Tony Nagle are fighting for the ball, neither has a clear shot, so Rodolfo Ducos, riding behind them with David Wilkins, should call Peter off, since he believes that he will win the ride off. Ali Abidi riding at the back should call Rodolfo off since he has the clearest shot of all and can pass it forward.

Leave it and take the man. *In A black 2 calls 'Leave it . . . man', or 'Take the man' if he has time. Black 3 then calls to 2 to 'Leave it'. In B black 2 calls, and all attacking players when called off try to ensure that the path to the goal is clear. Note black 1 does not push his opponent over into the goal.*

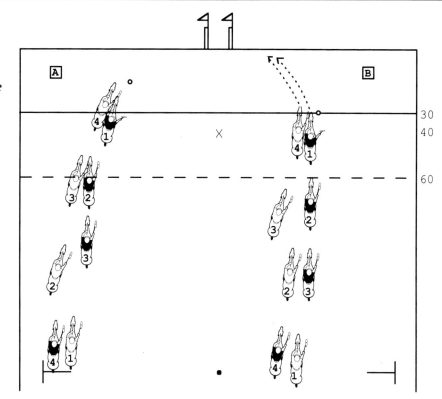

'The Ball'

When you hear this you should immediately race to the ball and hit it as quickly as possible.

'Leave it'

If ever you are called to 'Leave it', you must leave the ball. The player behind you can assess the situation and it is better to be called off, and then ride flat out towards the goal for a pass, than to hit the ball and be ridden off the next shot, thus losing possession.

Often, when playing, I will call a player two players in front to 'Leave it' because the next player will set up a play in a more advantageous way. These decisions are made on the spur of the moment, probably with little time. Your reaction to the call 'Leave it' is crucial and might result in a goal-scoring opportunity which would otherwise be lost.

Never call a player to leave the ball when he is going for a goal shot if there is any doubt that you might not get the shot yourself, particularly in tight play where the vital seconds that elapse between his shot and yours could result in your being hooked or prevented from making the shot by the opposition.

'Mine'

If two players are going for the ball the player most advantageously placed should call 'Mine', while the other player immediately goes for a pass or takes a man.

'Yours'	If you are the player in front with no one to pass to and your team-mate close behind you has a certain shot, shout 'Yours', thus telling him to hit it while you leave it and ride off the opposition who is going in defence of his pass.
'The Boards' or 'Centre', 'Open' or 'Tail', 'Abierto' or 'Cola'	These are the calls, made by the player following the back who is going to hit the ball, for directional backhands when there is any doubt about the direction in which he should hit it. Use these sparingly as the other team can hear them and it helps their anticipation too.
'Over here' and 'Back it'	These are calls for passes in different directions – 'Over here' is used by a player who is well to the side of the player with the ball and may not have been noticed, but has got himself into an advantageous position to set up a play. 'Back it' is a call for a backhand towards the caller and should be accompanied by a directional instruction if any doubt exists.
'Hook him'	This means that you should try desperately for the hook – it could be vital for your team's defence. Always be alert to the possibility of a hook. It may result in possession for your team.
Name the player	You should always name the player to receive a pass if there is any doubt.

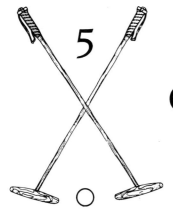

5

CAPTAINING THE TEAM

FORMING A TEAM

WITH YOUR KNOWLEDGE of the players available, the basis of forming a team should be to put the right players in the right places. Too many teams are put on the ground with three backs and a number 2, or perhaps three number 3 players and a patron or whoever else is available, just because they are the best.

A good team is one with a natural number 1, even if he is not the best player available; a number 2 who is playing most of his polo in that position at the time and is playing well; a number 3 who is the main pivot man and the thinker behind the team; and good, safe number 4, preferably with a long hit, who can also hit the ball to the right place.

The essence of good polo is not necessarily to hit the ball 100 yards – to hit it 50 yards in the right direction is far better, and it is more important to hit the ball with consistency. If you are going to hit it 100 yards one minute and 20 yards sideways the next, it is hopeless for your team to try to anticipate any shot you may make. If you hit the ball consistently 20 yards sideways, however, at least your team-mates will know where to go to pick up the pass – and you will have changed the line.

Ensure that your team is put together with the correct handicap to compete in the tournament that you are entering. If the handicap of a team member has recently been adjusted, the team may still qualify and play off a higher handicap. The handicap you play off must be correct at the time, and the difference between the total handicap of your team and that of the other team recorded correctly on the scoreboard prior to the start of the game.

THE CAPTAIN'S PREPARATION

As captain the preparation you make off the ground will be of vital importance in playing a better team game. It could give you the edge if your team's reactions are automatic and very sharp. Take the trouble to set out a horse list and ensure that you are not playing all your weak horses in the same chukka. You should consider all the horses very carefully and ensure that the number 1 and number 2 play their worst horses in different chukkas and the number 3 and number 4 also do likewise.

It is a good idea to award each horse in the game rating marks of 1 to 5 and then calculate the total rating for each chukka. You can then see at a glance if any chukka is way too high while another is too low. I believe that the best horse should be kept until the last chukka in the game; however, if you are not very confident, there is a lot to be said for riding your best and easiest horse in the first chukka to settle yourself down and get into the game straight away.

In a four- or five-chukka match it is essential to start fast and go hard, because you won't have much time to make up lost ground towards the end of the game. In the USA it is customary in the six-chukka matches they play to start a little slower and pour on the power towards the end.

In England we currently play quite a lot of 'American' tournaments. These are matches in which three teams play two chukkas against each other to find one winner out of three. When planning how to use your ponies in an American tournament, remember that the team who wins the tournament must win the first two chukkas, so you should always play your best ponies in the first two chukkas. The exception is if the second team you play is much better than the first.

MATCH PREPARATION

Always ensure that all your team are at the ground early and have sufficient time to warm up properly before a match. You should be there with at least half an hour to spare, allowing for a short discussion with them before the game.

Good organisation off the ground is essential to the success of the team on the ground. Always be precise with your pony arrangements and make sure that your grooms are organised to produce the ponies exactly where you want them before you need them. Make sure that a spare pony is ready at all times in case any one of the team gets into difficulties or has a lame pony, and see that all your players have spare sticks available in the middle of the ground – it is always closer to go to the middle than to the far end.

Before the game starts, ensure that the handicap put up on the board is correct. After the end of the first chukka, a handicap discrepancy cannot be changed. Remember that, in England, in a four-chukka game, two-thirds of the difference between the two teams in handicap should be awarded to the team with the lowest handicap. In other words,

$$\text{Handicap award} = \frac{\text{No. of chukkas to be played}}{\text{Maximum no. of chukkas possible}} \times \frac{\text{Difference between the}}{\text{teams' handicaps.}}$$

In the six-chukka matches of the USA the handicaps will reflect the full difference between the two teams; in a four-chukka game, however, they award two-thirds of the difference to the team with the lowest handicap, always rounding the figure up or down to the nearest goal. They do not award half-goals in the USA, whereas in England, and in much of the rest of the world, half a goal is awarded for any portion of a goal. The basic reason for playing four- instead of six-chukka matches is the shortage of pony power and therefore the half-goal is a good thing as it eliminates extra time and so lessens the stress on the horses.

Inspire the team to dominate their opponents at all times, both physically and mentally. For the sake of clarity, name the player to receive a pass and encourage your players to clear a channel towards the goal so that you or possibly your back will have a clear pathway through.

It is essential as the captain of the team for you to give your team constructive help to build their confidence. Defamatory criticism destroys both concentration and confidence.

You must encourage your team members to relax under pressure and play hard until after the final bell regardless of the score. Use clear and crisp calling during the game and encourage them to talk to each other so that they know automatically what will happen next and they then have the advantage of better anticipation. Finally, remember after the game to thank both the opposition and the umpires, and be prepared to make a thank-you speech if it is an invitational match and yours is the guest team.

TACTICS IN THE GAME

Tactics to be used in the game should be decided in a team discussion well before the game. The captain should always sit down with his team around a theory board to discuss the various positions for the set plays, the basic clearances from different positions on the ground, and the different plays that are available from various circumstances that arise in the game. As a result of this discussion the members of the team will begin to think together and will react automatically to any situation that might occur while they are playing. This is apparent when watching a team, whose members have been well coached, as they play together, because the game flows so much better.

The Anti-clockwise Game Strategy

It is a definite advantage if the attacking team plays the game in an anti-clockwise direction around the ground, thus allowing you to retain possession of the ball on the stick side and forcing the defending team to ride you off the line before they can get the ball. The minute the ball goes clockwise around the ground, the line is open to the defending team to meet the ball or hook the attacking player's stick, because they have easy access to the ball on the offside. They also have the right to play the ball backhand on the nearside, and therefore can readily gain

The anti-clockwise game. *If the ball travels around the ground anti-clockwise, the team in possession, with the ball on their stick side, have the advantage of the line. This illustrates two consecutive plays with white attacking. White 3 and 2 are controlling their players off the ball. In the second play, black 4 flies straight down the ground in anticipation instead of closing with white 1, and clears the ball under the neck. Note the direction the players run in anticipation as soon as they see that black 4 should hit the first shot. Black 3 always follows 4, and must try to prevent white 1 from hitting the ball if his 4 misses. The black line shows the direction the ball will travel, and the players should fly on to the anticipated line. This is the way to improve both the game and the ability of the players.*

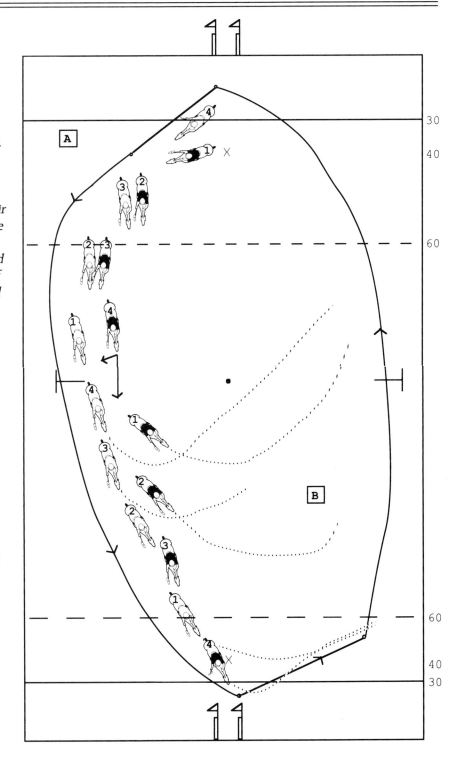

possession from the centre of the ground instead of from the more difficult area around the outside.

If, for instance, the attacker is riding off his opponent and taking the ball on the nearside up towards the defending player and the defending opponent pulls out of the ride-off, the attacker must immediately switch sides because the defender in front of him has the right to come in and meet the ball on the stick side or hook the attacker's stick. If the attacker maintains his position, with the ball on his nearside, he will immediately be fouling that defending player.

Taking the ball anti-clockwise round the ground makes it extremely difficult for the defending players to be able to meet the ball. They anticipate that the line between the ball and their goal will be the line on which the ball may be hit and, if you take it slightly wide to the right, the line will be on their offside and they will be unable to come in and meet the ball correctly. Also, because the defending team has a natural urge to protect the inside of the ground, they will ride the attacking team off from the centre, and therefore allow them to hit the ball on their stick side.

In the normal flow of the game it is not until the ball is centred towards the goal that the advantage switches to the defending team because of the change in the line – centring the ball puts it into the path of the defending players. They can then clear the ball, also in an anti-clockwise direction around the ground.

The development of this anti-clockwise pattern of the game has played a major part in the growth of the faster game in Argentina. It is true that the natural ability of the South American players to hit the ball when riding at speed seems to be greater too – they start to play polo when very young, and it is relatively common for players aged under twenty to be playing on 5- to 8-goal handicaps. But the combination of the two factors has made their high-goal polo currently faster than that of any other country.

Special Tactics

If you play as a team, particularly if there is one strong player in the opposing team, you will have the benefit of team *versus* individual strength, and in most cases, the team who play as a team will win. At the same time you should endeavour to apply as much pressure to the good player in the other team as possible.

Special tactics are required to beat a better team. As captain you should encourage your players to mark the man very tightly. They should ride the man first, then hit the ball. You should try to use quick changes of direction and choppy play to upset your opponents' rhythm. You must give everything all the time, as in any play of course, but you must ride even harder than normal, without becoming dangerous.

Always get your team to control the ground that is important to you. On defence it is the area around your goal, and on attack it is the area

Control the Ground.

a *Black controls the ground in attack. If black 2 hits to the line v-v, black get a goal shot. If he hits w-w, white 4 will claim the line, because black 1 has gone well ahead in anticipation, and cannot achieve the line w-w without fouling.*

b *Black 4 must take the first shot on his nearside. He may then cross the line if he has sufficient speed and distance, to hit at P under the neck. White 1 must fly along the curved line E-F to try and prevent that, then try to hook the nearside shot at F. If this is possible black 4 must check a little and ride off white 1 before hitting the under-the-neck shot. Black 3 follows 4. Black 2 flies along G-H, for a pass. Black 1 flies over the halfway line to pick up the line between the ball and the goal halfway to the 60-yard line. The alternative play: the ball backed to Q might allow black 3 to turn on to the new line, but if white 3 was quick to anticipate, he could claim the line and hook at Q, and white would thus gain possession. Note the positions of the umpires – one next to the play to check distance, and one on the line.*

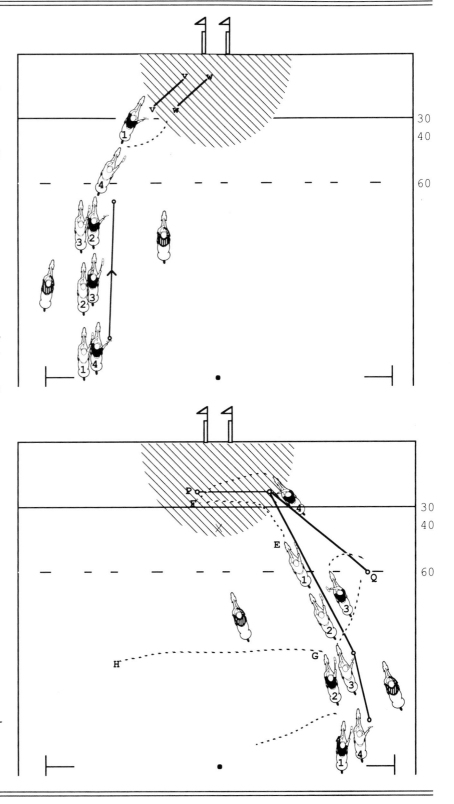

around your opponents' goal. If you can't control the ball, try to control the man and you will be taken to the ball.

The opposing team will probably try to match their best player with your strongest rider, or the best player in your team. Depending on the flow of the game, you should possibly have your strongest rider, though not your best player, marking that man all the time. If he is well mounted, he will sometimes be able to ride their good player away from the anticipated line of the ball, and your team will be more successful in dominating the game.

THE FOUR 'Ps' OF POLO

The principles of polo are four 'Ps', all achieved by maximum use of anticipation. They are: position, possession, pace and penetration.

Position

As the team captain, ensure that your team are always in their correct positions during the set plays and particularly going back to the half-way line for the throw-in. Give them confidence, with firm, crisp instructions which will sharpen them ready for the next fray. If you are losing, try to work out what your team can do to change the run of play. If you are winning, maintain the team's confidence and keep the pressure on the opposition. It is amazing what can happen in half a chukka of polo if your concentration slips.

Ensure that your team don't stand flat-footed while defending a penalty. Move early and make sure that when defending a 30- or 40-yard hit, the organisation is 100 per cent for one player to go across from right to left, defending with his offside towards *the striker*, and for another player just to come out next to the left-hand post in case the ball is running straight towards him. He may be able to meet it without danger to the player who is coming across. Take care that both players know what they are doing – several good players have been hurt in this manner, and the player who comes quickly must be able to stop if the other one calls 'Mine'.

In a 60-yard penalty all the team members should be on the move as the ball is hit. It is difficult to get your horse moving from a standstill, but certainly if he is already moving with impulsion he can change direction more quickly.

Stay in your position for as much of the game as possible. Whenever, say, the back finds himself at number 1, he will be ineffective and basically will not be mentally adjusted to that position. If he is worth four goals at back, he is possibly only worth one or two at number 1, and the same rule can apply to any other player in the team who is out of position. For that period of time or that play, the team is under-rated by the difference in the value of the handicaps of the players concerned. Revert to your correct position as soon as the change in play allows, but make sure that you don't leave your man if you are going back in defence.

While playing on the ground, always count your heads and ensure that you are riding with the correct man in the opposing team. If there are two blues and only one green in front of you, and you are green, you must rush back to cover the other blue. If the same is true but you are blue, with the ball in front of you, pick up the first green who tries to come past you because he is rushing back to pick up the man whom you will have spare.

Ride your man on attack to clear the way through for your number 3, but always pick up your man immediately in defence. Don't forget to take the man before the ball. If you are marking a much better player, stay with him all the time and try to control him – he will take you to the ball.

Possession

It is crucial in polo to retain possession of the ball – without the ball, you lose the game. Attack strongly when the ball comes loose, and if you are in doubt about the line, take the man. If he is coming down the line and you have the ball on your nearside, be prepared to hook the opponent's stick to control the ball rather than take the ball first. Ensure that you always know where the ball is in tight play and call to each other if necessary. Control your man as you are going to the ball, and know precisely where you are going to hit it at least 5–10 yards before you get there. You will then have time to set yourself up properly for the shot.

If you pass 10 yards in front and to the stick side of your team-mate, he will run on to the ball and pick it up with the least possible interference from the defending team. Always play to your own team. It is pointless to hit the ball if the other team are going to hit it back over the top of you. Even in a tight defensive situation, if you keep your head and play the ball in the right direction, you will probably retain possession of it.

If you are being ridden over the top of the ball, first try to control your man and then the ball into a position where you can get the good shot away. Hit the ball early and hit it hard if possible. It gives the defending team less time to ride into a defending position and dominate your players. If the ball is in a difficult situation, try to control it, or change the line so that you can get a good shot away to your team.

The use of the cut backhand in defence should be for short passes just in front of a team-mate who has already ridden on a line. Don't forget that the minute you open up the ball with a sliced backhand, you permit the other team to come in and hook your player's stick or to meet the ball, depending on their position. The tailed backhand is, in my view, the preferred shot as it sets up your team to take the ball around the ground.

Remember that the player without the ball creates the opportunity for continued possession. He should ride along the line he anticipates the ball will follow when you hit it, and go to a position where he is free to pick up a pass rather than allow himself to be hard-ridden by his opponent.

If you are running down the ground and all of your players in front of you are hard-ridden by their opposite numbers while you are relatively free, play the ball short of the next pair of players and a little wide on the stick side to ensure that you can retain possession, thus giving your team more time to ride their opponents off the ground or ride into a position to accept a pass from you.

Ensure that your numbers 1 and 2 are riding out the plays, not anticipating the back shots and turning early. While they ride out their plays, the number 3 should always anticipate the back shot and turn early so that he can achieve position and therefore possession of the ball.

It is essential that your numbers 1 and 2 make the opposing *back* and the *number 3* hit at maximum speed under pressure at all times, with the aim of reducing their accuracy and distance. Turn the ball only when you know you have time and, if the ground is bumpy and rough, don't dribble unless you have to, and then hit the ball away as soon as possible.

Centre the ball as early as possible after you go over the half-way line. This gives the eventual goal shot a far greater chance of success than if you have to take the ball down the outside of the ground and centre it as you go over the 60-yard line, or from the corner. To centre the ball on the 60-yard line also gives the defending team considerably greater opportunity to clear the ball because of the line suddenly becoming more or less across rather than down the ground.

You must retain possession near the goal. You have to get the ball through the goal, whereas the other team have the whole field to which they can clear the ball. Your numbers 1 and 2 must push hard, but not follow the player in front so closely that they miss their next shot.

When going for the goal shot, endeavour to hit the ball to the far post rather than the near one. Your aiming point should be 2 yards inside the far post. You will thus give the ball the maximum chance of going through the goal. The better players always hit the ball outside the far post if they hit it wide, whereas the worst players always hit wide outside the near post.

Remember to cut or pull the ball under the neck while riding your pony straight past the ball. Do not turn your pony towards the goal while making the goal shot. When going for the under-the-neck shot, you should put your arm in the 'one' position opposite the far goal post to enable you to get the right swing down through the ball. Take great care to ride to the ball properly for your goal shot, making sure you hit the ball before you turn the horse towards the goal. Most players, because they see the goal coming up, tend to ride too close or forget about riding precisely to the ball. Watch the ball, not the goal!

You should always know where the goal is and watch the ball for the last 10 yards before you hit it. You will possibly be hitting your goal shot at a faster speed than you normally hit the ball, so always swing crisply and firmly, never with a half-tap shot. Always play the ball by swinging down the line of the ball so that, if it should bounce, you will hit the ball on the cane. When the ground is rough, play a full shot rather than a half-shot, because if the ball bounces you can quickly adjust a full shot whereas you will always miss it with a half-shot.

Pace

Pace is the result of possession of the ball and your ability to play the game 'flat out'. To ensure that you are able to hit the ball at top speed, you must stick and ball regularly at a fast pace, otherwise when you come to make that shot at goal you will be going faster than is customary and you will mistime the ball. Practise hitting the ball as fast as you can from end to end of the ground and scoring through half-width goals. This will give you the confidence to hit goals in the match without worrying that you might miss.

If you always play with pace and drive, you will achieve the penetration required to get the ball to the other end of the ground and score. It is obvious, if the ball travels at speeds of up to 100 miles an hour and your maximum speed is about 40 miles an hour, that if you pass the ball from player to player, to get it from one end of the ground to the other, it will cover the distance in half the time and so dramatically increase the speed of the game.

Players should pass the ball on the forehand rather than the backhand if possible. When the ball goes wide, the good player will consider the under-the-neck shot if his angle is right. Always play the back shot if you are the number 1 and you have approached too wide of the goal. The benefit of centring the ball early will be appreciated when the player arrives for the goal shot.

If the number 2 can see the number 1 going for a back shot to centre the ball towards the goal, he should first ride towards the number 1 in preparation for the shot and then be able to turn along the new line properly. He should not just ride straight to the centre of the goal, because the defending *back*, coming along the new line and anticipating the centring shot, will have possession of the line and be able to clear the ball without difficulty. If the number 2 rides correctly, he should be able to pick up *the back*, ride him off the line and play a relatively easy nearside shot at goal.

Penetration

If your team lacks the penetration required, it may be because your number 1 is not staying in position. He must stay up, and when he comes back into the game, because of a change of play, the number 2 must immediately switch and play the number 1 position. It is essential for your team to have a number 1 in position all the time. If the number 1 is not there and the ball comes up, he is responsible for the lack of penetration. If the number 1 stays in position and the ball doesn't come, it certainly isn't his fault. So that the team does not lose possession of the ball in the middle of the game, your number 2 must ride harder to dominate his man and make the hole for the number 3 to get the ball through to the number 1.

Remember the importance of the art of anticipation. Your anticipation, depending on your position at the time and who has the next shot at the ball, should take you to a line somewhere between the ball and whatever goal it will travel towards, if you are in front of the play. The person on a handy pony can turn inside the player on a fast pony – his anticipation will get him to the ball quicker, while the player on the fast pony will go twice as far in the wrong direction. Always look to see who is going to hit the ball next, anticipate where it will go and, if possible, be there first.

THE WILL TO WIN

Never check up until the ball has gone either through the goal or wide over the back line. In many cases a player going towards the back line will check up when the ball is still 5 yards from the line because he thinks it is going over. Always endeavour to save the ball – it could be your opportunity to score. You never know when the ball may hit a divot, stop dead, bump sideways, do anything. If you are there and give it your best shot, you sometimes make a scoring opportunity out of a move which was otherwise lost.

If things are not going right in the game and your team members are not hitting well, they are probably hitting late. If they are being beaten for the ball, they must anticipate faster, ride harder and think much more quickly. As captain, ensure that your team are playing in their correct positions and, if in doubt, try another line-up for a while to see whether the team operates more fluently.

In every game you should play with good sportsmanship, and always make sure that your team has the will to win and gives everything from the throw-in to the final bell, regardless of whether you are winning or losing. Polo is a game which can be played to any level of commitment. Having made the decision to play, you owe it to the rest of the team always to give the utmost in your endeavour to win the game. At the same time you must remain calm, firm and kind to your horse, fair to the other team, and polite to the umpire, and always play to enjoy the game. It is harder to lose gracefully than to win, so after the game discuss with the umpires and the other team any fouls you weren't sure of – players and umpires will always try to clarify and explain a foul, particularly over a sociable beer.

Finally, try to make sure that your team enjoys the game, because enjoyment and playing for fun are what basic polo is all about. Too many people these days are so filled with the will to win that they forget about actually enjoying the game. This, in my view, is of paramount importance and should be retained above everything else as your main reason to play.

6

UMPIRING

ALL TOURNAMENT GAMES are umpired by two umpires and controlled by a referee from the side line. The two umpires are in control of the game at all times and only in dispute do they refer to the referee who, from the side line, makes an arbitrary decision depending on what he has seen; if he has not seen anything, he may call the umpires to the side of the ground and ask them why they blew the whistle. He must decide either a foul or no foul on what he hears from both umpires. If the referee did not see what happened and the umpires cannot decide in the discussion, no foul should be awarded and the ball should be thrown in.

When umpiring a game of polo, remember that you must exert control over the game with firmness, use your whistle correctly, blow it hard so the players hear it, and blow it immediately you see a foul or immediately you have decided that the advantage rule has not worked. The advantage rule is not written; it is simply a guideline for the umpires. If the team fouled retains possession and is not at a disadvantage, and the foul was not severe, play should be allowed to proceed. Remember that if the team fouled have still got control of the ball, to blow the whistle may be detrimental to them, and the advantage rule is important to the continuity of the game.

If you see what you think may be a foul, after considering the advantage, blow the whistle. You can only be wrong and that is no bad thing. It is much better to blow the whistle and be wrong than not to blow the whistle at all and be wrong. If possession changes rapidly, especially as a result of a foul, the umpire should blow a late whistle.

An umpire will rapidly lose the respect of the players if he repeatedly fails to blow the whistle, whereas an umpire who blows the whistle, even if he is wrong, still retains control of the game. The umpires must concentrate on the game at all times, and one should be on the line of play so that he can evaluate who is on the line of the play correctly, while the other should be beside the line of the play so that he can evaluate distance correctly. Thus, between them, they will be able to establish whether any play was dangerous or not and therefore a foul or not.

Umpires should keep up with the game. To be a player and have the whistle blow when the umpire sits on half-way and you are 5 yards from the goal is ridiculous. Make sure that, when you are umpiring on the ground, you keep up to within 20 or 30 yards of the ball and this will put you in an excellent position to evaluate any of the quick changes of play that occur, particularly in high-goal polo.

Be relaxed out on the ground, but absolutely firm, and do not tolerate any back chat or cheek from the players that may undermine your authority. If necessary, warn the players at the beginning of the game, before you throw the ball in, against appealing. This will eliminate the necessity to warn them again during the game and, if appealing takes place, you can then penalise the offender(s) straight away. It is important, for the image of the game, to be firm with a player who repeatedly appeals for fouls.

A good umpire retains the respect of the players by his concentration on the game and his ability to blow the fouls immediately they occur. Check the relative position of your co-umpire during the various set plays on the ground. Ensure that for penalties 3 and 2 one umpire is placed on the back line to make certain the defending team carry out the penalty correctly, while the other goes behind the striker as he hits the ball, to confirm a decision on whether a goal has been scored or not.

Make sure during hit-outs that one umpire is in position near the goal and the other out on the 60-yard line, wide to avoid being trapped by the players as they come out from the back line.

Learn the signs to consult the referee from the middle of the ground by putting your hand up. The referee should answer with his hand up if he sees a foul, and point in the direction in which the foul should be given. If in doubt, he will proceed to walk down the stand. You then canter over to the half-way line to consult him.

The HPA's instructions to umpires appear in the Appendix, and the theory diagrams from pages 188–227 show the correct positions of the umpires.

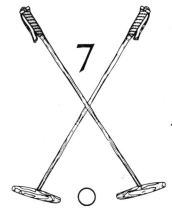

7

ARENA POLO

A RENA POLO has long been a very important complementary game to outdoor polo in the USA, where it has been the basis of collegiate polo – many of their twenty-five polo-playing universities and schools have excellent arena facilities. Some of the larger cities have established full-sized indoor polo arenas, with seating for up to 4000 spectators, who come to watch the top professionals play in organised competitive leagues during a three-month arena polo season.

During the last ten years, the L.A. Equestrian Centre led the upsurge in arena polo and its equidome became the home of the National Polo League, established by Dr Robert Walton and his family. An unfortunate break-up took the League to Houston in Texas, but the American Polo League was formed, under the captaincy of Tom Goodspeed, and its all-star cast of Rennie Tongg from Hawaii, 'Smokin'' Joe Henderson, originally from South Africa, and Dan Healy. The L.A. Colts became the first professional polo team, and a new spectator sport was born.

The polo school, established at the same time, at its peak had 150 students on its roll, and many famous names took their first polo strokes at the equidome. More recently, having run into consistent financial difficulty, the LAEC was taken over by Gibraltar Savings, and the pro team – still captained by Tom Goodspeed and ably supported by 'Smokin'' Joe Henderson, with a new number 1 each season – became the Los Angeles Stars, and won the 1989 Professional Arena Polo League. 'Smokin'' Joe became the first arena 10-goal player in thirty years, and only the third in the 100-year history of arena polo. He began his polo career only in 1984 and, even though he is a natural athlete, he has achieved an amazing goal – the maximum rating – in an unbelievably short time. Sadly, at the beginning of 1990, the LAEC polo programme was closed after the Cadillac sponsors decided to switch from polo to golf, and the Houston Arena will probably take control of the Arena Polo League.

Indoor polo at the Inter-nation Horse Show in the NEC Centre, Birmingham.

With the continued importance of arena polo at college level, there will be an increasing demand for the further expansion of arena polo facilities, and recent developments here in England auger well for the early establishment of international arena polo. The British HPA have just published their first Arena Rules, incorporating the USPA rules, with one or two important changes, and outlining the game very clearly; these are reproduced in full in the Appendix.

ARENA SURFACES

The mixture of sand and topsoil widely used in the USA as arena surface material has proved to be consistently satisfactory, provided a loamy topsoil is available without too much clay. However, polo is being played on many different surfaces in the existing show-jumping arenas – mostly indoor – which are scattered throughout the UK and Europe, and with the growth in general equestrian sport, these facilities will increase in number. Considerable work has been and is being done on surfaces that have been compounded using silica sand. This is a very fine white sand which packs down quite hard but does not cake or go really gluey if it becomes too wet. Combined with various additives and binding agents, several different surfaces are now available that are suitable for both polo and general equestrian use. Some of the most recent combinations are proving to be as good if not better for fast sports such as racing, because they can be prevented from freezing in cold weather and they will drain more quickly than normal turf after heavy rain.

THE BENEFITS OF ARENA POLO

Arena polo can be played on two ponies, thus making it available to a much larger group of players. One pony can very easily play two chukkas or, if fit, possibly three chukkas of arena polo, whereas the maximum allowed in outdoor polo is two, and one is preferable.

Ponies that don't handle quite so well outdoors are often very good to play in an arena, and a horse that is not quite sound on hard ground, in the galloping conditions of outdoor polo, may prove to be sound enough to play very good indoor or arena polo. It is more important for the indoor pony to handle well rather than gallop fast – his turning ability could be crucial. These things make the cost of arena polo tiny in comparison with the outdoor game, and with the cost of an arena not much more than the cost of a good outdoor field – on some surfaces such as clay possibly much less – a number of existing clubs will construct arena facilities over the next few years and new clubs based only on arena polo will become established.

The basic tactics of indoor polo vary from the outdoor game in that players should alternate very quickly. If one player is going up, another should be going back; and the player in possession at any time should possibly have a player in front to pass to and one behind who is going to back him up.

While the back stays more defensive, he should be quick to alternate, but the number 1 should not let himself come right to the back of the game too often. It is better for him to work at the number 1 or 2 position, with the back staying deeper.

One of the chief benefits of arena polo is that the learner cannot get too far away from the game and therefore is always involved. Because of the confined space, it is not so essential for the player to be a good rider, and confidence is more easily gained in the arena, because it is enclosed, than on a big field. It is also considerably easier to instruct your team-mates and learning players in an indoor arena because they don't get quite so far away.

Arena polo is, in most cases, ideal for making young ponies. It keeps them involved in the game, prevents them running away, makes them face up to a quick mêlée of horses and much more rapidly accustoms them to the rough and tumble of polo. It is essential to keep a young horse calm at all times in indoor or arena polo, and time should be taken to settle him down if he gets upset during a practice game. If a pony begins to get nervous and unsettled each time you take him into the arena, it may be better to school him outside for a few days and then rest him for a while.

A match can be umpired by two umpires, if the arena is large enough, with a referee in the stand. However, one umpire is quite able to cope in a smaller arena – the tournament committee makes the decision on this point. Remember at all times that the umpire is in sole control of the game and any decision made by him should be adhered to without dispute. As in outdoor polo, the umpire's decision is final and can be discussed only by the captain of the team if he needs to know who fouled, or what the foul was given for.

During the next few years, because of the evolution of the arena game in the UK and Europe, the rules are bound to be amended from time to time. Care should be taken to ascertain any recent changes to these rules if a polo club association is establishing an arena facility for the first time.

8
ESTABLISHING A POLO CLUB

POLO LEARNERS who are interested in playing the sport but have no appropriate organisation anywhere near them may want to consider putting together a club for themselves. The establishment of a polo club is not difficult and, given that half a dozen people need to organise somewhere where they can play together, it takes only one person to get things started. If you begin in a small way and gradually build up the interest of the players, you will find that their interest is infectious and an increasing number of people will be attracted to your club.

It is probable that, with the current interest in Pony Club polo in England and the resulting dramatic improvement in its standard, in ten years' time the standard of polo in England will be much higher. Because of the widely growing interest in the sport and the fact that more children are being initiated into it at an ever younger age, we may see the present dominance of the polo world by Argentina diminishing in the foreseeable future. It is certainly pleasing to see the emergence in English high-goal polo of several good players aged under twenty-five. They are playing exceptionally well and have a lot of potential, so let's hope they get the breaks in the game.

With enthusiasm for equestrian sports increasing all over the world, the benefits of polo as a family game cannot be over-emphasised. Young children can play – in Argentina they begin swinging a mini-stick when they start to walk – and love the sport. In England evidence of this is very apparent in the Pony Club polo already mentioned. The first polo that these children play is on ponies of Shetland size and upwards that are possibly not even trained to accept a polo stick, but the children out on the ground thoroughly enjoy the camaraderie and the competitive spirit of the game. If instruction is given on how to handle the polo stick and how to teach their ponies to stick and ball, in no time at all these ponies can be encouraged to play the game and everyone will thoroughly enjoy it.

The two essential requirements for the establishment of a small polo organisation are a place to play and horses to play on. A flat field of 350 × 350 yards is ideal and allows for a full-sized field and a practice area, but it doesn't have to be absolutely flat: if it rises a little towards one end or one side, it can still provide enjoyable polo. A minimum of approximately 10 acres is adequate (a regulation full-size polo field is 12 acres), but it is possible to have a very enjoyable game on a considerably smaller field – we play three-a-side on about 5 acres, and it is great fun. If a field is of sufficient size is not readily available, an arena 300 × 150 feet, as described in Chapter 7, could be considered: this has been used successfully in the USA as the basis on which the university polo circuit has been built.

I remember being involved in the staging of an excellent 12-goal tournament on a field that was 220 yards long and 120 yards wide, in Holland. It was a lovely field, surrounded by trees, and we had crowds approaching 3000 watching the games. It was one of the most successful and enjoyable tournaments I've had the pleasure to become involved with.

Once you have organised a field for your polo club, you need to turn your attention to the ponies. The new club members can use the horses they have already, given that they are 14–16 hands and not too highly bred. Somebody who already knows the game and is a reasonable coach should be approached to show them how to swing their sticks properly and teach their ponies to accept both the stick and ball in the right manner.

Initially you may find that more enjoyment is gained by using a soft, plastic ball than the ordinary hard polo ball, which requires a reasonably flat and mown surface to enable players, and especially learners, to hit successfully. A plastic ball, on the other hand, will travel on most unmown surfaces quite effectively.

As your club becomes established, you may want to augment your horses with well-trained polo ponies. Remember, however, that when trained polo ponies are introduced into such an organisation, they can prove to be so much better than the local horses being used that, of course, they make it very difficult for players on those horses to win the ball from them. This problem was particularly noticeable when Argentinian ponies were introduced into Nigerian polo, for naturally the game played on the local ponies was much slower than that achieved on Argentinian imports. In a large and thriving club this can cause unexpected problems, and the organising committee should be well aware of the fact. Members who bring in specially trained ponies proceed to win all the tournaments, and this can create a lot of ill feeling and dissatisfaction among the other members of the club. The possibility of occasional tournaments for locally-bred horses only may be an idea worth considering.

Another way of arranging a supply of ponies for a new polo club is for a patron or a sponsor to put together a group of horses – a minimum of twelve and ideally about sixteen – which would then be available to learner players at a rental which would cover the cost of their maintenance plus their depreciation. The club would immediately be able to stage polo games, and thus create spectator interest as well. Gradually members would become keen enough to buy their own ponies – either from the club or independently – and make the arrangements to keep them at the club themselves.

A further method of organising horses is for two or three people to own two ponies each and arrange matters on a collective basis so that, if six-chukka matches are played, one player can play each of the six ponies, or possibly two players can play three chukkas each, at any time. If two players share four ponies and four-chukka matches are played, they can play alternately and can organise quite a cheap set-up which is convenient to both parties.

When putting together the organisation to run a polo club, it should be borne in mind that up to fifty ponies will eventually be needed for about twenty members. And twenty to thirty members would be enough for the normal ground to cope with, playing up to three times a week, though this would depend on the type of soil upon which the ground is based. A clay field will dry out and bake very hard in hot weather, but in wet weather it can be difficult to play because it can become squashy – the ponies leave deep footprints. On the other hand, a sandy loam ground seems to tolerate a lot of wear and tear without too much damage to the surface, provided it has been well consolidated over a period of time. If the field has been well established in ordinary pasture for some years, and was well worked and flattened before planting, it will be possible to mow and roll it and play excellent polo on it. It is advisable to oversow it with grass seed in the late autumn to thicken up the sward. For information on installing a top-quality polo ground, see page 246.

In New Zealand the Rangitiki Club used to play once a week on a Saturday afternoon. This did not provide enough polo for young players to make significant progress, and the club has since added more grounds and playing facilities. Remember that a club should play at least twice a week to enable the potential of young players to be realised. It also gives a boost to club spirit if you play regularly, two or three times each week. This seems to build a better and more active club, especially with the pace of life these days. Thus, when setting up a club, the potential for expansion needs to be considered if a choice of land is available, for the club will probably grow quickly after it has become established.

Initially, interested members can be invited to ring up and book their polo with an individual we shall call 'the polo manager'. The polo manager of any club is responsible to its members for organising the day-to-day running of polo and the maintenance of the ground. In a small club which plays polo twice a week, it is only a part-time job for one person and involves scarcely any managerial expenses. In a large English club, however, where we play polo four times a week, the establishment of an office is required with a secretary and ground staff who are capable of putting the grounds back together for the next day's play.

As your club grows, it is possible, in these days of highly sophisticated telecommunications, to organise your office around a facsimile machine and a very good telephone answering system. Provided the members ring up to book their polo by a given time, the office can be run by a part-time secretary.

As well as the polo manager, the club will need a chairman. He will arrange the fixtures for the polo season, setting up inter-club tournaments and invitational matches for teams from other clubs, and various display matches for sponsors or for charity.

In the original establishment of your polo club, consideration should be given to the contact you will have with the governing body – the polo association – which oversees and controls polo within a country. In England the Hurlingham Polo Association (HPA) is responsible, as the governing body of the sport, for the overall supervision of the individual clubs which are affiliated to it. The HPA also puts together the annual list of official fixtures – the tournaments run by the clubs, to which HPA playing members have the right to enter teams. Obviously a private club can do whatever it likes and organise its own polo. However, clubs affiliated to the HPA get assistance for expansion projects and maintenance of their facilities, and their club members get a handicap which is registered with the HPA and is recognised throughout the world. This enables them to travel abroad and play polo anywhere.

There are certain countries which, basing their handicap on the English standard, will rate their players possibly two or even three goals higher, thus enabling them to differentiate between the abilities of local players and to lift their national polo to a reasonable standard. Increased handicaps make it considerably more enjoyable from the point of view of sponsors and spectators. In Singapore, for instance, there were a number of players who were starting to learn to ride and play polo at the same time, and to enable them to differentiate between the abilities of various learner players, a local handicap of −4 was established. I remember winning a tournament over there and one of my team members coming to me thoroughly thrilled that his handicap would be raised from −4 to −2!

SPONSORSHIP

The polo world has changed considerably in the last few years and is increasingly used by commercial concerns, because of its ambiance and spectator appeal, as a venue for product exposure or business entertainment. Thus we have seen – particularly in England and the USA – a

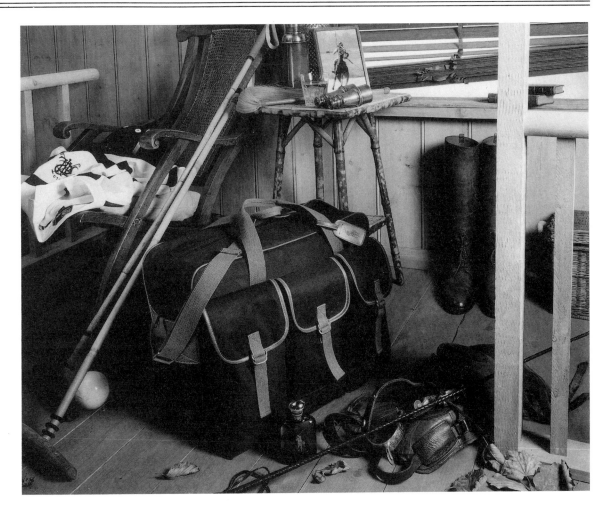

Publicity and sponsorship are becoming more prominent in the world of polo. Seen here is a publicity shot for Ralph Lauren using new and old polo equipment.

vast increase in sponsorship interest, with polo tournaments and games being sponsored for quite large sums of money by companies who can benefit from the image that the game has created.

In England the expansion of the sport would certainly not have been nearly as rapid without sponsorship as it has been over the last few years. Polo as a game appeals to the aesthetic senses of sporting spectators. It is conducted with all the elegance and ceremony of the best English tradition, in surroundings which are ideal for relaxation and enjoyment. Lovely wide open spaces, fields in immaculate condition, thoroughbred animals turned out to perfection, ready to pit their strength and ability against each other in a head-to-head confrontation, all together create an image which is truly spectacular and has brought pleasure to polo aficionados throughout the world. The elegance of both horse and rider and the *haute couture* image of the social spectator have combined to attract the most upmarket sponsors, and names such as Cartier, Piaget, Rolls-Royce, Mercedes and BMW, Lloyds of London and Coutts Bank are rubbing shoulders with the international set of polo players and spectators on the turf of English polo clubs these days. Players, spectators and the sport in general have benefited immensely from the assistance that this sponsorship has provided.

In the establishment of a polo club, consideration should be given to the advantages that sponsorship may provide once the club has grown to the point where the facilities for the players and spectators are satisfactory to cope with the particular requirements of sponsors. Financial benefits to the club and individual sponsorship of teams provide an injection of funds which all go towards reducing the cost of polo to the players and providing increased facilities for spectators – and this can only be good for the sport.

INSTALLATION AND CARE OF A TOP-QUALITY POLO GROUND

In these days of international players and high-goal polo, a very good playing surface will be required if good players are to be attracted to your club. Should you decide to provide a top-quality match-polo ground, considerable trouble should be taken both with the levelling of the playing surface and with the drainage. The natural drainage properties of the soil will depend upon its type and will determine whether additional drainage facilities, providing a reasonably dry surface within two days of heavy rain, need to be installed.

When all the earth works have been completed, the area should be sown with grass seed, your choice of which will depend on the climate and the qualities of the soil. In England, on reasonably loamy soil, three types of rye and 10 per cent of a fine lawn grass seed are recommended to provide the basic mixture for a new polo field. In the hotter countries of the world, Bermuda grass has proved to be an ideal surface for polo. The Royal Palm Polo Club in Florida even established a turf nursery which was found to be the best method of maintaining the playing surface.

A club recently established in England on substantially clay-type soil used a mixture of 70 per cent perennial rye grasses, 15 per cent creeping red fescue, 10 per cent barren parapatensis and 5 per cent highland browntop lawn grass. This establishment has particular problems with drainage and the consolidation of the ground after play, which causes considerable damage in damp conditions. Frequent top dressings with sand have resulted in gradual improvement of the playing surface, but treating the ground in this way is a very time-consuming and expensive business, so it is advisable to try to avoid a clay soil if the choice is available.

Once the grass cover has been established on the field for some two months, a top dressing of a general-purpose fertiliser, at the rate of 1 cwt to the acre, is recommended. As soon as the field is dry enough – it is essential not to go on to it with any heavy machinery while the

Creating your own polo fields. In the early stages . . .

. . . and nearly there.

ground is still moist – the grass should be mowed. Your aim should be to strengthen the grass roots and so form a mat of strong turf to withstand the rigours of polo, and careful mowing helps do this. The initial work should always be done in parallel lines up and down the ground to maintain in the direction of the intended line of play any wheelmarks that might be put into slightly soft spots. I have seen a field virtually ruined because heavy machinery used to mow the grass in the initial mowing left wheelmarks every 10 feet across it: the field became

Irrigation is very important. The irrigation system in front of the Royal Box on Guards Number One ground is shown here.

almost unplayable because of this unfortunate occurrence. Great care should therefore be taken to ascertain that absolutely no damage is done when this initial work is carried out on a new ground.

A light tractor with wide tyres is essential for normal maintenance work on a grass surface such as a polo field. Considerable research has been done recently on the grass management of golf courses, and it would be a wise move to consult the turf manager of your nearest golf course for his ideas.

If the weather becomes hot and dry in the polo season, it is essential to consider in the long-term some form of irrigation for the polo field. According to several polo managers, the ideal polo-field irrigation system is the boom spray system. This consists of either two or three booms, with a sufficient spread to cover the whole of the polo field, attached to in excess of 300 yards of hose which is coiled around a giant drum. The spray booms are pulled right down the length of the field and the action of the water drives a series of gears which wind the hose back around the drum as the field is being irrigated. This pulls the boom back along the field and the speed at which the boom is pulled back controls the amount of water released. Depending on given conditions, and the prevailing laws regarding irrigation, it is customary to put on the equivalent of from ½ to 1 inch of rainfall at each irrigation.

DAILY MAINTENANCE OF THE POLO FIELD AFTER PLAY

If manpower is available, there is nothing better than a gang of people with long-handled forks for 'treading in' divots kicked out by the horses during play. If the fork is used in the right manner the surface will be returned to its original state. Lift the turf which has been driven into the ground halfway, at the same time treading in around the piece of turf and forcing the ground back into its original shape, then replace the piece of turf in the hole.

If this is done on a loamy surface and followed by rolling with a light roller, the surface can be kept in the best possible condition. In certain conditions, harrowing with a wire-mesh harrow is greatly beneficial in filling up the small holes which will gradually appear if the ground staff are not available to put the field back by hand.

In cases of exceptional damage, there is very little else that can be done other than going over the ground with a mixture of sand, soil and grass seed, and filling up the really bad holes by hand.

If a spiking machine is available, some benefit could be achieved by spiking the ground in two different directions – the last way being lengthways down the ground in the direction of play. Followed by rolling and irrigation, this could be the best mechanical method of repairing a badly worn ground. However, a machine recently imported from Australia, which has been developed to 'tread in' mechanically, may prove to be a good way of treating a ground at the end of the season. Depending on the state of the ground after spiking, a very light harrowing – again with the wire-mesh harrow mentioned before – may well prove beneficial before the rolling. If the ground is too compacted, omit the rolling for as long as possible and reduce the number of rolls per season.

A 'rest' period is advisable on badly damaged ground to let the grass seed establish, but, of course, that depends on the playing itinerary of the club. If it is possible to play a field only once a week, it is ideal for the ground, you can play matches all the time and the surface still can be maintained to a very high standard.

For the club with only one field, reasonably frequent harrowing – again with the light harrow – can help to keep the surface reasonably smooth. The reasonably frequent use of a special wide high-speed roto-roller mower, hydraulically operated on the back of a tractor, is the best way of keeping the grass mown and the surface rolled and consolidated at the same time.

For the club that is just beginning, it is most important to keep a playing surface which encourages the players to come and enjoy the facilities. In this connection an arena is, without question, of substantial advantage when only one playing field is available. A polo club is put together for the benefit of its members; they need to enjoy the polo that they play there and therefore they need adequate playing facilities; they also need the spice of competition against other clubs, if it can be arranged. But, above all, polo is a game to be played for the enjoyment of both player and spectator, and everything should be designed with that in mind.

In this book on polo, I have tried to cover all of the most important aspects of the game very fully and have touched on a number of others, which together make up this enthralling and exciting sport. I hope that having read it, you will, like thousands of people around the world, be tempted to try the game for yourselves, and I am confident that the 'polo bug' will do the rest.

My family and I have enjoyed some of our happiest moments in polo – both on and off the field – and I hope that all of you who take it up will experience the enjoyment and pleasure which the game can provide.

The four Grace sisters – Janey, Pippa, Katie and Victoria – celebrating their win in the National Women's Tournament at Ascot Park, 1990.

THE RULES OF POLO*

1 GENERAL RULES

Height of Ponies

1 – Ponies of any height may be played.

Size of Grounds

2 – (a) A full-sized ground shall not exceed 300 yards in length by 200 yards in width, if unboarded; and 300 yards in length by 160 yards in width, if boarded.

(b) The goals shall not be less than 250 yards apart, and each goal shall be 8 yards wide.

(c) The goal posts shall be at least 10 feet high, and light enough to break if collided with.

(d) The boards shall not exceed 11 inches in height.

Size of Ball

3 – The size of the ball shall not exceed $3\frac{1}{2}$ inches in diameter, and the weight of the ball shall be within the limits of $4\frac{1}{4}$ to $4\frac{3}{4}$ ounces.

Qualifications of Players

4 – (a) The number of players is limited to 4 a side in all games and matches.

(b) No player may play under the influence of stimulative drugs.

(c) No player shall play with his left hand.

Notes:

(1) No person shall play in any tournament or advertised match conducted by an Affiliated Club or Association in the British Isles unless:

(a) He is an Associate Member of the HPA.

(b) He has lodged a signed declaration, either with his Club or the HPA, to be bound by the rules, regulations, orders and directives of the HPA.

(c) He is listed in the Association's current handicap list,
or has been allotted a handicap by the Association's Handicap Committee during the current season,
or his handicap has been confirmed by the Honorary Secretary of the Association.

(2) Please refer to the Rules for Official Tournaments in the *HPA Year Book*, page 105.

Substitution

5 – (a) A player may only play in one team in the same tournament and in a tournament with the same 'control number' in the fixture list, except as stated in (e) below.

(b) Substitutes must be qualified to play in the tournament and the team must remain qualified after the substitution has been made.

(c) A player who has taken part in one or more of the earlier rounds of a tournament, who is unable to play in a later round or rounds, may be replaced by a substitute. A member of a team who is unable to play in the earlier rounds of a tournament may also be replaced by a substitute.

(d) A player may be substituted for another during a match only if the latter player through sickness, accident or duty is unable to continue. If the substitute is of the same or lower handicap the score will not be altered; however, if he is of a higher handicap the score will be immediately altered to reflect the increased aggregate handicap of the side irrespective of the period of play in which the substitution occurred.

(e) A Tournament Committee may agree to *any* player being used as a substitute provided:

(i) They consider there is no suitable player (see Note 1) available who has not already played in the tournament or has been knocked out of a tournament with the same control number and is not due to play any further matches therein.

* Reproduced from *The Hurlingham Polo Association Year Book 1991*, with kind permission. The *Year Book* shows examples of the line and right of way as specific illustrations of these rules. An abridged version of the rules appears here; a complete, annually updated copy can be obtained from The Hurlingham Polo Association, Winterlake, Kirtlington, Oxford OX5 3HG.

(ii) They are satisfied that there is a *bona fide* need for a substitute.

(iii) The total handicap of the team requiring a substitute will not be increased thereby, except in the circumstances described in (d) above. If a second substitute is brought into a team, it shall be the handicap the last time the team played which shall count.

(iv) In matches with an international flavour the Captain of the opposing team's side agrees.

Notes on Substitution Rules:

(1) A player shall be regarded as 'suitable' if his handicap is not more than two goals less than the handicap of the player he is replacing.

(2) If a player is brought in, in the case of an emergency for the completion of one match, he shall not be disqualified from continuing with his original team; he may continue to play with that team provided the original player is still not available and his own team is not still in the tournament.

(3) If a player is late and the game is started with a substitute, the late player may replace the substitute after the first chukka, but not thereafter.

(4) In the prospectus of a tournament with a subsidiary, it should be clearly stated whether or not both count as one tournament for the purposes of these rules.

Qualifications of Ponies

6 – (a) Ponies of any height may be played.

(b) A pony blind in one eye may not be played (see Field Rule 3).

(c) A pony may not be played which is not under proper control (see Field Rule 3).

(d) In high and medium-goal tournaments, a pony played by one team cannot be played by any other team in the same tournament.

Notes:

(1) Attention is drawn to the Directive on the Misuse of Drugs and the Welfare of Ponies on page 260.

(2) In the British Isles all polo ponies must have a current certificate of vaccination.

Umpires, Referees and Goal Judges

7 – (a) The Rules shall be administered in a match by two Umpires, who shall be mounted to enable them to keep close to the play, and a Referee who shall remain off the field of play in a central position. By mutual agreement between Captains of teams, one Umpire and if desired, also the Referee, may be dispensed with. The decision of the Umpire shall be final, except where there are two and they disagree, in which case the decision of the Referee shall be final.

(b) In important matches Goal Judges should be appointed each of whom shall give testimony to the Umpires at the latter's request in respect to goals or other points of the game near his goal, but the Umpires shall make all decisions.

(c) The above Officials shall be nominated by the Committee conducting the tournament or match except in international matches when they shall be mutually agreed upon.

(d) Captains shall have the sole right to discuss with the Umpire or Umpires questions arising during the game. No player shall appeal in any manner to the Umpire or Umpires for fouls. This does not preclude a Captain from discussing any matter with the Umpire.

(e) The authority of the above Officials shall extend from the time the match is due to start until the end of the game. All questions arising at other times may be referred by the Captains to the Committee conducting the tournament or match and its decision shall be final.

Note: In the British Isles, except in international matches, every possible effort will be made to appoint at least one British Umpire. It is recommended that the Referee is also Bristish, and should be a regular past or present player in polo at least to the level being refereed.

Timekeeper and Scorer

8 – An official Timekeeper and Scorer shall be employed in all games and matches.

Doctors and Veterinarians

9 – At all organised polo games there will be a doctor and/or paramedic and a veterinary surgeon either present or on immediate call. A wagon equipped with a screen must also be provided.

Duration of Play

10 – (a) The duration of play is 42 minutes divided into 6 periods of 7 minutes each. The number of minutes played in a period, or periods played in a match, may be reduced by the Committee conducting the tournament or match. In all matches there shall be a half-time interval of 5 minutes. All other intervals between periods shall be of 3 minutes' duration.

Handicap Calculation

(b) In all matches played under handicap conditions the higher handicapped team shall concede to the lower handicapped team the difference in the handicaps divided by six and multiplied by the number of periods of play of the match. All fractions of a goal shall count as 'half-a-goal'. Mistakes in handicaps or in computing goal allowances must be challenged before a match begins, and no objection can be entertained afterwards.

Play Continuous

(c) With the exception of the said intervals, play shall be continuous, and no time shall be taken off for changing ponies during a period, except as legislated for in Field Rule 23.

Termination of Period

(d) Each period of play, except the last, shall terminate after the expiration of the prescribed time (designated by the ringing of the bell or other signal) as soon as the ball goes out of play or hits the boards.

A bell or other signal will be sounded 30 seconds after the first bell or signal, if the ball is still in play, and the period will terminate at the first sound of the second bell or other signal, although the ball is still in play, wherever the ball may be.

Penalty Exacted Next Period

(e) If a foul is given after the first stroke of the 7-minute bell, the Umpire's whistle terminates the period, and the penalty shall be exacted at the beginning of the next period, except in the event of a tie in the last period when the penalty shall be exacted at once, and the period continued until the ball goes out of play or hits the boards or the 30-second bell is sounded.

Game Stopped

(f) The game can be stopped in two different ways:

(i) Where the time during which the game is stopped is *not* to be counted as part of the playing time of the period (i.e. where the clock is to be stopped). To indicate this to the Timekeeper the Umpire should blow one firm blast. This way is used for fouls, Penalty 7 and under Field Rules 11, 14, 21 and 23. The ball is dead until the Umpire says 'Play', and the ball is hit or hit at.

(ii) Where the time during which the game is stopped is to be counted as part of the playing time of the period (i.e. where the clock is *not* to be stopped). This occurs when the ball goes out of play, through the goal or over the boards, side or back lines (unless hit over the back line by a defender). As a rule the game will automatically stop, but if it continues (e.g. if the ball is hit straight into play after crossing the back or side lines), the Umpire should blow two sharp blasts. This will tell the Timekeeper not to deduct time.

Last Period

(g) The last period shall terminate, although the ball is still in play, at the first stroke of the 7-minute bell, wherever the ball may be, except in the case of a tie.

(h) In the case of a tie the last period shall be prolonged till the ball goes out of play or hits the boards, or till the 30-second bell rings, and if still a tie, after an interval of 5 minutes the game shall be started from where the ball went out of play and be continued in periods of the usual duration, with the usual intervals, until one side obtains a goal, which shall determine the match.

Widened Goals

(i) In the event of a tie at the end of the final period of a match goals will be widened for the ensuing periods:

(i) If the tournament conditions state that this will be so, or

(ii) If the Captains of both teams concerned request that they should be.

In any event goals will be widened if no goal has been scored by the end of the first period of extra time.

Rules for Widened Goals:

(1) Width of goals to be doubled to 16 yards by moving goal posts 4 yards outwards.

(2) After a 5-minute interval ends shall be changed and the ball thrown in from the centre in the first of the extra chukkas.

Note: Committees are advised to put in the sockets to hold the goal posts at the 4-yard extensions before the tournament begins.

Prolongation in Case of Penalty

(j) In the event of a penalty being awarded within 20 seconds of the end of the match, the Timekeeper shall allow 20 seconds' play from the time the ball is hit, or hit at, in carrying out the penalty, before he rings the final (7 minute) bell. If a goal is scored after the ball has been put into play, the final bell shall be rung, if the original regular time (7 minutes) has expired. The match shall terminate as usual on the first stroke of the final (7 minute) bell.

Unfinished Match

(k) Once a match has started it shall be played to a finish unless stopped by the Umpire for some unavoidable cause, which prevents a finish the same day, such as darkness or the weather, in which case it shall be resumed at the point at which it has stopped, as to score, period and position of the ball, at the earliest convenient time, to be decided upon by the Committee conducting the tournament.

How a Game is Won

11 – The side that scores most goals wins the game.

Polo Helmet or Cap

12 – No one shall be allowed to play unless he wears a protective polo helmet or polo cap, either of which must be worn with a chin strap.

Confusing Colours

13 – If in the opinion of the Tournament Committee the colours of two competing teams are so alike as to lead to confusion, the team lower in the draw shall be instructed to play in some other colours.

FIELD RULES
Definition of Foul

1 – Any infringement of the Field Rules constitutes a foul and the Umpire may stop the game.

Dead Ball

2 – The Umpire shall carry a whistle, which he shall blow when he wishes to stop the game. When he does so the ball is dead until he says 'Play', and the time is dead and not counted in the playing time of the period, except as legislated for in General Rule 10 (f).

Note: If a whistle is blown for a foul at approximately the same time as a goal is scored:

    (i) The goal will be disallowed if the foul was against the attacking side and the foul is confirmed.

    (ii) The goal will be allowed if the foul was against the attacking side and the foul is over-ruled; or if the foul was against the defending side whether or not the foul is confirmed.

Disqualified Ponies

3 – A pony blind of an eye may not be played; a pony showing vice, or not under proper control, shall not be allowed in the game.

Note: In the British Isles all polo ponies must have a current certificate of flu vaccination.

Equipment for Ponies

4 – (a) Protection of ponies by boots or bandages on all four legs is compulsory.

    (b) Blinkers are not allowed, nor any form of noseband which obstructs the vision.

    (c) Rimmed shoes are allowed, but the rim may only be on the inside of the shoe.

    (d) Frost nails and screws are not allowed, but a calkin, fixed or movable, is permissible, provided this is placed only at the heels of the hind shoes. The fixed or movable calkin shall be limited in size to a half inch cube.

    (e) Hackamores or bitless bridles will not be used in matches or tournaments.

Note: The movable calkin is allowed so that when it becomes worn it can be replaced by a fresh one without re-shoeing. The essence of this permission is that the movable calkin should resemble, as far as possible, the recognised form of fixed calkin, and it does not permit the fixing of any fancy shaped spike, nor the placing of the calkin anywhere except at the heels of the hind shoes.

Disqualified Equipment for Players

5 – (a) Sharp spurs are not allowed.

    (b) No player may wear buckles or studs on the upper part of his polo boots or knee pads in such a way as could damage another player's boots or breeches.

Safety Zone

6 – (a) No person is allowed on the ground during play for any purpose whatever except the players and the Umpires. A player requiring a stick, pony or other assistance from an outside person must ride to the boards, side or back lines, to procure it. No person may come on to the ground to assist him.

    (b) No person is allowed within the safety zone during play except those playing, Umpires, Referee, Goal Judges, Manager and Stickholders.

Note: The Safety Zone is an area including the field of play, the ground within about 10 yards of the boards and the ground within about 30 yards of the goal line.

Start of Game

7 – At the beginning of the game the two teams shall line up in the middle of the ground, each team being on its own side of the half-way line. The Umpire shall bowl the ball underhand and hard between the opposing ranks of players, from a distance of not less than 5 yards, the players remaining stationary until the ball has left his hand.

How a Goal is Scored

8 – A goal is scored when a ball passes between the goal posts and over and clear of the goal line. If a ball is hit above the top of the goal posts, but in the opinion of the Umpire between those posts produced, it shall count as a goal.

Changing of Ends

9 – (a) Ends shall be changed every goal except where a goal is awarded under Penalty 1. Ends shall also be changed if no goals have been hit by half-time (in a seven or five period match, after the fourth or third period respectively), and play shall be re-started at a position corresponding to the change of ends. After a goal has been hit, the game shall be re-started from the middle of the ground as prescribed by Field Rule 7. The players shall be allowed a reasonable time in which to reach the middle of the ground at a slow trot and take up their positions.

Wrong Line-up

(b) If the Umpire inadvertently permits lining up the wrong way the responsibility rests with him, and there is no redress; but if at the end of the period no goal has been scored the ends shall then be changed.

Attackers Hit Behind

10 – (a) The ball must go over and be clear of the back line to be out.

(b) When the ball is hit behind the back line by the attacking side, it shall be hit in by the defenders from the spot where it crossed the line, but at least 4 yards from the goal posts or boards, when the Umpire says 'Play'. None of the attacking side shall be within 30 yards of the back line until the ball is hit or hit at; the defenders being free to place themselves where they choose.

Unnecessary Delay

(c) The defenders shall give the attacking side reasonable time to get into position, but there shall be no unnecessary delay in hitting in. In the event of unnecessary delay the Umpires shall call on the offending side to hit in at once. If the Umpire's request is not complied with, he shall bowl in the ball underhand and hard, at the spot where the ball crossed the back line and at right angles to it.

Defenders Hit Behind

11 – If the ball is hit behind the back line by one of the defending side, either directly or after glancing off his own pony, or after glancing off the side boards, Penalty 6 shall be exacted. If the ball strikes any other player or his pony before going behind it, it shall be hit in in accordance with Field Rule 10.

Ball Hit Out

12 – (a) The ball must go over and clear the side lines or boards to be out.

(b) When the ball is hit over the boards or side line, it must be bowled, underhand and hard, by the Umpire into the ground from a point just inside the boards or lines where it went out, on an imaginary line parallel to the two goal lines, and between the opposing ranks of players, each side being on its own side of the imaginary line. No player may stand within 10 yards of the side lines or boards. Players must remain stationary until the ball has left the Umpire's hand. A reasonable time must be allowed players in which to line up.

Restarting after an Interval

13 – On play being resumed after an interval, the ball shall be put in play in the normal manner which would have been followed had there been no interval, i.e. in

accordance with Field Rules 9, 10, 12 or 26, as the case may be. If the ball hits the side boards without going over them at the end of the previous period, it shall be treated as though it had been hit over them as laid down in Field Rule 12. The Umpire must not wait for players who are late.

Note: General Rule 10 (e) deals with resuming play when a period ends with a foul.

Damaged Ball

14 – If the ball be damaged or trodden into the ground, the Umpire shall, at his discretion, stop the game and re-start it with a new ball, in the manner prescribed in Field Rule 26.

Note: It is desirable that the game shall be stopped and the ball changed when the damaged ball is in such a position that neither side is favoured thereby.

Carrying the ball

15 – A player may not catch, kick or hit the ball with anything but his stick. He may block with any part of his body but not with an open hand. He may not carry the ball intentionally. If the ball becomes lodged against a player, his pony or its equipment, in such a way that it cannot be dropped immediately, the Umpire shall blow his whistle and restart the game in accordance with Field Rule 26 at the point where it was first carried.

CROSSING

16 – The Right of Way

(a) (i) At each moment of the game there shall exist a Right of Way, which shall be considered to extend ahead of the player entitled to it, and in the direction in which he is riding.

No player shall enter or cross this Right of Way except at such a distance that not the slightest risk of a collision or danger to either player is involved.

(ii) The Right of Way, which is defined in paras. (c) to (e) below, is not to be confused with the line of the ball and does not depend on who last hit it.

The Line of the Ball

(b) (i) The line of the ball is the line of its course or that line produced at any moment.

(ii) If the line of the ball changes unexpectedly, for example when a ball glances off a pony, and as a result the Right of Way changes, the player who had the Right of Way must be given room to continue a short distance on his original Right of Way.

(iii) When a dead ball has been put into play through being hit at and missed the line of the ball is considered to be the direction in which the player was riding when he hit at it.

(iv) If the ball becomes stationary while remaining in play, the line of the ball is that line upon which it was travelling before stopping.

Player Riding in the Direction the Ball is Travelling

(c) (i) A player following the ball on its exact line and taking it on his offside, is entitled to the Right of Way over all other players.

(ii) Where no player is riding on the exact line of the ball, the Right of Way belongs to the player following it on the smallest angle, provided he does not contravene Clause (f).

(iii) Two players when following the exact line of the ball attempting to ride one another off, share the Right of Way over all other players.

(iv) A player riding in the direction the ball is travelling at an angle to its line, has the Right of Way over a player riding to meet the ball at an angle to its line, irrespective of the width of the angle provided he does not contravene Clause (f).

(v) No player shall be deemed to have the Right of Way by reason of his being the last striker if he has deviated from pursuing the exact line of the ball.

Equal Angles

(d) In the rare case of two players riding in the general direction of the ball at exactly equal angles to it on opposite sides of its line, the Right of Way belongs to that player who has the line of the ball on his offside. The same rule applies as between players meeting the ball at exactly equal angles from opposite sides of its line.

Player Meeting the Ball

(e) (i) A player who rides to meet the ball on its exact line has the Right of Way over all players riding at an angle from any direction.

(ii) As between players riding to meet the ball, that player has the Right of Way whose course is at the least angle to its line.

Player to Take the Ball on Offside

(f) The Right of Way entitles a player to take the ball on the offside of his pony. If he places himself to hit it on the nearside and thereby in any way endangers another player who would otherwise have been clear, he loses the Right of Way and must give way to this other player.

(g) When two players are riding from exactly opposite directions to hit the ball, each shall take it on the offside of his pony. If a collision appears probable the player who has the Right of Way must be given way to.

Checking

(h) (i) No player may check or pull up either on or across the Right of Way if by so doing he runs the slightest risk of collision with the player entitled to it.

(ii) If a player enters safely on the Right of Way and does not check, a player must not ride into him from behind, but must take the ball on the nearside of his own pony.

(iii) If a player with possession of the ball or right to the line of the ball on his offside, checks his speed to such an extent that an opposing player may enter the line and take the ball on his offside, without, in the opinion of the Umpires, creating any danger to the checking player, if that player were to *maintain* his reduced speed, then no foul shall be deemed to have occurred, even if the checking player subsequently increases his speed. Umpires are advised that if the checking player slows to a walk or stops completely, under this directive, it is almost impossible for any danger to occur and therefore no foul is committed.

Dangerous Riding

17 – A player may ride off an opponent, but he may not ride dangerously, as for example:

(a) Bumping at an angle dangerous to a player, or his pony.

(b) Zigzagging in front of another player riding at a gallop, in such a way as to cause the latter to check his pace or risk a fall.

(c) Pulling across or over a pony's legs in such a manner as to risk tripping the pony, etc.

(d) Riding an opponent across the Right of Way.

(e) Riding at an opponent in such a manner as to intimidate and cause him to pull out, or miss his stroke, although no foul or cross actually occurs.

(f) 'Sandwiching', i.e. two players of the same team riding off an opponent at the same time.

Use of the Whip

18 – The whip may not be used unnecessarily or excessively.

Rough Handling

19 – No player shall seize with the hand, strike, or push with the head, hand, forearm or elbow, but a player may push with his arm, above the elbow, provided the elbow be kept close to the side.

Misuse of the Stick

20 – (a) No player may hook an opponent's stick, unless

he is on the same side of the opponent's pony as the ball, or in a direct line behind, and his stick is neither over nor under the body nor across the legs of an opponent's pony, nor may any player hook or strike at an opponent's stick unless all of the opponent's stick is below the opponent's shoulder level. The stick may not be hooked or struck unless the opponent is in the act of striking at the ball.

(b) No player may reach immediately over and across or under and across any part of an opponent's pony to strike at the ball, nor may he hit into or amongst the legs of an opponent's pony, but if a player rides from behind into the backhander of the player who has the Right of Way, he does so at his own risk and there is no foul.

(c) No player may intentionally strike his pony with his polo stick.

(d) No player may use his stick dangerously, or hold it in such a way as to interfere with another player or his pony.

(e) No player may knowingly strike the ball after the whistle.

Note: If a hit occurs after the whistle for a foul, the Umpire may increase the severity of the penalty if the hit is by a member of the fouling team, or cancel the penalty or decrease its severity if the hit is by a member of the team fouled.

Loss of Headgear

21 – If a player loses his headgear the Umpire shall stop the game to enable him to recover it, but not until an opportunity occurs that neither side is favoured.

Dismounted Player

22 – No dismounted player may hit the ball or interfere in the game.

Accident or Injury

23 – (a) If a pony falls or goes lame, or if a player or pony be injured, or in the case of an accident to a pony's gear which in the opinion of the Umpire involves danger to the players or other players, the Umpire shall stop the game.

(b) If a player falls off his pony, the Umpire shall not stop the game, unless he is of the opinion that the player is injured. What constitutes a fall is left to the decision of the Umpire.

(c) When the game has been stopped in accordance with Clause (a) above, the Umpire shall re-start the game in the manner laid down in Field Rule 26, directly the player concerned is ready to resume play. The Umpire shall not wait for any other player who may not be present.

(d) If a player be injured, a period not exceeding 15 minutes shall be allowed for his recovery. If the injured player is unfit to play after 15 minutes, the game shall be restarted with a substitute in place of the injured player, unless Penalty 8 has been exacted. If, however, the injured player subsequently recovers he may replace the player who was substituted in his place, but the handicap of the higher handicapped player will be counted in accordance with General Rule 5 (d).

(e) In the event of a player being, or seeming to be, concussed, the following action will be taken. The Umpires, or if no Umpires are present, the senior player on the ground will stop the game and arrange for the player to see a doctor as soon as possible. The player will not be permitted to play again for a minimum of one week without a certificate of fitness from the official medical officer of his club. If no doctor is present when the accident occurs it will be the sole responsibility of the Umpire or the senior player present to decide if the player was actually concussed.

Disablement

24 – If a player be disabled by a foul so that he is unable to continue, Penalty 8 may be exacted, or the side which has been fouled shall have the option of providing a substitute. Penalty 1, 2 or 3 shall be exacted in any case.

When a Game is Not Stopped

25 – It shall be within the discretion of the Umpire not to stop the game for the purpose of inflicting a penalty, if the stopping of the game and the infliction of the penalty would be a disadvantage to the fouled side.

Re-starting When the Ball was Not Out

26 – If for any reason the game has to be stopped without the ball going out of play, it shall be re-started in the following manner. The Umpire shall stand at the spot where the ball was when the incident occurred, and facing the nearer side of the ground, but not nearer the boards or side lines than 20 yards. Both teams shall take up their positions, each team being on its own side of an imaginary line, parallel to the goal lines and extending through the Umpire to the sides of the ground. No player may stand within 5 yards of the Umpire. The Umpire shall bowl the ball, underhand and hard, between the opposing ranks of players, towards the nearer side of the ground, the players remaining stationary until the ball has left his hand.

Discretion of Umpires

27 – (a) Should any incident or question not provided for in the Rules of Polo, or the supplementary Rules of the Polo Association concerned, arise in a match, such incident or question shall be decided

by the Umpire or Umpires. If the Umpires disagree, the Referee's decision shall be final.

(b) There are degrees of dangerous play and unfair play which give the advantage to the side fouling. The Penalty to be inflicted is left to the discretion of the Umpire or Umpires and shall only be referred to the Referee in the event of the Umpires disagreeing on the penalty.

PENALTIES

Note: In all free hits the ball shall be considered in play the moment it has been either hit or hit at and missed.

Penalty Goal F.R. 16, 17, 19, 20, 24

1 – (a) If, in the opinion of the Umpire, a player commits a dangerous or deliberate foul in the vicinity of goal in order to save a goal, the side fouled shall be allowed one goal.

(b) The game shall be re-started at a spot 10 yards from the middle of the fouler's goal in the manner prescribed in Field Rule 26. Ends shall not be changed.

30-Yard Hit F.R. 16, 17, 19, 20, 24

2 – (a) A free hit at the ball from a spot 30 yards from the goal line of the other side fouling opposite the middle of the goal or, if preferred, from where the foul occurred (the choice to rest with the Captain of the side fouled); all the side fouling to be behind their back line until the ball is hit or hit at, but not between the goal posts, nor when the ball is brought into play may any of the side ride out from between the goal posts; none of the side fouled to be nearer the goal line or back line than the ball is, at the moment it is hit, or hit at. In the event of the Captain of the side fouled electing to take the penalty from the spot where the foul occurred none of the defending side to be within 30 yards of the ball, nor come out from between the goal posts.

(b) In carrying out Penalty 2, if the free hit would, in the opinion of the Umpire, have resulted in a goal, but is stopped by one of the side fouling coming out from between the goal posts, or crossing the back line before the ball was struck, such a shot is to count as a goal to the side fouled. If the player who stopped the ball did not infringe these rules, but another member of his side did, Penalty 7 (a) shall be exacted.

40-Yard Hit F.R. 16, 17, 19, 20, 24

3 – (a) A free hit at the ball from a spot 40 yards from the goal line of the side fouling opposite the middle of the goal; all the side fouling to be behind their back line until the ball is hit or hit at, but not between the goal posts, nor when the ball is brought into play may any of the side ride out from between the goal posts; none of the side fouled to be nearer the goal line or back line than the ball is at the moment it is hit or hit at.

(b) In carrying out Penalty 3, if the free hit would, in the opinion of the Umpire, have resulted in a goal, but is stopped by one of the side fouling coming out from between the goal posts, or crossing the back line before the ball was struck, such a shot is to count as a goal to the side fouled. If the player who stopped the ball did not infringe these rules, but another member of his side did, Penalty 7 (a) shall be exacted.

60-Yard Hit (Opposite Goal) F.R. 16, 17, 19, 20, 22

4 – A free hit at the ball from a spot 60 yards from the goal line of the side fouling opposite the middle of the goal, none of the side fouling to be within 30 yards of the ball, the side fouled being free to place themselves where they choose.

Free Hit from the Spot F.R. 6, 15, 16, 17, 19, 20, 22

5 – (a) A free hit at the ball from where it was when the foul took place, but not nearer the boards or side lines than 4 yards. None of the side fouling to be within 30 yards of the ball, the side fouled being free to place themselves where they choose.

Free Hit from the Centre

(b) A free hit at the ball from the centre of the ground, none of the side fouling to be within 30 yards of the ball, the side fouled being free to place themselves where they choose.

60-Yard Hit (Opposite Where Ball Crossed) F.R. 11

6 – A free hit at the ball from a spot 60 yards distant from the back line, opposite where the ball crossed it, but not nearer the boards or side lines than 4 yards. None of the side fouling to be within 30 yards of the ball; the side fouled being free to place themselves where they choose.

Another Hit Penalty 2, 3, 4, 5, or 6

7 – (a) If the side fouling fail to carry out Penalty 2, 3, 4, 5 or 6 correctly the side fouled shall be allowed another free hit at the ball, unless a goal has been scored or awarded. If both sides fail to carry out Penalty 2 or 3 correctly, another free hit must be taken by the side fouled, irrespective of the result of the previous free hit.

Hit in by Defenders Penalty 2 or 3

(b) If the side fouled fails to carry out Penalty 2 or 3 correctly, the defenders shall be allowed a hit in from the middle of their own goal. None of the attacking side shall be within 30 yards of the back line until the ball is hit, or hit at; the defenders are free to place themselves where they choose.

Hit in from 30-Yard Line F.R. 10, Penalty 7(b)

(c) If the attacking side fail to carry out Field Rule 10 correctly the defenders shall be allowed to hit in from the 30-yard line, from the spot opposite where the first hit was made or would have been made. None of the attackers shall be within 30 yards of the ball until it is hit or hit at; the defenders being free to place themselves where they choose. For infringement of Penalty 7 (b) or any further infringement of Penalty 7 (c) by the attacking side, the defenders shall be allowed another hit in from the 30-yard line.

Unnecessary Delay

(d) In the event of unnecessary delay by the side fouled when called on by the Umpire to take a penalty hit, the Umpire shall restart the game from the spot where the hit should have been taken in accordance with Field Rule 26.

Player to Retire F.R. 24

8 – Designation by the Captain of the side fouled of the player on the side fouling whose handicap is nearest above that of the disabled player, who shall retire from the game. If the handicap of the disabled player is higher than that of any of his opponents the player whose handicap is nearest below that of the disabled player may be designated. If there are two or more such players the Captain of the side fouled shall designate the one to retire. The game shall be continued with three players on each side, and if the side fouling refuses to continue the game, it shall thereby forfeit the match. This penalty does not apply to international matches.

Pony Disqualified F.R. 3

9 – (a) For infringement of Field Rule 3; the pony ordered off the ground by the Umpire and disqualified from being played again during the game or match.
Note: The case of a pony blind of an eye must be reported by the Umpire in writing to the Committee conducting the tournament who shall take all steps necessary to ensure that it shall not be played again in any tournament.

Pony Ordered Off F.R. 4

(b) For infringement of Field Rule 4; the pony ordered off the ground by the Umpire and disqualified from playing again until the offence has been removed.

Player Ordered Off F.R. 5

(c) For infringement of Field Rule 5; the player ordered off the ground by the Umpire and disqualified from playing again until he has removed the offence.

General Note: In all the above three cases play must be re-started immediately as prescribed in Field Rule 26 and the game shall continue while the player is changing his pony or removing the offence.

Player Excluded

10 – The Umpire may exclude a player from the game, in addition to any other penalty, in the case of a deliberate, dangerous foul, or conduct prejudicial to the game. Alternatively, for a less serious offence, he may exclude a player for the rest of the chukka in progress. The side to which the excluded player belonged shall continue with three players only, or forfeit the match.
Note: The circumstances which caused this penalty to be inflicted must be reported by the Umpire to the Committee conducting the tournament, to enable them to judge whether the case should be reported to higher authority.

Suggested Layout of a Polo Ground

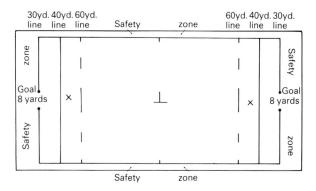

Length: 300 yards maximum, 250 yards minimum.
Breadth: 200 yards. (165 maximum if boarded).
Safety zone: at sides about 10 yards, at ends about 30 yards.
Markings on Ground: 30-yard line straight across ground – this helps Umpires in carrying out F.R. 10. At 40 yards a spot or small cross exactly opposite the middle of the goals, and at 60 yards a broken line is sufficient, but there should be a line exactly 4 yards long from boards inwards – this enables Umpires to place the ball 4 yards from side boards when required under Penalites 5 and 6.
Centre Line: a T in centre and marks on boards.

The figures 30, 40 and 60 should be painted on the boards, a mark being sufficient for the centre line.

Flags should then be used to show 30, 40 and 60 yards, but care should be taken to place them behind the side lines.

The goals must be 8 yards apart (16 yards when playing widened goals) and at least 10 feet high. They must be capable of collapsing should there be a collision.

Dimensions of a Polo Board:

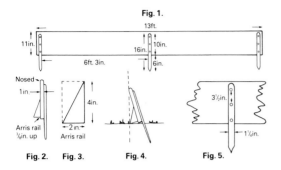

Fig. 1.

Fig. 2.   Fig. 3.   Fig. 4.   Fig. 5.

1 Back view of a section; length 13ft, height 11in, thickness 1in.
2 Side view of section, showing arris rail lifted by ⅜in.
3 Section of arris rail 4in × 2in.
4 Side view of board in position, showing effect of raising arris rail ⅜in. The ball after striking arris rail comes back into play, owing to angle.
5 Dimensions of iron peg 16in × 1¼in.

Polo boards cause less damage to ponies when in sections, as there is more give – also a splintered section can immediately be replaced whilst the game is in progress.

The boards may be curved inwards at the ends of the ground.

DIRECTIVE NUMBER 9001
MISUSE OF DRUGS – WELFARE OF PONIES
General
The Stewards have studied the recommendations of the Veterinary Officers' Committee and consider them a most valuable and authoritative guide to prevent the misuse of drugs (A) and for the welfare of ponies (B).

Implementation
The Stewards do not consider it practical for the HPA to form and instruct a centralised neutral body to implement these recommendations and that control, prevention and disciplinary action for the misuse of drugs or the abuse of ponies should be the responsibility of each individual Club, using its discretion on measures of control within the framwork of the Veterinarians' recommendations.

HPA Policy
(a) The Stewards draw particular attention to the list of permitted drugs listed in 'A' and emphasise that although some drugs banned in other horse sports may be appropriately used in moderation in connection with polo ponies, heart stimulants of any kind are NOT to be administered under any circumstances, due to the danger to both horse and rider.

(b) Both random and specific tests will be arranged by the HPA and the Clubs as considered necessary. The services of the Horseracing Forensic Laboratory will be used.
(c) **Disciplinary Action**. It is HPA policy that the abuse of drugs and of ponies is not to be tolerated by Clubs and it is considered that, where such abuse is discovered the firmest disciplinary action should be taken by the Club Committee concerned, depending on the severity of the abuse.
     (1) Warning.
     (2) Suspension for varying periods.
     (3) Referral to the Stewards for the most severe cases.
(d) **Right of Appeal**. The owner or rider penalised will have the right of appeal, through his Club Committee, to the Stewards.

A – MISUSE OF DRUGS
(1) The administration of any drug or substance which is not a normal constituent of horse food is banned with the exception of the permitted substances shown below.
(2) No medication involving injection (or syringes) will be used by anyone except a qualified vet or with permission from a club official on polo ponies in the precincts of a polo ground. (Directive April 1989).
(3) Permitted Substances:
     Phenylbutazone
     Flunixin
     Ventipulmin
     Sputulosin
     Visorbin
     Isoxuprin
     Regumate
     Antibiotics except procaine penicilin.
Note: The concentration in the blood plasma of phenylbutazone, with its active metabolite oxyphenbutazone, or of flunixin must be less than 10 microgrammes per ml of plasma. If they are used together the concentration of either must be less than 5 ug/ml. It is recommended that, to stay within these limits, a maximum dose of phenylbutazone is 2 grammes a day and the last dose should be given no later than 10 p.m. on the night before play. A recommended dose of flunixin is no more than 2×10 gramme sachets of Finadyne per day. In both cases the dose should be halved if both are given.

The following drugs will only be permitted if prior declaration of their administration has been made to the Club:
     Diuretics
     Local anaesthetics.

B – WELFARE OF PONIES
(1) On the polo ground, should any complaints be made regarding the condition of a particular

pony, the complaint should be referred to the polo manager who should then instruct the duty veterinary surgeon accompanied by two senior members of the Club Management to inspect the pony before any further action is taken.

(2) In view of the fact that, particularly early in the season, some ponies appear on the polo ground in poor bodily condition, it is recommended that a respresentative of the Club should informally inspect the pony lines to observe any ponies in a poor condition and then refer them to the veterinary surgeon if required.

(3) No ponies should be brought to the polo ground with an infectious or contagious disease.

(4) All ponies should have a valid vaccination certificate. At the beginning of each season they should be shown to the polo manager.

(5) Ponies seen with blood in their mouths or excess spur or whip marks should be reported to the Umpire or the Referee, who should then request that the pony be inspected by the veterinary surgeon.

(6) The withholding of water for an extended period of time is detrimental to the pony's health and should not be allowed.

(7) Any pony that is seen to be lame should be referred to the duty veterinary surgeon before resuming another chukka. (If a pony does resume play, it is suggested that a public announcement should be made). Lame ponies should not play.

(8) Poor or badly fitted tack which is causing physical damage to the pony is not allowed.

(9) In the event of a horse having to be 'put down' for humane reasons, the final decision will rest with the owner.

(10) No medication involving injection will be used by anyone except a qualified vet or with permission from a Club Official on polo ponies in the precincts of a polo ground.

2 NOTES FOR UMPIRES

THE REFEREE
Referee

General Rule 7 (a), states: The Rules shall be administered in a match by two Umpires, who shall be mounted to enable them to keep close to the play, and a Referee who shall remain off the field of play in a central position. By mutual agreement between Captains of teams, one Umpire and, if desired, also the Referee, may be dispensed with. The decision of the Umpire shall be final, except where there are two, and they disagree, in which case the decision of the Referee shall be final.

The task of the Referee is a very responsible one, and requires continual concentration throughout the game. In many matches he may never be asked for a decision; and then, suddenly, an occasion arises when the Umpires disagree and come to the Referee for a ruling, and a definite and final opinion must be given. The Referee should have had considerable experience of good polo, and, if possible, of umpiring. He should not only know the Rules well, but be able to refer to any Rule quickly. He should always have the Book of Rules beside him.

When the Umpires appeal to him to decide whether a foul occurred or not, the Referee should confine his decision to this point, as laid down in Field Rule 27 (b). The Referee should refrain from allocating a penalty unless specifically asked to do so.

The Referee should sit in a central position, at the side of the ground, *apart from distracting influences*, from which position he can see clearly and be easily accessible to the Umpires, who should know his exact position before play begins.

The Rules allow for a Referee when there is only one Umpire. In this case the Referee's duties are quite different; instead of arbitrating in case of disagreement between the Umpires he now has to act as a second Umpire to whom the mounted Umpire can appeal for assistance to decide cases in which he may not be able to see sufficiently clearly the degree of danger in a foul, etc.

Whenever possible the Referee should be a regular past or present player in polo at least to the level of the game he is refereeing. In the British Isles he should, where possible, be from the UK.

Hand Signals

The following hand signals are used in order to reduce the time taken in discussions between the Umpires and the Referee.

(a) The Umpires having consulted each other, turn towards the Referee and one of them raises his hand (this is to show that they disagree).

(b) If, in the Referee's opinion, no foul occurred, he will make the wash-out signal by a horizontal movement of both arms across his front.

(c) If he thinks a foul has occurred and it is obvious which side fouled, he will raise one hand above his head and point in the direction the hit is to be taken with the other.

(d) If he is in any doubt whatsoever about any aspect of the affair, he will stand up but will make no signal at all, upon which the Umpires will canter up to consult him.

(e) The Umpires may wish to consult him in any case, in which case they will naturally canter straight up to him without making any signals.

(f) There is no reason why the Umpires should not ask the Referee which side fouled if they are in any doubt.

THE UMPIRES
1 Ponies

Official and voluntary Umpires in every class of polo must

be adequately mounted. They should be sufficiently well mounted to enable them to keep close to the game without having to think of riding their ponies. The practice of Umpiring on young ponies in order to school them is strongly deprecated.

2 Umpires' Duties Before the Game Begins

(a) It is important that at advertised games at Polo Clubs, where public money is being taken, the game should start at the time advertised. Whilst this is really the business of the Polo Manager in a big Club, Umpires should be ready strictly on time and should ride out to the centre of the ground 2 minutes before the game is due to start.

(b) The Umpires should check the following points before throwing the ball in:
   (i) Who the Referee is and where he is sitting.
   (ii) That the Timekeeper and Goal Judges are in position.
   (iii) In handicap matches, that the handicap is correctly put up and that both sides are satisfied with it, General Rule 10 (b).
   (iv) That they both, as well as the Timekeeper, fully understand General Rule 10 (f).
   (v) That one of the Umpires should be prepared to toss for choice of goals on the arrival of the teams.

3 Positions

(a) *Division of Ground* Before going on the ground Umpires should mutually agree to take a side line and a back line each. It is suggested that they should change sides at half time or by matches, as, if a polo ground is correctly laid out, it means that one Umpire is facing the sun the whole afternoon.

   While it is obvious that one Umpire must be responsible for throwing in from one side line to the other, it must be clearly understood that the responsibility for blowing the whistle for an infringement of the Rules in any portion of the ground is co-equal.

   An Umpire on one side of the ground must not hesitate to blow his whistle if he sees a Rule being broken towards the other side of the ground, even in the near vicinity of the other Umpire, for that other Umpire may at the moment be unsighted by having ponies between him and the foul, or he may unavoidably miss it through being in the act of turning.

(b) *Hit-in* It is essential also that the one Umpire should be behind the back line when the ball is hit from behind. If an Umpire is standing behind a Player hitting in from behind he will see the exact line of the ball in whatever direction it is being hit and will get a very clear view of any opposing Player coming to meet the hit-in.

This meeting of the hit-in forms one of the most frequent causes of crossing, and it is important that the exact line of the ball should be observed; the other Umpire should be keeping his eye on the 30-yard line to see that the opponents of the side hitting in do not cross the line before the ball is hit or hit at.

(c) *Penalties 2 and 3* It is even more essential that one Umpire should be on the goal line in 30- and 40-yard hits, as the defending side may not cross the back line until the ball is hit or hit at, or come out between the goal posts. Infringement of this Rule has such strong penalties that it is obvious that an Umpire should be on the goal line, otherwise it will be impossible to detect this infringement.

(d) *Penalties 4 and 5 (a) and (b)* In the case of the 60-yard hits and the free hits (in the event of the latter being fairly near goal) it is also important that an Umpire should be close behind the line in the melees which frequently result from those penalties close in front of goal, the hooking of sticks on the wrong side often occurs, and the defenders may hit behind and it is difficult to see unless the Umpire is close.

(e) It follows that if these positions are mutually agreed to by the two Umpires, the general position of the two Umpires, whatever direction the game goes in, will be that one Umpire will be more or less at a short distance behind the game while the other is galloping level with it. It is considered that this is the ideal combination of the two positions to make certain of seeing every possible infringement of the Rules.

4 Use of Whistle – General Rule 10 (f)

(a) Be careful to use the whistle correctly. Remember there is a Timekeeper who has to stop the clock when you blow one firm blast, but who must not stop the clock when you blow two sharp blasts. Read General Rule 10 (f) carefully and note the occasions when to blow one firm blast and when to blow two sharp ones. In both cases the ball is dead until you say 'Play' (Field Rule 2), but in the latter case the time it is dead counts in the playing time of the period and in the former it does not; you must be very careful to blow the whistle in the correct manner. Although you should not normally blow the whistle when the attacking side hit behind, you must be on the lookout to do so if the defending side hit behind, as this will entitle the attackers to a 60-yard hit opposite where the ball crossed.

(b) The Umpire should carry his whistle in his hand ready for instant use and must make up his mind in a flash and blow without hesitation. Owing to the pace at which polo is played, any momentary delay is fatal, as situations change so rapidly that an Umpire may end by not blowing his whistle at all for a foul that he really meant to give. A small stick with a whistle fitted at one end is recommended.

(c) The Umpire having blown his whistle should quickly check with the other Umpire that he agrees there was a foul and to the proposed penalty. This can be done either verbally or preferably by a nod of the head or some other prearranged signal. It is most important that there should be no delay through long discussion.

The Umpire should then loudly and clearly announce the foul and penalty, thus 'Cross against Red, Free hit from the spot,' and without waiting canter to the spot where the foul occurred, drop the ball and go to his position. There is no necessity to state the number of the penalty awarded.

5 Concentration

Owing to the speed at which it is played, polo is the most difficult of all games to Umpire. The Umpire must be concentrated on the play every moment of the period; he should be watching the game so closely that he is certain of the line of the ball each time it has been hit, and, consequently, knows at a glance which Player has the Right of Way. He must further establish the direction of the Right of Way (in his mind) bearing in mind that it is very likely that the Right of Way and the line of the ball will not coincide. The moment the line of the ball is changed he must quickly know who is now entitled to the Right of Way and in what direction the new Right of Way lies. Attention is drawn to Field Rule 16 (b) (ii). It is the Umpire's job to see that the Player who has Right of Way is given sufficient room to pull up or turn when the Right of Way changes suddenly.

A common error among inexperienced Umpires is lack of concentration due to watching some brilliant individual or combined play, more from an appreciation of the Players' point of view than as an Umpire.

6 No Appealing – General Rule 7 (d)

Captains shall have the sole right to discuss with the Umpire or Umpires any matter arising during the game: but no Player shall appeal in any manner to the Umpire for fouls. This includes a Player holding up his stick, for which he may be penalised after a warning under Field Rule 27. If thought necessary a general caution to all Players should be given at the beginning of a match or chukka, after which an appeal for a foul may be penalised without further warning.

It is very necessary that there should be no hanging about or long discussions between Umpires, and the right of a Captain or a side to discuss matters with the Umpire does not include the right to challenge the Umpire's normal decisions.

Never get into an argument with the Players. It is unnecessary to discuss anything with the Players while playing; or explain reasons for giving any decisions; but, in the interests of the game, when it is finished a discussion of the game and the fouls that occurred will be found helpful, especially to young players.

7 Prolongation in the Event of a Tie – General Rule 10 (h)

Remember that if the game ends in a tie at the end of the final period the game must carry on after the bell is rung until the ball goes out of play or the 30-second bell is rung.

8 Allowing a Goal after Whistle

Read carefully the Note to Field Rule 2 as to when a goal may be allowed to stand after the whistle is blown for a foul.

9 Field Rules 3, 4 and 5

The method of dealing with offences under these Rules is given in detail in Penalties 9 (a), (b) and (c) respectively. These offences concern unmanageable ponies, blinkers, frost nails, sharp spurs and protruding buckles on boots and knee pads. The Umpire should ride up to the Captain of the team and direct him to tell the Player to change his pony or remove the offence.

Note that if a pony is disqualified (Penalty 9 (a)) or a Player is excluded (Penalty 10) a report is required from the Umpire.

10 Changing Ends – Field Rule 9

Remember that, if by half-time no goals have been scored, ends will be changed.

Remember also, that if a goal has been scored, it is laid down that teams should return to the centre at the pace of a slow trot. It will be found that, in an exciting match, when the score is level or nearly level and the last period is being played, one team or the other, or both, will gallop back to the centre to get the ball thrown in. Remember to stick to the trot when returning to the throw-in.

11 Crossing – Field Rule 16

(a) It is difficult to lay down an exact distance as to what constitutes a cross, but in all doubtful cases the pace at which the players are moving must be considered, or whether there was any danger involved, as on this depends the question whether the Player entitled to the Right of Way has to check to avoid a collision. The benefit of the doubt should be in favour of the man entitled to the Right of Way.

The good Umpire gets consistent in giving Penalties for crossing, and this is more appreciated by the Players than anything else.

(b) A frequent form of foul is committed by a Player swinging his pony across the Right of Way immediately before or after hitting at the ball.

This often occurs after taking a nearside back-hander. Another foul under this Rule is checking for a backhander (even when the striker is entitled to the Right of Way) when an opponent is following close behind in full pursuit. On the other hand, once a Player has safely taken over the Right of Way from another Player, the latter may not ride into the former from behind unless the former checks his pony.

(c) Umpires are apt to forget that a Player riding in the direction that the ball is travelling at an angle to its line, has the Right of Way over a Player riding to meet the ball at an angle to its line, irrespective of the width of the angle, provided he takes the ball on his offside.

It is only when a Player rides to meet the ball on its *exact* line that he has the Right of Way over all other Players riding at an angle from any direction.

12 Dangerous Angle – Field Rule 17 (a)

The Umpire when deciding whether a bump was made at a dangerous angle, should consider the speed at which the Player was riding and whether the bump could have caused the pony to fall, for example a bump behind the saddle at an acute angle.

Players should straighten out almost parallel with their opponents before riding them off.

13 Intimidation – Field Rule 17 (e)

This Rule should be carefully read and strictly enforced.

14 Misuse of Stick – Field Rule 19

The Rule states that the stick may be only hooked or struck when an adversary is *in the act* of striking at the ball and that a Player is not allowed to strike or hook an opponent's stick above the level of the shoulder.

It should be noted that no Player may strike at the ball among the legs of an adversary's pony and that the hind legs are included in this Rule. However, if a Player rides into the backhander of a Player entitled to the Right of Way, he does so at his own risk.

The same Rule states that no Player shall intentionally strike his pony with his polo stick. Under the HPA Rule a Player is prohibited from intentionally striking his pony with the shaft or even thumping it with the butt end of the handle.

Some examples of dangerous use of stick are:

(a) Taking a full swing at the ball from the throw-in or in a scrimmage in such a way as to endanger other Players.

(b) Striking hard into a group of ponies' legs during a scrimmage.

(c) Striking at the ball in the air so as to endanger other Players.

(d) Taking a full swing under a pony's neck in such a way as to endanger a Player riding alongside.

(e) Striking an opponent's stick in such a way as may cause injury to an opponent.

As a general rule Umpires are not sufficiently strict about giving these fouls.

15 Accident or Injury – Field Rule 23 (a)

This Rule states: 'If a pony falls or goes lame, or if a player or pony be injured, or in case of an accident to a pony's gear which, in the opinion of the Umpire, involves danger to a player, or other players, the Umpire shall stop the game.'

For example the following can be considered:
Broken martingale, if end trails on the ground.
Broken girth.
Broken reins, if single.
Broken headstall, allowing bit to fall out.
Loose bandages, or boots.
The game is not stopped for:
Broken martingale, if *not* dangerous.
Lost or broken leathers.
Broken curb chain.
Lost bandages or boots.
Responsibility for deciding what is or is not dangerous, however, must remain with the Umpire.

16 When the Game is not Stopped – Field Rule 24

'It shall be within the discretion of the Umpire not to stop the game for the purpose of inflicting a Penalty, if the stopping of the game and the infliction of the Penalty would be to the disadvantage of the side fouled.'

This is one of the most difficult Rules to apply, for if the Umpire refrains from blowing his whistle because he thinks the striker is bound to get a goal, it is perfectly all right if he gets the goal, but should he miss, it is both unfortunate and awkward.

N.B.: Note to Field Rule 2.

17 Discretion of Umpires – Field Rule 26

This Rule empowers Umpires to penalise all dangerous and unfair play and bad behaviour on the grounds that it is not mentioned in the Rules.

18 Penalties

(a) There are no less than five separate penalty hits (Penalties 2 to 5 (b)):
The 30-yard Hit.
The 40-yard Hit.
The 60-yard Hit.
The Free Hit from the Spot.
The Free Hit from the Centre of the Ground.

As regards the actual penalties themselves: there are eleven. Umpires must know these by heart, but there is no longer any need to know the numbers, since the Rules give the name of each penalty, which should be used in preference to the number.

Umpires must bear in mind that penalties should be both appropriate to the infringements which they penalise and consistent, in that the same penalty should always be awarded for infringements of similar type and gravity. Inconsistency is a major cause of friction between Players and Umpires.

(b) *Penalty 1*

The ruling of a Penalty Goal states: 'If, in the opinion of the Umpire, a Player commits a dangerous or deliberate foul in the vicinity of goal in order to save a goal, the side fouled shall be allowed one goal.'

The Umpire, having awarded a Penalty Goal, shall immediately instruct the Goal Judge to wave the white flag.

When throwing in from the spot 10 yards in front of the goal it is preferable that the ball should be thrown in towards the side of the ground where the foul took place.

A clear definition is sometimes asked for as to what 'vicinity' means in terms of distance from the goal.

The fact that the foul is considered to have been committed in order to save a goal obviously denotes that the Player fouled is in a position to score, and is therefore, in most cases, close to the goal. It is difficult to lay down any actual distance to cover 'vicinity,' but this Penalty Goal has seldom been given at distances exceeding the 40-yard line unless the Player fouled is more or less in front of goal and had an open run at the goal if he had not been fouled.

(c) *Penalty 2*

Remember that the wording for a 30-yard Hit is: 'A free hit at the ball from a spot 30 yards from the goal line of the side fouling, opposite the middle of the goal, or, if preferred, from where the foul occurred (the choice to rest with the Captain of the side fouled . . .)' . . . It is therefore clear that the Umpire, if the foul occurs anywhere nearer the goal than 30 yards, should immediately ride up to the Captain of the side fouled and offer him the choice of a free hit from 30 yards or from the place where the foul occurred; he should not decide this matter himself, and he should remember that in the latter case the fouling side may not be within 30 yards of the ball, nor may they come out between the goal posts.

(d) *Penalty 2 and 3*

It is of utmost importance to remember that in carrying out 30- or 40-yard Hits, if the hit would, in the opinion of the Umpires, have resulted in a goal, but is stopped by one of the side fouling coming out between the goal posts, or crossing the back line before the ball was struck, such a shot is to count as a goal to the side fouled. If the Player who stopped the ball did not infringe these Rules, but another member of the side did,

then the fouled side should be allowed another hit from the same position (Penalty 7 (a)).

This bears out the importance of one Umpire being on the goal-line.

(e) *Penalty 4 and 5 (a)*

Remember that, in 60-yard Hits and Free Hits from the spot and centre, the Umpires should see that the side fouling should stand back 30 yards from the ball before it is hit or hit at. In view of the fact that there are a large number of 60-yard Hits, Umpires can train their eyes very quickly as to what 30 yards is, as there is a 30-yard line marked on the ground as well as a 60-yard line.

Remember that a Free Hit (i.e. from where the foul took place) can be as severe as a 30- to 40-yard Hit, for it is clear that if an infringement of the Rules takes place, say, 15 yards in front of the goal for which the Umpire decides that a Free Hit is suitable, the side fouling must be 30 yards from the ball when it is hit or hit at, and will, therefore, be 15 yards behind the goal, thus making the goal almost a certainty; and if an infringement occurs calling for the exercise of a 60-yard Hit opposite goal or a Free Hit from where the foul took place, at a point nearer the goal line than 60 yards, then a Free Hit from the spot should generally be given and the side fouled get the benefit of having the better chance of hitting a goal than if they had been given Penalty 4 and taken back to 60 yards. However, the gravity of the infringement must be the deciding factor in the Umpire's decision.

(f) *Penalty 5 (b)*

Umpires should bear in mind that the object in having both Penalty 5 (a), a free hit from the spot, and Penalty 5 (b), a free hit from the centre of the ground, is to give Umpires alternative penalties which may be awarded at their discretion. In awarding these and other penalties the gravity of the infringement, where it took place and the direction of play must decide the severity of the penalty. Thus a Penalty 5 (b) may be awarded where a free hit from the spot is considered inadequate and a 60-yard Hit would be too severe.

For example, where the attacking side commits an infringement near the defenders' back line the Umpires should award either a free hit from the spot or a free hit from the centre depending upon the gravity of the infringement. They also have the more severe options of Penalties 4, 3 or 2 but would only award one of these in the case of a serious foul. Alternatively, where a defending team commits a minor or accidental infringement just within its own half then a free hit from the spot may be more appropriate than a Penalty 4.

Additionally, without overriding their general discretion Umpires should take into account the direction of play when an infringement occurs. As a general rule if the attacking team is fouled it should at least be taken forward to the next most severe penalty, whilst if a defending Player is fouled a free hit from the spot will often be appropriate.

19 Unnecessary Delay

(a) Your attention is drawn to Penalty 7 (d) 'Unnecessary Delay'. The HPA has decided that it will include 'teeing-up' and circling.

(b) 'Teeing-up' whether by the striker or another Player, or both, will be taken to mean either making a 'tee' or rolling the ball on to an existing 'tee' (e.g., hoofprint).

(c) The ball may be moved by a Player, but once it is lying on a flat surface of reasonable area it is ready to hit.

(d) The Umpire will allow reasonable time for this (say 2 or 3 seconds) and he will say 'Play' as soon as he can, and will do so in any case if the Player tries to 'tee-up'. If the striker does not then *immediately* begin to take the hit, the Umpire will blow his whistle and act as in Penalty 7 (d).

(e) As soon as the ball is touched or hit in any way after the order 'Play', this will be taken to be the free hit.

(f) You are reminded that delay is sometimes caused deliberately, not only for the sake of 'teeing-up', but also to allow a pony to be changed, etc. For this reason, the practice of circling to get on the right leading leg, or any reason, is also to be disallowed, either at the beginning of the run-up or at the end of it.

(g) Umpires' attention is drawn to the rule that the interval between chukkas is 3 minutes. It is accepted that the 5 minute interval at half-time is not always enforceable due to the practice of 'treading in'.

20 Nearside Offences

Taking the Ball on the Nearside
The relevant Rules on the subject are Field Rule 16(f) (Player to take the ball on offside) which reads as follows:

(a) 'The Right of Way entitles a player to take the ball on the off side of his pony. If he places himself to hit it on the nearside and thereby in any way endangers another player who would otherwise have been clear, he loses the Right of Way and must give way to this other player.'
and Field Rule 17 (Dangerous Riding):

(b) 'Zigzagging in front of another player riding at a gallop in such a way as to cause the latter to check his pace or risk a fall.'

(c) 'Pulling across or over a pony's legs in such a manner as to risk tripping the pony etc.'

There is nothing in the Rules to prevent a player taking the ball on the nearside provided, as in any other manoeuvre, he does not endanger another player by doing so. It must be remembered that in high goal polo, the pace is faster than in low and medium, and the faster the horse is going, the longer it takes him to pull up. The safety distance in high goal polo is therefore greater than in low.

This manoeuvre can, of course, be penalised under Rule 16(f) or 17(b) and (c). Umpires are therefore directed that a player may move over and take the ball on the nearside, provided there is sufficient distance between him and the other player not to endanger the latter; the important words being in 16(f) '... and thereby endangers another player'. The other guiding principle is that the faster the polo, the greater the safety distance that must be allowed.

It is, of course, a foul to take the ball on the nearside if an opponent is meeting it correctly, Rule 16 (g).

21 Damaged Ball

(a) Example. The ball splits into two parts and one part goes through the goal. If it is clear that the larger part of the ball goes through the goal the Umpires will normally award a goal. If the parts are about equal, the Umpires have to use their discretion and decide one way or the other. If a goal is not awarded, Field Rule 14 may be applied.

(b) Example. The ball splits or breaks up when struck in the course of a penalty being taken. Umpires, in this case, should allow the penalty to be taken again. But presumably they may decide the ball has not broken up sufficiently and that the larger part is still in play or has gone through or past the goal.

22 Throw-ins

(a) '*Throw-ins*' from the *Centre*.
   (i) Keep the players behind the mark.
   (ii) Stop them charging the Umpire.
   (iii) Keep 10 yards back from the mark.

(b) '*Throw-ins*' from the *Side*.
   (i) Place your horse's *hind* legs on the side line.
   (ii) Keep the players a further 5 yards away.
   (iii) Keep them still.

(c) The ball should be thrown in under-arm and hard.

The Goal Judges

The duty of signalling goals each end is usually undertaken by a member of the ground staff, and this duty is generally efficiently carried out.

General Rule 7 (b) reads: 'In important matches Goal Judges shall be appointed each of whom shall give testimony to the Umpires at the latter's request in respect of goals or other points of the game near his goal, but the Umpires shall make all decisions.'

A flag should be waved, when a goal is scored, until acknowledged by the Timekeeper.

This flag should be *kept down and furled* until a goal is scored.

Remember, an Umpire may order a Goal Judge to signal a goal for Penalty 1 without the ball having actually passed through the goal.

When the ball is hit behind, a Goal Judge should quickly place a new ball on the spot where it crossed the line, remembering that it must not be nearer than 4 yards to the goal posts or the side boards.

Remember, the Umpires may at any moment ask the Goal Judge's opinion on the question of whether the defending side hit the ball behind the goal-line or on other points of the game near the goal. They, however, make decisions.

Sometimes the ball rolls only a few inches over the goal-line between the posts, or is hit back again by a defender just as it has crossed the line. This must be carefully watched for.

Goal Judges should wear white coats (long ones are not recommended), and keep out of the way of the players.

It is recommended that in important matches two Goal Judges should be appointed each end. They should be polo players, and energetic.

Many polo players and Umpires will remember difficult situations when a goal has been shot at from an acute angle, particularly if the ball has passed above the level of the goal posts. The normal single Goal Judge standing well back behind the centre of the goal, may be in doubt whether it was a goal, but must either signal a goal or not. The Umpire, whose decision is final, can intervene but may or may not have been in a position to see more clearly than the Goal Judge.

If two Goal Judges are posted each end such a situation should not occur. They can stand together behind the goal when the game is running towards the other goal; but the moment an attack on their goal is coming, one of them should always keep moving, so as to keep the approaching ball in view through the goal posts, particularly when it is actually struck at goal.

3 ARENA RULES

1 – Facilities

    (a) *Playing Arena*

        (i) A playing area of 300 feet in length by 150 feet in width is considered ideal for Arena Polo. The indicated minimum recommended size is 150 feet in length by 75 feet in width; this size would only be suitable for two-a-side.

        (ii) Goals shall be centred at opposite ends of the Arena and shall be 10 feet in width by 12 feet in height, inside measurement. In smaller Arenas the goal size may be reduced, but not to less than 8 feet in width by 10 feet in height. (1.1)

        (iii) The Arena shall be clearly marked at the centre with a 'T' and at points 15 yards and 25 yards perpendicular to each goal.

    (b) *Balls*

    The ball shall be not less than 12.5 inches or more than 15 inches in circumference and the weight not less than 170 grams or more than 182 grams. In a bounce test from 9 feet on concrete at 70 degrees F, the rebound shall be a minimum of 54 inches and maximum of 64 inches at the inflation rate specified by the manufacturer. This provides for a hard and lively ball.

2 – Mounts and Equipment

    (a) A mount is a horse or pony of any breed and size.

    (b) A mount blind in an eye may not be played.

    (c) A mount showing vice or not under proper control shall be excluded from the game.

    (d) Protection of ponies by boots or bandages on all four legs is compulsory.

    (e) Blinkers are not allowed, nor any form of nose-band which obstructs the vision.

    (f) Rimmed shoes are allowed, but the rim may only be on the inside of the shoe.

    (g) Frost nails, screws, calkins and studs are not allowed.

    (h) No mount may be played by more than one team in any event. (2.1)

3 – Players and Alternatives

    (a) There shall normally be three players in each team, designated at Number 1, Number 2 and Number 3. Each team may designate one or more alternative players. It is possible to play two-a-side.

        (i) Players shall not appear in any event in other than proper uniform including a protective polo helmet or polo cap, either of which must be worn with a chin strap.

        (ii) A player shall not use sharp spurs nor any gear with protruding buckles or studs.

        (iii) If in the opinion of the Tournament Committee the colours of two competing teams are so alike as to lead to confusion the team lower in the draw or second named in a league competition shall be instructed to play in some other colours.

    (b) A player may be substituted for another during an event if the latter player is, for any reason, unable to finish the event. Any such substitution must be made prior to the commencement of a period except as provided in Rule 16(h) relating to an injured player.

(c) In all cases of substitution, the substitute must be qualified to play in the event and the team must remain qualified for the event after the substitution has been made. The handicap of the player having the higher handicap shall be counted in any game in which a substitution occurs.

(d) In case a player is disabled so as to be unable to continue, the team shall have the option of providing a qualified alternative. If an alternate is needed and not available, a player may be removed from the opposing team by the Umpire, thereby equalizing the number of players on each team, and the game continued. (3.1) If the disablement is as a result of a foul, the Captain of the team fouled shall have the right to nominate the player from the opposing team whose handicap is nearest above that of the disabled player, who shall retire from the game.

(e) A team shall present itself to play at the time scheduled by the Committee.

(f) No player shall play for more than one team in any event.

(g) No person shall play in any tournament or advertised match conducted by an Affiliated Club or Association in the British Isles unless:

　(i) He is an Associate Member of the HPA.

　(ii) He has lodged a signed declaration, either with his Club or the HPA, to be bound by the rules, regulations, orders and directives of the HPA.

　(iii) He is listed in the Association's current handicap list,

　(or) has been allotted a handicap by the Association's Handicap Committee during the current season,

　(or) his handicap has been confirmed by the Honorary Secretary of the Association.

(h) No player may play under the influence of stimulative drugs.

(i) No individual shall participate as a player or official in any match if physically impaired (e.g., sick, hurt) before or during a match and such impairment endangers the safety of the individual or others. This rule is to be strictly enforced by the Umpires and the Tournament Committee.

(j) A player registered with the HPA is eligible to play in any match, game or tournament event except that: a player with a handicap of −1 may not play above the 8-goal level, and −2 may not play above the 4-goal level. (3.2)

(k) In no case may the handicap of any individual player exceed the upper handicap limit of the event, and in HPA official tournaments with an upper limit above 4 goals, may not exceed ¾ of the upper handicap limit. (3.2)

4 – Officials

(a) *Tournament Committee*

　(i) Each HPA event will be conducted by a Committee appointed by the Association or by the Host Club which shall be responsible for all aspects of the event including scheduling, conducting the draw, appointment of officials, and resolution of all questions which arise at times other than when the Umpire is in charge. (4.1)

　(ii) It is recognised that some limitations may from time to time exist which make it impossible or impractical for the Committee to fully comply with the Rules of Arena Polo. In such cases, the Committee shall spell out such exceptions prior to the event. The Committee shall make every effort to comply with the intent of these Rules if an exception must be made. (4.2)

　(iii) The Committee may impose penalties, including Penalty 8 or 9 and/or recommend discipline by the Executive Committee of the Association for actions before, during or after a game.

(b) *Umpire and Referee*

　(i) Every tournament game shall have two Umpires and a Referee or just one Umpire at the discretion of the Committee. (4.3)

　(ii) The authority of the Umpire and/or Referee shall extend from the time each game is scheduled to start until its end.

　(iii) The Umpire shall be responsible for enforcing the Rules and maintaining proper control over players and teams during the game.

　(iv) Subject to Rule 18, all decisions of the Umpire, or agreed decisions of two Umpires, shall be final.

　(v) In the event two Umpires are serving and they disagree, the Referee shall decide which Umpire's opinion is to prevail or call no foul.

　(vi) Should any incident or question not provided for in these Rules arise during a game, such incident or question shall be decided by the Umpire.

　(vii) Umpires must wear a protective polo helmet, polo cap or hard hat to BS 4492, either of which must be worn with a chin strap.

(c) *Timekeeper*

　(i) The Timekeeper shall be appointed by the Committee whose reponsibility it shall be to keep track of time elapsed during and between periods of the game.

　(ii) The Timekeeper shall signal the expiration of time to the officials. (4.4)

　(iii) The authority of the Timekeeper shall be subordinate to that of the Umpire.

(d) *Scorekeeper*
  (i) The Scorekeeper shall be appointed by the Committee whose responsibility it shall be to keep track of goals scored, including goals by handicap or penalty.
  (ii) The Scorekeeper shall fill out any forms or score sheets required by the Committee following the game or event.
  (iii) The authority of the Scorekeeper shall be subordinate to that of the Umpire.

(e) *Goal Judges*
  Goal Judges may be appointed who shall give testimony to the Umpire at the latter's request as to goals scored or other points of the game near the goal, but the Umpire shall make the final decision.

(f) *Team Captains*
  (i) Each team shall designate one player as Captain who shall have the sole right to discuss with the Umpire questions arising during the game, except as provided in Rule 16.
  (ii) In the event of a protest other than that made by a Team Captain, or a continuing and/or argumentative protest by a Team Captain, after due warning by the Umpire, any further protest may subject the team to a penalty. (4.5)

5 – Length and Number of Periods

(a) A regulation game shall be four periods of 7 minutes each with intervals of 4 minutes after each period except the second period. There will be a 6 minute interval after the second period.

(b) Each period of play, except the last, shall terminate after the expiration of the prescribed time (designated by the ringing of the bell or other signal) as soon as the ball goes out of play. A bell or other signal will be sounded 30 seconds after the first bell or signal, if the ball is still in play, and the period will terminate at the first sound of the second bell or other signal, although the ball is still in play, wherever the ball may be. The last period will terminate even though the ball is still in play, at the first stroke of the 7-minute bell, wherever the ball may be, except in the case of a tie.

(c) In the case of a tie the last period shall be prolonged until the ball goes out of play, or until the 30-second bell rings, and, if there is still a tie, after an interval of 10 minutes, the game shall be started from where the ball went out of play and continued in periods of the usual duration, with the usual intervals, until one side obtains a goal, which will determine the match.

6 – Scoring

(a) A goal counts one point.

(b) In order to score a goal, the ball must pass between the goal posts and across a line drawn between those posts at the mouth of the goal, over and clear of the goal line and beneath the top of the goal. (6.1)

(c) Where play is stopped in the belief that a goal has been scored, and it is subsequently ruled that no goal has been scored, play shall be resumed by a bowl in at the 15-yard mark with the nearer goal to the Umpire's right.

(d) Goals awarded by handicap or penalty shall count as goals scored.

(e) The team which scored the most goals shall win the game.

(f) Following a goal, play is resumed by a bowl in at the centre of the Arena.

(g) If a goal is scored at approximately the same time a foul is called:
  (i) The goal shall be counted unless the foul was called on the attacking team and is confirmed. The play will then continue from the 15-yard line as Penalty 1.
  (ii) The goal shall not be counted, and the game resumed by the appropriate penalty hit, if the foul was called against the attacking team and is confirmed.
  (iii) If a goal is scored at approximately the same time as the whistle blows for a time out (official's or player's) the goal shall be counted and play resumed at the centre of the Arena. (6.2)

7 – Dead Ball

(a) When a ball is broken or trodden into the ground in such a manner as to be unserviceable, or when it strikes the Umpire or Umpire's mount so as, in the Umpire's opinion, to affect the flow of the play, the Umpire shall stop the game, take time out and bowl the ball towards the kneeboards between the players at the point where the event occurred but not closer than 15 yards from the goal.

(b) If the ball becomes lodged against a player, mount, or equipment and cannot be dropped immediately, the ball shall be declared dead and bowled in at the point where it first became lodged but not closer than 15 yards from the goal.

(c) If the ball becomes involved in a melee such that neither team can properly make a play, the Umpire may blow the ball dead and bowl the ball in at a point where it was blown dead. The bowl in shall not be closer than 15 yards from the goal.

(d) If the ball is driven outside or leaves the Arena, whether or not it bounces back into the playing area, while the game is in progress, the Umpire shall stop play and the clock. Play is resumed by a bowl in at the point nearest to where the ball left the arena but not closer than 15 yards from the goal. (7.1)

(e) At any time the Umpire blows the whistle the ball is dead and no further play may be made by any player. Play is resumed by a free hit or a bowl in as specified elsewhere in these Rules.

(f) If a foul is called and overruled, and no goal scored, play shall be resumed by a bowl in at the point of the alleged infraction, but not closer than 15 yards from either goal.

8 – Starting of Game and Periods

(a) The Umpire shall toss a coin before the game, in the presence of the Captains of the opposing teams, first designating which Captain shall call. The winner of the toss shall have the choice of which goal to defend. Ends shall be changed after each period of play. In the event of an extra period, the ends shall be changed in the same manner as after each other period. (See Rule 5 (c))

(b) The Umpire shall start play in any period by bowling the ball underhand, on the ground, between the teams which shall be lined up in parallel lines at the centre of the Arena, each team on the side of the centre line nearer the goal it is defending, behind the cross of the 'T' and at least 3 yards from the Umpire.

(c) The timer shall start the clock at the moment the ball leaves the Umpire's hand.

9 – Penalties

(a) A violation of these Rules may be penalised by the Umpire in accordance with its severity, its location, and its effect on the game, by awarding to the offended team one of the following penalties:

Penalty 1

The team fouled shall be awarded a goal. On resumption of play, the Umpire shall bowl the ball in towards the sideboards at a point 15 yards in front of the centre of the goal defended by the fouling team. The fouling team's goal shall be to the Umpire's right.

Penalty 2

A free hit at the ball by the team fouled from a spot 15 yards in front of the mouth of the goal undefended by the fouling team, all players to be behind the point from where the free hit is made until the ball is hit or hit at. No opponent shall be within 5 yards of the player making the hit. Play shall continue in the event no goal is scored on the free hit.

Penalty 3

A free hit at the ball by the team fouled from a spot 25 yards in front of the mouth of the goal undefended by the fouling team, all players to be behind the point from where the free hit is made until the ball is hit or hit at. No opponent shall be

within 5 yards of the player making the hit. Play shall continue in the event no goal is scored on the free hit.

Penalty 4

A free hit at the ball by the team fouled from a spot 25 yards in front of the mouth of the goal defended by the fouling team, all players to be behind the point from where the free hit is made until the ball is hit or hit at, except one of the fouling team, who may be placed between the mouth of the goal and the 25-yard line. No opponent shall be within 5 yards of the player making the hit. Play shall continue in the event that no goal is scored on the free hit.

Penalty 5

A free hit at the ball by the team fouled from the centre of the ground, none of the side fouling to be within 5 yards of the ball, the side fouled being free to place themselves where they choose.

Penalty 6

A free hit at the ball from where it was when the foul took place, but not nearer the edge of the ground than 4 yards. None of the side fouling to be within 5 yards of the ball, the side fouled being free to place themselves where they choose.

Penalty 7

(i) In the event of a failure to correctly carry out the above Penalties 2, 3 or 4 by the fouling team, another free hit shall be granted to the hitter at the same place originally called for in the penalty awarded, if a goal has not been scored. However, if, in the opinion of the Umpire, the original free hit would have resulted in a goal, but was missed or blocked because of failure of the fouling team to correctly carry out the penalty, Penalty 1 shall be awarded the team making the free hit.

(ii) In the case of a failure to correctly carry out Penalties 2, 3 or 4, by the team fouled, the ball shall be bowled in at the centre of the Arena; or in the case of Penalties 5 or 6 where the foul occurred.

(iii) In the case of a failure to correctly carry out Penalties 2, 3, 4, 5 or 6 by both teams, another free hit shall be granted the hitter from the same spot regardless of whether a goal was scored.

(iv) In the case of a failure to correctly carry out Penalties 5 or 6 by the fouling team, another free hit shall be granted the hitter.

Penalty 8

The Umpire may remove a player from all or any part of the remainder of the game in addition to any other penalty in case of a deliberate or dangerous foul, or conduct prejudicial to the game.

Penalty 9

The match shall be forfeited. (9.1)

Penalty 10

(a) The player or mount shall be disqualified. If the disqualification is for illegal equipment, the player or mount may return when the offending equipment is removed.

(b) On Penalties 2, 3 or 4 the team fouled may only hit the ball once and may not hit or hit at it again until the ball hits the wall, an opposing pony or player, or until an opposing player hits or hits at the ball. If the hitter misses the ball completely, the team hitting may not hit or hit at the ball until it has been hit or hit at by a member of the opposing team. On Penalties 5 and 6 the hitter may only hit or hit at the ball once, thereafter any player may hit or hit at the ball. In the event the hitter misses the ball completely, it remains in play and the line of the ball is defined in Rule 11 (b). (9.2)

(c) On Penalties 2, 3, 4, 5, 6 or 7 play shall begin and the clock started when the Umpire calls 'Play' and the ball is hit or hit at. The hitter must hit or hit at the ball promptly after the call of 'Play' and if he does not, Penalty 7(b) may be called against him. (9.3)

(d) On Penalties 2, 3, or 4 there shall be no contact between any player and opponent until the ball is hit or hit at. This does not apply to Penalties 5 or 6.

10 – Calling of Fouls by Umpire

(a) The Umpire may declare any violation of Rules of Play a foul when seen or, when not seen, upon evidence satisfactory to the Umpire.

(b) When a foul is called, the Umpire shall stop the game, call time out and announce the foul to the players.

(c) If both teams commit a personal foul at approximately the same time, no free hit is taken and the ball is bowled in at the point where play was stopped.

(d) The following penalties may be exacted for violation of specific Rules:

Rule Violated	Penalty Exacted
2b,c,d,e	10
2f	9
3ai,ii	10
3c,e,f,g	9
4fi,ii	1,2,3,4,5,6,8,9
7e	1,2,3,4,5,6,8,9
12	1,2,3,4,5,6,8
13	1,2,3,4,5,6,8
14	1,2,3,4,5,6,8
15	1,2,3,4,5,6,8
16b,i,j	1,2,3,4,5,6,8

11 – Line of the Ball

(a) The line of the ball (hereafter referred to as 'line') is the line of its course or that line produced forward or backward at any moment.

(b) When the ball is put into play by a free hit a line is created when the ball is hit and assumes a direction. If the ball is hit at and missed, a line is established at the time of the stroke forward and backward to the centre of the goal.

(c) When the ball is put into play by a bowl in, a line is created at the instant the ball leaves the Umpire's hand.

(d) Should the ball become stationary while still in play the line remains the last line travelled before the ball became stationary except as provided in Rule 11 (b).

(e) At any time the ball changes direction, from whatever cause, a new line is immediately established and a new Right of Way (Rule 12) as determined by the new line may be created.

12 – Right of Way

(a) At each moment of the game there shall exist as between any two or more players in the proximity of the ball a Right of Way, which gives to the player entitled to it the right to proceed in the direction in which the player is riding.

(b) No player may enter, cross, or obstruct the Right of Way of the player entitled to it unless at such a distance that no risk of collision or danger to either player is involved.

(c) When the line of the ball changes and, as a result, the Right of Way changes, a player must be granted the necessary time to clear the new Right of Way. A player clearing the Right of Way may make no offensive or defensive play in doing so.

(d) Subject to Rule 12(g) no player may have the ball other than on the offside or the offside of the player's course, if in so doing an opponent is endangered who could have safely attempted a play had the original player kept the ball on the offside, or the offside of that player's course. This subsection takes precedence over 12(e) and 12(f).

(e) Subject to Rule 12(g) each of two players, when one is following and the other meeting the ball, must ride with the line of the ball on the offside until they have passed. (12.1)

(f) As between two players when both are following or both are meeting the ball:

(i) The player riding parallel to or at the lesser angle to the line of the ball has the Right of Way over the player riding at the greater angle to the line of the ball.

(ii) In the case of two players on opposite sides of the line of the ball at equal angles to the line of the ball, both players have a Right of Way up to the line of the ball or until the angle of one becomes less than the angle of the other.

   (iii) A player waiting on the projected line for the ball must yield the Right of Way to a player following the course the ball has already travelled.

(g) Subject to Rule 12(i), when playing the ball along the side or end wall, if the distance of the ball from the wall does not permit an offside play, a player who is both at the least angle to the line of the ball and following the direction of the ball shall have the Right of Way even though playing the ball on the nearside.

(h) Subject to Rule 12(i), the player with the Right of Way may play the ball at any speed and any player approaching from the rear must make a play from the nearside. However, a player may not check suddenly so as to cause a following player to collide. (12.2)

(i) Two players riding together on, or at an angle to, the line have the Right of Way over a single player riding at an equal or greater angle to the line regardless of whether the players are meeting or following the direction of travel of the ball.

13 – Dangerous Riding

(a) Careless or dangerous riding or lack of consideration for the safety of other players, regardless of team, is a foul.

(b) The following are examples of riding prohibited under this rule:

   (i) Bumping at an angle or speed dangerous to a player or to a mount. (13.1)

   (ii) Running into or over the rear quarters of another mount.

   (iii) Pulling up, on or across the Right of Way of another player.

   (iv) Zigzagging in front of another player.

   (v) Riding an opponent dangerously across the Right of Way of another player.

   (vi) Running the head of a horse into an opposing player.

   (vii) Riding an opponent's mount dangerously into the side or end walls.

   (viii) Two team-mates simultaneously making a play against a single opponent. (13.2)

   (ix) Riding one's mount into the stroke of another player. (13.3)

14 – Improper Play

(a) A player shall not strike an adversary's or a team-mates's mount with hands, whip or stick.

(b) A player shall not strike the ball or interfere in the game when dismounted.

(c) A player shall not seize with the hand, strike or push with the head, hand, arm or elbow, an opponent, but a player may push with the shoulder, provided the elbow is kept close to the side.

(d) A player may not hold the ball in the hand, arm or lap: nor kick or hit at the ball with any part of the person in such a way as to direct its course. The ball, however, may be blocked with any part of the person or mount.

(e) No player may appeal in any manner to the Umpire for a foul. This does not preclude a Captain from discussing any matter with the Umpire.

(f) A player may not dismount while the ball is in play. (14.1)

15 – Use of the Stick

(a) A player may hook or strike the stick of an opponent with his stick provided that:

   (i) (1) The opponent is in the act of striking at the ball, including both the upward and downward phases of the stroke; or

   (2) The opponent is attempting to hook the hitter, in which case the hitter may strike the opponent's stick.

   (ii) The player is on the same side of the opponent as the ball or in a direct line behind.

   (iii) The contact is made below the level of the mount's back. (15.1)

(b) A player may not reach over, under, in front of, or behind another's mount.

(c) A player may not strike another's mount with the stick. (15.2)

(d) In any bowl in, players shall hold the stick with the head below the level of the mount's back. (15.3)

(e) All players shall carry the stick in the right hand.

(f) A player shall not intentionally strike his own mount with the stick. This includes using any portion of the stick as an aid in managing the mount.

(g) No player may use the stick carelessly or dangerously, for example:

   (i) Taking a full swing in close quarters.

   (ii) Hooking, striking or slashing an opponent's stick with unnecessary force.

   (iii) Carrying the stick in such a way that it might become entangled in a player or mount's equipment. (15.4)

   (iv) Using the stick to hit or hit at the ball in the air. (15.5)

(h) A player striking at a ball assumes the full responsibility for using the stick safely, but swinging at it in close quarters will not be permitted.

(i) A player is at all times responsible for the consequences of the stroke including backswing, stroke, and follow-through. (15.4)

(j) No player may swing the stick in 'windmill' fashion as in appealing for a foul.